How is Language Possible?

How
is Language
Possible
?

Philosophical Reflections
on the Evolution of Language
and Knowledge

J. N. HATTIANGADI

Open  Court

La Salle, Illinois

OPEN COURT and the above logo are registered in the U.S. Patent and Trademark Office.

© 1987 by Open Court Publishing Company.
First printing 1987.

Printed and bound in the United States of America.

Library of Congress Cataloging-in-Publication Data

Hattiangadi, J. N.
How is language possible? : philosophical reflections on the evolution of
language and knowledge / J.N. Hattiangadi.
p.   cm.
Bibliography: p.
Includes index.
ISBN 0-8126-9044-3 : $29.95.   ISBN 0-8126-9045-1 (pbk.) : $13.95
1. Languages—Philosophy. 2. Linguistic change. 3. Language and languages—Origin.
4. Semantics (Philosophy) 5. Language acquisition. I. Title.
P106.H354 1987
401—dc19

87-25290
CIP

Contents

Acknowledgements

This book owes so much to so many that I have to select for mention here only those who have had the most influence on it. Some have made suggestions, which I have adopted, others have engaged in discussions, perhaps long ago, that I remember stirring me up, still others have helped me to rewrite and rethink it better, and still others have helped me with the writing, editing, and format of the book. Some have done several of these things for me. I am grateful to all of the following and many more for their help: J. O. Wisdom, C. G. Hempel, R. Grandy, I. Lakatos, T. S. Kuhn, I. C. Jarvie, P. Feyerabend, R. Butts, C. Hooker, E. Akin, S. Nathanson, R. A. Cobb, J. Agassi, G. F. Cowley, P. Urbach, K. R. Popper, P. Jack, M. Bakan, L. Briskman, D. Miller, G. Saulitis, P. Hébert, J. Bent, J. Saindon, M. Haynes, A. Cohen, B. Baigrie, N. Ziv, J. Kramps, C. Erneling, D. R. Steele, P. J. Griffiths, and the secretarial services of York University (Arts) who helped me with the production of typescript several times.

I also wish to thank the following for allowing me to use, in whole or in part, material previously published with them:

I thank Nicholas Rescher for allowing me to use material in Chapters 3 and 4 which was previously summarised in *American Philosophical Quarterly,* 1979. Much of Chapter 5 was part of my doctoral dissertation at Princeton University 1970, and I thank University Microfilms for allowing me to use it. Chapter 7 overlaps considerably with "The Structure of Problems" *Philosophy of the Social Sciences,* 1978–79, and I thank my co-editors, Ian Jarvie and John O'Neill for allowing me to use the material. Chapter 8 contains section B which overlaps with "Knowing That and How" in *Methodology and Science,* 1984, whose editor P. H. Esser has kindly permitted me to use it. *Word* (1984) Chapter 9, was revised with Noam Ziv and published under the same title. I thank Noam and the editor of *Word* for allowing me to publish the original chapter. Chapter 10 is a version of a paper based on an earlier draft chapter which included 9 and 10. It was published by *Philosophy Forum* in 1973.

And my warmest thanks go to Mira and Anandi who have been partners in this venture, sometimes without their knowledge, and sometimes in spite of great inconvenience.

Introduction

Philosophy and Science

The title of this book might well remind the reader of Kant, who is best known for asking questions of this form. Such is Kant's influence that I would be naive to deny it. But it is nevertheless my belief that my answer is quite unlike those given by Kant to similar questions.

Kant described questions of this form as proper to philosophy, whereas science asks more factual questions. Philosophy therefore establishes possibilities and conceivabilities (and impossibilities and inconceivabilities, too). In contrast to this, science describes what is the case, by strict attention to fact.

The idea of a philosophy which need concern itself with no factual detail was a liberating influence on philosophy. But the philosophy it let loose turned out to be far from liberal, and prompted Kant, who was an Enlightened philosopher, to say that with friends such as those who spoke for him he did not need enemies.

So powerful was Kant's idea of a prior subject, freed from any need to address factual detail, that it continues to flourish long after philosophers have ceased to invoke Kant. While philosophers are disagreed on everything else, most are agreed that in philosophy one studies the framework of knowledge, and not any body of facts, which are left to the different natural and social sciences, the arts, and the technologies.

How is empirical knowledge possible? Kant thought that if a mind must know something in the world by or through sense perception, then that which is known must be similar to our idea of it. This thought is Berkeley's, but it was given a profound new twist by Kant, who suggested that certain features of the objects known to us are features not of the objects in themselves, apart from our knowledge of them, but of the objects as they appear to us. Eddington explicated this thought with the elegant metaphor of the mind as a fishing net—we cast the net into the sea; the scientist studies the fish picked up, and notices a minimum size—a fact, about those fish, no doubt. But the size of the mesh in the net determines this, and not what is out there in the ocean.

Kant's method is to establish the only possible way in which objects can be seen, thought of, and spoken about, to establish the transcendental truths, as the philosophical truths are called.

Scientists, and particularly mathematicians, discovered many intriguing ways of showing how the mind can think in manners not dreamt of in Kant's philosophy. Kant thought that the truths of mathematics were necessary truths because that is the only way we can perceive things. Abstracted from perceptual intuition were the pure intuitions of Time and Space, from which we could derive the idea of succession and Arithmetic in the first case, and Geometry in the second.

But Russell and Whitehead derived mathematics from logic, without any need for those intuitions. This was a blow to Kant's system of ideas. Einstein's theory of the structure of space-time was another blow to the Kantian idea of a transcendental method.

Out of the ruins of transcendental philosophy there arose language philosophy. Where Kant asked how knowledge is possible, this new philosophy asks—how is truth possible? For a statement to be like something in the world, the world must have a language-like structure. True statements correspond to facts. This modern Kantianism is no less remarkable than the old one.

"1.1. The world is all that is the case.

1.2. The world is a collection of facts, not of things."

Thus began Wittgenstein's *Tractatus Logico-Philosophicus*. It investigated the very possibility of language, and concluded that its very possibility required that the world have a linguistic structure, to the extent that we can speak of it at all.

Moreover, the structure of the world which reflects the structure of language cannot be spoken of, for to speak truly or falsely is to use the similarity of structure. Thus the task of philosophy, which is to investigate the framework (or structure) of the world and of language simultaneously, is impossible within language. Whereof one cannot speak thereof one must be silent, he said, though only at the end of a long series of impossible assertions.

The study of language, then, has come to be the study of the framework of our thought because what can be thought at all can be said (another of Wittgenstein's aphorisms). If we think that we think something propositional which cannot be said, then we are not really thinking at all.

The picture theory of meaning and truth, as this has been called, was shown by Tarski to be in error. It is *not* necessary for the universe of discourse to consist of facts in order for statements about objects in it to be true or false. Apologists for Wittgenstein's *Tractatus* may say that Tarski's theory does not give us an ontology. But that is exactly the point. Tarski's theory frees us from the need to postulate that for language to represent the world truly or falsely, the world must be a collection of facts and not of things.

Wittgenstein subsequently abandoned the idea of a structural similarity between the world and language, but perversely maintained its corollary to the end of his life, namely that in language we find a framework for description, so that the philosopher who tries to describe the framework as if it were factual speaks nonsense. Philosophy properly pursued has the task of showing how the nonsense of philosophy, which is beguiling, is patent nonsense. Philosophy leaves everything as it is, he thought to the end.

This essay is an attempt to rescue language from philosophy. It asks 'How is language possible?' while supposing that the answer might possibly bear upon matters of factual detail, which is, of course, the way in which language needs rescue.

Central to my enterprise is the thought that 'How is such and so possible?', is a central sort of question *in science*. Kant's antinomies are the form in which problems can also present themselves *to the scientist*. If scientists go on to the detailed study of facts, then it is because, given alternative possible resolutions of antinomies, they have to investigate the details to see which alternative is better. Science flourishes where the facts speak equivocally, and the dispute is theoretically still open (even if all or almost all intellectuals think that one of the possibilities is clearly the best).

This collapses the distinction between the framework and detail. In the end, Kant was in error because the transcendental questions he discussed are capable of being evaluated empirically (as Einstein has demonstrated to us in one instance). With the benefit of hindsight it is easy to improve upon Kant.

Language philosophers do not regard empirical questions as relevant to philosophy. Empiricism in this century is the philosophy that everyone else should pay attention to the facts.

Among logicians there is the quaint myth that the study of logic can establish metaphysical truths. Among Ordinary Language Philosophers, whose philosophy of language, at any rate, is far from ordinary, there is the wonderful illusion that they can pronounce without regard to factual responsibility.

I suspect that Wittgenstein thought that language has certain features which represent the framework of our knowledge because he thought *something* must be part of the framework, and he could not see what else it could be, but language. But this is to presuppose the view that every detail is part of a framework, which cannot itself be studied in detail.

If there is one thing that I believe is clear, it is that one can study any features of language with due attention to detail. My only regret is that, trained as I am as a philosopher, I have not been sufficiently adept at seeing where so many more details might have refined, improved or overthrown so many of my own pet hypotheses.

Enlightenment

It was characteristic of the eighteenth century that the Encyclopedists did not want to accept traditions that did not stand up to the light of Reason.

Their thought was *radical,* because they questioned the very roots of human practice.

When the reaction set in (in England and Scotland, for example) there was launched a staunch defence of traditions as greater than what can be comprehended by Reason. This political difference of opinion between Radicals and Conservatives profoundly affected the political development of Europe, and all the countries which came into contact with European thought and political practice.

In this century, the issue has not gone away. We have, at one end, the radical theories of language, theories which try to defend language as an expression of human rationality, such as in the writings of the early Wittgenstein, and in those of Chomsky, or in the writings of those who, in the more traditional Whig spirit, would improve on language in the light of what has been rationally concluded—Bertrand Russell, or George Bernard Shaw, for example, or many of those followers of Russell in philosophy who constructed and studied artificial languages.

The conservative—even Tory—conception of language as a tradition finds its defence among functionalists in anthropology, the first and greatest of these being, perhaps, Durkheim, and in more recent years in the writings of Wittgenstein in his 'later' period.

Being able to see two philosophical perspectives in language against the background of the intellectual and political controversies of Scotland, England, and France in the eighteenth century does not help us resolve any issues. On the contrary, it alerts us to more difficulties for either view that we might not have seen before noticing their historical setting. What the historical background does give us is a classification of theories of language. We can ask: a) Is it a radical theory? b) Is it a conservative theory? Is it neither?

Of those which are neither, I suggest that there is one clear type which may be called romantic theories. These theories are inspired by Herder's comment that thought takes place in language and a language is always located in a community. Reason, it would seem to follow, is communally based. Language, in this approach, is a natural outgrowth from the activity of people. Folk art and folklore are the foundation of the communal mind, the source of language. Language transcends Reason, but it is not just any tradition either.

In political terms, this may be distinguished from radicalism, and conservatism, and can be described as 'groupism' or 'communalism', the most popular forms being national communalism or international communalism (or socialism). In the theory of language this point of view is represented in the study of languages from a socio-economic perspective, which would regard both logical analysis and functional description as superficial.

The point of view offered in this book is a hybrid—it is none of these, but tries to accommodate every insight that we can find. Its distinctive feature, that we may identify as a type, if we insist, is that it is *evolutionary*. It takes as its task to understand how language could have arisen at all (this is where it comes closest to the third point of view). It studies language as a tradition also, and how we must be subject to it to make ourselves understood to each other. In this respect it is like conservative or functionalist theories of language. But its distinguishing feature is that it puts Reason, in a certain limited way, as the engine of a certain kind of linguistic change, namely in our ability to become more and more articulate in time. In this respect it is like the first.

If, however, we were to press the point, I would have to concede that my views are perhaps closest to the first point of view. I believe that language like philosophy is part of both framework and detail, and can be therefore studied philosophically and empirically. My view, therefore, can also be described by unsympathetic critics as a most extreme kind of scientism.

Science and Philosophy

The great problems of modern philosophy arose when modern mathematical physics tore asunder the harmonious conception of the world of previous ages. Modern philosophy flourished because science could not resolve the difficulties it had created. The rise of modern biology has shown us how we can begin to bring harmony into the world picture once again. This, fundamentally, is why I urge empiricism within philosophy also—because the gaps created by the rise of physical theories can be filled by biological theories. We do not need prior philosophy. I shall sketch each of these points, and draw upon them to describe certain distinctive features of human beings, and languages, which are important features of my study.

The classical world and the scholastic world were not without difficulties and disputes, but Aristotle's considerable influence showed in the conception of a harmonious universe. The kind of harmony I have in mind is between knower and known, which might not have been appreciated quite as much until modern physics shattered it.

The classical description of things as falling into kinds or sorts, each of which has its essence or form in it, makes it easy to understand how a soul can grasp it epistemically. But with the rise of modern mathematical physics, this harmony is lost. The physics of Galileo and Descartes describes a mathematical world in which familiar sorts of things around us have a physical explanation which is quite different from their appearance. This creates serious difficulties: 1) It raises a serious difficulty about the very possibility of the knowledge of the physical world. 2) Another difficulty concerns the existence of active and knowing beings in a world which is supposed to consist of only inert mathematical objects. How does matter interact with and/or create such beings? 3) Moreover, the physical world is governed by laws, particularly laws of the conservation of mass and of momentum, and in modern terminology, of the conservation of energy. How is this compatible with our conception of ourselves as making choices, of having moral autonomy and of being responsible for our actions?

In the first couple of centuries following the scientific revolution the statement that we could understand human knowledge, human minds, and freedom in material terms was a mere programme, a hope. Since the nineteenth century revolution in biology, with the elaboration and development of Darwinian natural selection, Mendelian genetics, and the new 'trigger' model in physiology (and in modern times the development of thermodynamics, quantum physics and molecular biology) it seems that we can begin to make a new harmonious sense of the world without recourse to a prior philosophy to fill the gap.

The full elaboration of this perspective would require another book, but its presence can nevertheless be felt throughout this one. Philosophers asked how the world must be that we can understand it. We learn in biology that if we understand how *we* have evolved from our ancestors we can understand how it is that *we* can have an understanding of our world. Our minds are imperfect products of the evolutionary process, in ways not much different from the way genetic control of cellular development is an evolutionary product, though at a much different time.

In brief, modern biology gives us a much more interesting picture of ourselves as organisms then we have ever had, so that we may begin to see how the philosophical gap between matter and mind, knower and known, subject and thing can be bridged without sacrificing our intellectual standards.

Central to this biological picture are two models of biology—the neo-Darwinian conception of the evolution of species and the 'trigger' model of action patterns. Both of these models play a large part in my exploration of language. But the 'trigger' model is less known and less remarked upon, so I shall introduce some of its features here which I hope will help us with the study of language and of language use.

As I see it, the significant feature of modern biological thought that has not been utilized by philosophers to resolve their difficulties has been the analysis of the 'trigger' mechanism in living systems. This model presupposes the existence of routine actions as templates for the action patterns of organisms. In the case of all living forms, we must imagine the normal state to be one of routine or routinized responses, with variation and improvisation being the rare or unusual occurance (that may often be understood in terms of *other* routines).

In the case of organisms, the eruption of a certain action is prompted by a trigger which releases the action. But in social matters there are routines governed by more complex relations than the trigger model suggests. Grammar in language is interpreted in this book as a social routine, a template which allows us to communicate routinely. Speculation and theorizing are the activities, I suggest, that create the need for improvement in language, and thus for the modification of linguistic templates. These modifications are in turn fossilized and become new patterns for us to use in our effort to communicate. Human language, no less than human knowledge, is a product of our evolution—not only the genetic and social evolution of millions of years, but also the more remarkable cultural evolution of recent times.

1
Problems Regarding
Natural Languages

A. Four Problems of the Growth of Language

This book is an attempt to solve an array of problems, or riddles, which form a complex and interrelated system. Its claim to novelty lies primarily in the attempt to solve this large group of problems in one sweep. The task of actually establishing some solution beyond doubt, or even one small part of one solution, will not be attempted; nor do I believe that it is feasible.

The problem-complex may be introduced by considering four riddles or problems which, among others, will later be considered more fully. These problems are: the problem of self-perpetuation of language, the problem of linguistic change, the problem of language learning, and the problem of relativity and reality. They are only stated in this chapter in a preliminary way and will be taken up later in the text. The problems and the summary of my views which follow are in turn only preliminary and together they will serve as an introduction to other problems in the book.[1]

i. The Problem of the Self-Perpetuation of Language

There is an extensive literature on the relative determination of social institutions by individuals and by society. But language is one institution in which the tension between these two entities comes to a head, and it is hard to state precisely the right relationships between them.

If anything about language is evident it is that it perpetuates itself in whatever form it exists, even as we use it. Every individual must learn the language that others speak if he is to communicate in that language. This means that he must learn a language whose conventions are already established or 'given'. Yet clearly language was not created for us by some deity; it is strictly a human product, created by us. This is puzzling. For how can something be at once created and given?

To fully appreciate this difficulty imagine what would happen if someone in an intelligent prelinguistic society suddenly started speaking English. Not a single one of his fellow tribesmen—be they ever so pregnant with linguistic potential—would be able to understand a word he says, because they do not know the conventions which govern this language. Nor could our talker *explain* these conventions to his people unless they already understood the very language made possible by such conventions. How, then, does a language ever become established?[2]

ii. The Problem of Linguistic Change

A second problem, which is not unrelated, concerns not so much an overview of language as a social institution, but rather the inner structure of the language itself. The meanings of words are fixed by usage or convention, as are the modes of combining them to mean what we intend by our sentences. Since we depend upon these conventions in order to communicate, they cannot be changed by any individual arbitrarily, except to the extent that one can indicate one's meaning, usually with the help of the conventions already available.

Nevertheless we know that widespread conceptual changes in meanings of words, even basic words, are not uncommon.[3] And it has been persuasively argued that new concepts which come about during revolutions in our ideas are not reducible to (or definable in terms of) concepts which predate them. We also know that grammars evolve, unless they are grammars of 'dead' languages. How can the view that linguistic conventions must be fixed before communication is possible accommodate the fact that these conventions change?

iii. The Problem of Language Learning

The problem of change is also related to the problem of learning a language. How can we learn the same vast language with the same grammatical and syntactic conventions if no two of us are exposed to exactly the same pieces of evidence to tell us what this language is?[4] How can we guess the same language if each one of us has only partial and meagre clues to tell us what this vast system of language is?

iv. The Problem of Reality and Relativity

This concerns the relation of language to reality. The system of concepts together with the grammar of a language comprise a system which enables us to learn about the world. But what can we learn about that world in any language?

A comparison of languages from different parts of the world suggests that there are basic differences between the world views that are captured by, or presupposed within, different languages.[5] Not all these presupposed views can be right. In fact, almost all such views would be mistaken, even if they contained many truths, and even if we found it hard to state them. This would seem to suggest that our own views more than likely presuppose a false basic understanding, which we can never correct.

Yet, few would doubt that translations between diverse languages are possible. However difficult communication might be, it can be established between any two linguistic communities. Even if there is some initial misunderstanding between cultures, the fact that we can come to appreciate this fact shows that we do gain understanding after all. We also seem to have some objective knowledge in science, which seems less language-dependent than this view would seem to allow.

How can objective science, or interlinguistic translation transcend the "absolute presuppositions" (Collingwood's phrase) of a language in a given time frame?[6] How is this possible if different languages have different absolute presuppositions about reality?

B. Some Isolated Solutions

Each of these problems can be solved by various means. Each solution, however, is usually satisfactory only so long as we do not ask how it fares with respect to other problems, including those I have stated. So my task, the task of finding a view that is generally satisfactory, is not an easy one. Let me illustrate this by presenting some solutions to each of the above problems, and the difficulties faced by each. If these discussions appear to be somewhat sketchy, the reader must await later chapters where they are dealt with more fully.

i. The Problem of Self-Perpetuation: Behaviourism and Functionalism

One way of dealing with this question is to deny that it is of any importance. The term 'language', we might hold, is an abstraction which does not correspond to one thing, but describes rather loosely behaviour of a verbal kind. Whatever similarity there is between the speech habits of community members can be understood in terms of the system of rewards for conformity within that society and the prediliction of members to respond to operant conditioning. The first person who speaks (if such an identification can be made) is simply an example to be imitated by the other members of the community, more or less faithfully, depending on the rewards for accuracy.

Verbal behaviour, then, is to be understood solely in terms of individual responses to stimuli as determined by operant conditioning. But this cannot account for the following sort of circumstance: different speakers who may have very different linguistic 'inputs' (evidence or conditioning) are nevertheless able to pick out very nearly the same (potentially infinite) set of expressions as 'grammatical'. And they pick them out of the infinitely many possible different combinations of words in a language. A mere statistical account cannot explain how verbal expressions that are novel to two speakers can be understood by them in the same manner (i.e., as exemplifying the same grammar). This point has been made most forcefully by Chomsky.[7]

The problem of self-perpetuation can also be solved by upholding an extreme form of functionalism (as in anthropology). We might regard linguistic experience as a social fact whose significance is established entirely within a social context, and which is hence entirely beyond the power of an individual to change. Thus, one may use words idiosyncratically, but what the words themselves mean depends on what people generally use them for. Such is, for example, the view of Wittgenstein. To understand an expression is in the end to see how it fits into 'a form of life', to see how it functions in complex social situations.

Any form of functionalism faces the grave difficulty, pointed out by Ernest Gellner, that it fails to explain how institutions evolve.[8] This is also one of our central concerns. The widespread influence of Wittgenstein's approach to language and indeed his whole philosophy can only be explained by the fact that most philosophers believe that scientific language and ordinary language exist in quarantined compartments. But science and common sense are not so far from each other as this view implies. And once we see just how mistaken this view is, we see that the existence of conceptual revolutions, and their influence on language, poses a great difficulty for Wittgenstein's point of view.

ii. The Problem of Linguistic Change: Organismic Theory

One interesting solution to the problem of linguistic change or evolution is to accord language the status of an organism. Thus all linguistic change (like the evolution of grammar, or that of phonetics) will depend upon irreducibly internal organising features. In this way we seek for a morphogenesis of language, much the same as a morphogenetic study of animals or plants. While such a view gives an excellent account of the autonomy of language and of its systematic character, which are exhibited in the very manner of its change, the fact of human adaptation poses a difficulty for it. If we regard language as an organism which grows solely of its own accord, it seems incredible that we, through whom language evolves, have derived such adaptive benefit from its growth. There must be at least some linguistic change which corresponds to our evolving social needs. Moreover, such a view is not compatible with the fact that conceptual revolutions, which affect the meanings of words in a language, are not governed solely by linguistic laws. They often come about entirely through the efforts of individual thinkers.[9] Such language growth, which represents a response to conceptual revolution, would seem to refute an organismic theory of language.

iii. The Problem of Language Learning: Chomsky's Theory

Today a most brilliant solution to the problem of linguistic learning can be found in the writings of Noam Chomsky.[10] Though it is a version of essentialism, in its details it is a very novel solution. And yet it is unsatisfactory when considered in a broader context.

The basic principle Chomsky evokes to explain linguistic learning is that of the existence in each and all of us of an "essence" of language, usually called 'Universal Grammar'. This is the basis of all language. It never changes. (Hence, all linguistic change must be in the superficial levels of language and not in its most basic structure). All learning is determined by our Universal Grammar, for this Universal Grammar is such that if we are given a certain amount of exposure to a language, we are able to determine its whole grammar.

Interesting as this view is, and for all the linguistic evidence which can inevitably be found to confirm it, it suffers the defect of all essentialistic theories, namely, it is not compatible with the neo-Darwinian view of the evolution of man or of life. The very notion of species-defining essences which is central to Chomsky's theory is incompatible with our understanding of the evolutionary mechanism. Chomsky's theory is therefore untenable, unless it can provide a superior, non-Darwinian explanation for the evolution of species.

iv. The Problem of Relativity and Reality: Relativism and Formal Semantics

This problem can be solved in at least two ways, each of which, again, seems satisfactory only to the extent that we do not take more general considerations into account. One way of resolving the problem of relativity and reality is simply to accept that each language embodies a point of view which it must always presuppose, which makes it inherently impossible to translate exactly from one language to another, or to understand reality within a language. In any language, then, we are imprisoned by the most basic point of view which informs the language. While there may be a measure of truth in this statement as a description of the way things are, if we compare two languages in the abstract, we do know that each language is capable of considerable modification, so that it may well be able to simulate the effect of a very different language. In this case the moot question is whether a language can escape or transcend any of its own basic presuppositions. Here the evidence suggests that it can do so.

An analysis of a Western European language (such as a linguistic analysis of ordinary English, as practiced in Oxford) would show that a great many things to which we implicitly assent in our everyday talk are quite at odds with what scientists tell us about the world. For example, some physicists deny the primacy of individuals and assert the primacy of fields in which there are only apparent individuals. This is at odds with what Strawson persuasively describes as the implicit metaphysics of ordinary English.[11] It would seem to follow that it is possible to overcome linguistic limits, and, therefore, that it is also possible to translate from one language to any other, provided that each is allowed to modify itself appropriately.

The other way of approaching the riddle of relativity and reality is to deny that languages have points of view. According to this theory, meanings do not exist, except insofar as they can be understood in terms of 'reference', the reference of a word being those objects which it truly describes. Such an austere position has been taken by W. V. Quine.[12] We could add, with Frege, that the reference of a word is determined by its sense, to obtain a less austere point of view which admits of something besides reference. Following Hintikka, we could take the meaning or sense of a word to be the class of its referents in every possible world.[13] In this way we allow for the possibility that expressions with the same reference can have different meanings. For though the actual objects referred to may be the same, they may well refer to different objects in worlds other than the actual one.

Such views have the charm of simplicity. This general approach is also one of the most precisely conceptualized theories available, and any adequate theory of meaning would perhaps have to incorporate such a view in some form or another. Yet, to understand meaning either as reference, or merely as something which yields reference as a function, is to ignore the simple fact that we can learn language. As it happens I am not acquainted with a single electron, nor with a single dolphin. Yet I know what the key words mean. How is this possible? Nor are there more than a handful of universal words in the English language whose entire reference classes are known to me. Does it follow that I know no universal words well enough to use them correctly? Nor do I know of any possible world other than ours, let alone *all* worlds. All of these views are epistemologically unsatisfactory, however pleasing they may be from a formal point of view.[14]

Language is a tool for understanding the world. But if we adopt the point of view of the formal semanticist, then it would be just as hard, or harder, to determine the meaning of any simple concrete statement, as it would be to determine the truth of any metaphysical statement, however abstract it may be.

What we should conclude from all this is that a study of language from a general point of view should be most rewarding, for no cut-and-dried answers to many interesting questions are available. While the short and undeveloped criticisms sketched above can be answered by any of the views sketched, they do suggest that a better view might emerge from a concentrated study of the many different problems.

But these problems, and the further problems that solutions to each of them generate, take us deeper and deeper into details which are difficult to synthesize effectively. This alone should justify an attempt to find one solution to all these different problems. I am also convinced, though by no means irrevocably so, that as a general solution the following view is superior to any of those sketched above.

My aim in the further introductory remarks that follow, however, is to sketch only as much of my own view as is necessary to orient the reader, who will find this position more carefully worked out later in the book.

C. Grammatical Change Due to Revolutions in Thought

When new ideas are proposed, we use language. There is no better way to convey ideas. So it comes as a surprise to find that some new ideas have changed the very language in which they are expressed. The phenomenon is surprising and needs to be elaborated before I can propose a statement and resolution of some puzzles about it.

When Einstein proposed his special theory of relativity, he introduced some radically new versions of the concepts of 'mass', 'velocity', 'length', and 'time'. We know about his revolutionary ideas concerning time. For example, we know that, according to this theory, a twin who travels rapidly in space will return to earth as a young man, thousands of years after the other twin has died. Each twin 'has his own time'. We know also that we can no longer speak of length—say the length of an object—absolutely, but must speak of it as relative to some coordinate system. Hence the *property* of being one foot long has now become the *relation* of being one foot long in a certain co-ordinate system.

We know this and we have learned to accept it. But there is a genuinely surprising aspect to such changes in our language if we think of the implication that Einstein's theory has for grammar. Once upon a time, if we asked 'How much does thirty miles per hour weigh for a hundredweight at the earth's surface?', we would have been asking a meaningless question. How can *speed* have *weight*? This is a 'category mistake', and a particularly blatant one at that. Every concept belongs to but one of many proper categories, and a meaningful sentence can combine expressions from different categories only in certain grammatically acceptable ways. For example, a verb is modified by an adverb, and not an adjective, as set out here.

But it is an astonishing fact that the question regarding the weight of thirty miles per hour is not only meaningful but has a perfectly good and computable answer!

Einstein's theory yields a very well-known equation—$E = mc^2$—which asserts that mass and energy are equivalent and hence interconvertible at a certain rate. But when a body's velocity increases by thirty miles per hour, this represents additional kinetic energy, which, when put into the equation, will give a certain equivalent mass. Any mass at the earth's surface, as we know, has weight, which can be calculated by applying the gravitational constant. So we can calculate the additional weight of thirty miles per hour when an object accelerates by that amount.[15]

One is tempted to suspect foul play here. Perhaps Einstein did not really mean to assert the *equivalence* of mass and energy, but something else. But as a matter of fact, we can find the mass of certain energies in the following way: take some particles and keep accelerating them, measuring their impact at greater and greater speeds. *The mass increases.* And even more spectacular is the conversion of mass to energy. Who in the mid-twentieth century has not heard of the atomic bomb, which uses just a little mass to create a lot of energy? In fact, though all of us know about nuclear energy generally, we do not comprehend all that is meant by the equivalence of mass and energy.

So we must agree that speeds have mass, no matter how violently this may clash with our intuition about the fitness of expressions. Nor is this the only departure from our grammatical intuitions that modern physics requires. Suppose I were to ask 'How often is that chair?' or 'How frequent is this desk?' You would have a right to be puzzled. How can a chair be often, a desk frequent? An adverb cannot modify a noun, but only a verb or an adjective.

Now if I had asked instead 'How frequent is that baby?' then there is little difficulty in framing an answer. 'Four times a day, doctor, and very painfully' would have been a good answer. That is because we know what the baby is doing, frequently. But how can a thing be 'often'—what could it possibly be *doing* as it exists? It turns out, however, that all matter has wavelike characteristics. What does this mean? Simply that all matter is a little bit like a cyclic happening, like a repeated refrain in a song. And matter, therefore, has a frequency or a rate of repetition—an idea first investigated by Louis de Broglie.

Physics, then, tells us that there is something called wave–particle duality. Few realize what a truly revolutionary idea this is. What does it mean? Simply this: that things sometimes behave like repetitious events, or "waves", and waves sometimes behave like things. One does not realize how peculiar this is until it is described in ordinary language: what one is really being told is that there is no fundamental difference between things and events— that there is no great difference between nouns and verbs. Hence, it *does* make sense for an adverb to modify a noun after all. Equally, some adjectives can meaningfully qualify some verbs. A chair is a little like an event after all. And my scribbling on this paper, which is an event, has substance, though perhaps not the substance that I intend it to have.

Of course, we do not have to speak thus. We can ignore science and speak as if we are unaware of what modern physics tells us. But does anyone have the foresight, or the temerity, to say that we shall never change our language and begin to utter such strange locutions? Two hundred years from now? Four thousand years from now? Perhaps one day we will not distinguish things from events by grammatical means, but will rely instead on explicit differentiation by conceptual means. An interesting question to raise is the following: Have any of the languages that we know today ever changed in response to an idea like the one we are here considering? Later I shall suggest that this has happened within historical record.

D. The Possibility of Change:
The Meaning of a Word is a Set of Theories

Let us look at some general questions which emerge, and which are quite puzzling. I shall divide the questions into two groups.

1. How is such change in language possible? If language alone can be used to communicate a theory, how can the theory change the very language that expresses it?

2. How can we possibly understand a new theory if even its language is new? This question is puzzling because:

(a) we would first need to understand the new language to understand the theory which is expressed in it, and

(b) it would seem that we also need first to understand the new theory before we can understand the modifications made in the language. This is paradoxical, as both of them cannot be first.

The central hypothesis which I shall propose to solve both these problems is this: *the meaning of a word is a set of theories.*

Usually one thinks of theories as they are expressed by sentences, which in turn are composed of words. And the words are supposed to have meanings, that is to say ideas, which are a little bit like Platonic forms. Such ideas can be understood or intuited directly, somehow.

Consider an alternative to this view. Consider for a moment that the building blocks of language are not words, with their respective sense, but rather that these building blocks are theories, or beliefs, or expectations— or something like that. Think of words or combinations of words which could form predicates as 'crystallizations' of theories, the meaning of each word being composed of a vast number of theories. Then we can think of a sound as attaching to some crystallization to form a meaningful word. Each meaningful sound can then combine with other meaningful sounds, or phrases, to form sentences in the usual way. Sentences will make sense according to the manner in which words are combined in them, following traditional word usage and grammar.

Let us consider a particular word, for example the word 'red'. What does this mean, in my view? It means a great many theories—every theory, in fact, which is expressed by sentences like 'If anything were red it would be F' (where F is some predicate or relation which we happen to believe, whether explicitly or implicitly). Thus, if I believe that anything red would anger a bull, then this is part of what I mean by red, even if the belief is quite mistaken. Also, if I am superstitious and believe mistakenly that red things bring me good luck on Thursdays, then this also is part of what I mean by the word 'red'. At the same time, what merely happens to be red, such as the fact that so–and–so is wearing a red necktie, is not usually part of what one means by the word 'red'.

The total meaning of the word 'red' will include a great many theories. The word, therefore, has somewhat different meanings for different people, even if they share a vast number of beliefs about red things, and, therefore, some common elements of the meaning.

In this view, each sentence expresses a theory. But all the beliefs expressed in all the sentences ever used by us are only the tip of the iceberg: the vast majority of theories are submerged in the meanings of words, and in the manner in which we traditionally combine them to form sentences. Imagine that a word does not have for its meaning any of the following:

1. an abstract something called an 'idea' for which the word stands (a fairly common view);
2. the uses to which the word can be put (Wittgenstein's theory);
3. the syntactic and other rules governing the use of the word (structuralist and Chomskian theories at one time).

Rather the meaning of a word would be something like this: the word would mean (for you) all those things that you believe would be true of anything were it to be truly described by the word in question.

How does this help us to solve the difficulties or puzzles which are raised by the change of meaning in language brought about by a theory of physics? Let us take the first of our two puzzles about language learning. How can a theory change the very language which is used to express it? This first question is puzzling because to state anything we must presuppose a language. And we cannot change it because we are presupposing it. Or so it seems.

The mechanism for effecting the change in language is a very simple one: when new theories are introduced, they can stand in logical relationships of various kinds to our older theories. For example, they can entail earlier theories. Or they can contradict them. Or they can be independent of them. Suppose we have a theory about matter which we believe to be the best solution to some puzzling problem in physics. We may, therefore, think that it is the best hypothesis available—especially if it makes startling predictions which turn out to be true. Such was the case when Einstein's theory was proposed.

A theory like this may well contradict an earlier theory, a deeply entrenched theory which is part of the meanings of our words, perhaps even presupposed in our grammatical categories. When such a situation arises, we see that something must give way. If we absolutely cannot find a better theory than Einstein's, then we must begin to accept the fact that our speech, our *everyday* speech, is obsolete. We may continue to speak as we do, but with a mental proviso that all this is only *a manner of speaking*. Strictly speaking, we would say, "this is not what I mean"—and then we would try to express ourselves by means of some new words and combinations of words. Thus new theories can bring forth changes in concepts because they *contradict* theories embedded in the meanings of old words. So, if meanings consist of theories, we can see how language can be influenced by theories: the mechanism is a logical one.

Let us turn to the second question: how can we understand a new theory if we first have to understand the meanings of the words whose meanings we cannot understand without first understanding the new theory? The answer is simple: we understand both in terms of problems. By studying the problem, or the intellectual purpose for which a theory is proposed, we can see why one may be obliged to adopt a very new position, once one finds that none of the familiar old theories are of much use. When we see how the new theory can solve such a difficult problem we shall also begin to understand how the meanings of contentious new words are to be understood. Thus to understand the meaning of physical words, we must study physical theories, and the problems or riddles that they are designed to solve. Similarly, to understand the jargon of economics we must understand some economics. And so on.

Those of us who first studied any subject from the kind of textbook which begins with definitions have experienced a sense of frustration over not understanding what the definitions were all about. But once we master a subject, it is not at all hard to read a book which begins with definitions. The reason for this is simply that technical definitions make sense only against a background of understanding which beginners do not, and cannot, have. In short, understanding the technical language of a subject requires that we understand its theories, and to understand its theories we need to understand the language: we understand both by looking for the problems which the theories solve by using the modified language.

We can learn a subject only by pulling ourselves up by our boot-straps. First, we understand the problem, for which we propose a theory; this gives us some new words; in these words we state a new problem; this problem is solved by a new theory; the new theory gives us some more technical language. And so on.

This account can be generalized to all language learning, for all language is learned in this manner. A child learns the meaning of all words just as a student at university learns the meaning of the technical words of his subject— all language-learning is closely bound up with learning about the world generally, and vice versa. Each stage in the understanding of the language is reached against a background of some general understanding. But as our language is enriched, so is our ability to understand yet more. And so theory and language are closely intertwined in learning. In fact, if I am right, language learning cannot be entirely separated from general cognitive development.

The everyday understanding of the world, which we take for granted as adults, must have once seemed as impossible as the most difficult concepts in an entirely alien subject seem to us now. At such a time, learning the appropriate point of view and the concepts associated with that view must have been analogous to studying economic theories and their technical terms for the first time (or any other subject for that matter).

A corollary of my view is this: before any language is learned a child must entertain theories. This might seem strange, if we think of children believing in theories like Einstein's theory of relativity. But by the word 'theory' here, I refer to all those *expectations* a child has, which it may be born with, or which it may acquire in the first year after birth, before or during the beginning of language-learning. Many of these expectations are independent of language at first, and perhaps some remain independent all through life. Such a background of expectations (theories) interacts with and infuses our language.

E. Conceptual Change: An Intellectual Evolution

So far, the issue we have dealt with has had to do mostly with the meanings of words, and how we learn them. But even our customary *usage* or word combinations reveal unsuspected theories trapped in them. Words which are closely and regularly associated mask certain expectations. For example, we speak of uncontrollable anger, but rarely of inanimate anger or unplugged anger, or intestate anger. Why? Because of the sort of thing we take anger to be: to speak of controlling it makes sense, but not of plugging it, or willing it to someone else after death. But we have seen how even grammatical categories, such as the difference between verbs and nouns, depend fundamentally on our understanding of the world. No doubt we do not always recognize this background of theory, at least not until an Einstein comes along to show us that we do have such an understanding by showing us that it is wrong. In other words, even the rules governing word usage which we call 'grammatical rules', such as the one distinguishing nouns from verbs, are not exempt from possessing a theoretical background. Even they mask hidden points of view, which we recognize, if at all, only after they are challenged by the growth of knowledge.

The discovery that grammatical structure presupposes a world-view was discovered by the great linguists-cum-anthropologists Edward Sapir and Benjamin Lee Whorf.[16] When he studied the Hopi language Whorf found that there was an enormous gap between the point of view presupposed by this language and the one we are used to in English or French.

He showed how, to take one example among many, Hopi tenses are different from ours and so exhibit a different conception of time. He also showed how Hopi understanding of plurals differs from our own. He even noticed that the distinction between verbs and nouns, or between words and sentences, applies only to some languages, and not, as we might think, to all languages.

Benjamin Lee Whorf came to agree fully with Sapir on this aspect of language, and in one of his famous papers even took the following statement of Sapir's as his motto.[17]

> Human beings do not live in the objective world alone, nor alone in the world of social activity as ordinarily understood, but are very much at the mercy of the particular language which has become the medium of

expression of their society. It is quite an illusion to imagine that one adjusts to reality essentially without the use of language and that language is merely an incidental means of solving specific problems of communication or reflection. The fact of the matter is that the "real world" is to a large extent built up out of the language habits of the group. . . . We see and hear and otherwise experience very largely as we do because the language habits of our community predispose certain choices of interpretation.

The grammar of a language depends on presupposed theories. But we must not think that grammar is simply an expression of the latest world view. A language often has grammatical structures which may depend upon views long discarded. Thus gender, or tenses, may well reveal a point of view which none of us accepts today. Such grammatical forms, like the lapels on our coats, or like our neckties, or our habit of shaking hands, were once perfectly meaningful, but have since become dysfunctional and in turn have since acquired new functions. In short, grammar can be either the expression of our basic categories, or, more usually, *the scars left within language by the old revolutions in our thought.*

What this last suggestion amounts to is that meanings, grammar, and other structural features of language must be understood historically, or in terms of the evolution of language. In itself, there is nothing new about such a view. Since the nineteenth century it has been a commonplace to regard language as a product of grammatical evolution. If there is anything in my proposal that is new, it is simply this: in the history or evolution of language the active and progressive element is, and always has been, intellectual endeavour. The concepts of our language, the grammatical structure evident in it, and the customary combinations of words we find in it, are all the product of intellectual effort. That is my view. Let us look at some other views.

Some regard language as a game in which we passively follow certain conventions or rules. Some regard language as an activity in which we conform to established word usage in order to do socially functional things. Some regard language as an activity in which we imitate our elders passively, sometimes stupidly, and often unsuccessfully. Some regard language as an organism which evolves in accordance with its own principles. Some regard language as a behaviour which is natural and genetically determined, as blossoming is to a flowerbud. And so on.

All such views either see our own function in language as a basically passive one, or else they deny the separate reality of language. Language happens to us. We merely follow rules, or blossom forth, or whatever. Or else there is no independent or autonomous thing like language, but just verbal behaviour, or just 'intentionality'. The trouble with all such views—and this includes every theory of language available—is that they cannot even explain how a marvellously complex language like English or Konkani could possibly have come into existence.

For it is quite impossible that a complex social institution like the English language could have sprung up suddenly out of nothing. Imagine that someone suddenly learnt how to speak when no one else around her did. Who would she tell about her discovery? No one would expect speech, or understand it, and so there could be no linguistic communication. The discovery would die with the discoverer. Thus, language, when it was first invented, and at every stage as it became more complex, has needed our active involvement for its modification. Moreover, we must play with language in order to understand each other's attempted modifications.

The evolution of language must therefore be one in which we have constantly risen above language as we have tried to master it and to use it to understand the world. Although we are products of the past, and of our traditions in particular, we rise above language by our very attempt to use it to understand the world. At the same time, we are not able to do without it. We have to fall back on language to make ourselves clear to each other.

F. *Conclusion*

How can different individuals learn the same complex language of infinite (potential) size if they have only finite evidence, which, moreover, does not coincide? As Chomsky suggests it is the fact that we have similar innate equipment, together with a similar linguistic environment, that leads to our possession of similar languages. But, unlike Chomsky, we need not postulate the existence of a miraculous universal grammar. Rather, our understanding of language is *approximate*. I do not believe that we ever do understand the *same* languages, but only *largely similar* ones. This, of course, raises the question of how people with different but similar languages can communicate. The solution to this mystery will be left for a later chapter.

How can we escape the absolute presuppositions of our own language? Of course this question is important if we are ever to solve the problem by the solution to the third problem above. If two people can transcend their languages, then they may be able to understand each other even if their languages are not exactly the same.

In my view, transcending the presuppositions of the language is far from extraordinary: it is commonplace. *Every child learning a language is constantly transcending the presupposed views of its own language.* The key to this process is the peculiar ability of a language to allow us to entertain views which are contrary to its own presuppositions. The means by which this is accomplished is the institutionalization of forms of speech, divorcing them somewhat from their original significance. It is this which allows us to transcend our languages, to understand each other.

These problems, the sketch of my views, and the sketch of my solution to the problems, are only introductory, and are intended to orient, so that the reader is not lost when matters of detail are taken up.

2
The Desiderata for a Theory of Language

A. Four Desiderata for a Theory of Language

What would we require of a good theory of the growth of language? For every discipline that deals with language, the criteria for an adequate theory are different. There are many disciplines in which the study of language figures prominently, such as anthropology, logic, sociology, aesthetics, literary criticism, philosophy, to name a few. But the riddles or problems that prompt this study do not fall squarely into any one of these subjects, nor into a simple combination of them. Neither does it fall within linguistics, at least as it has been studied so far. Let me begin, therefore, by laying down some *desiderata* for a good theory of the growth of language which may serve as a point of departure. Later, as we see what difficulties we face in meeting these desiderata, we will have to recognize and meet more desiderata. The first set of four desiderata which have been chosen are closely related to the two riddles which prompted this study of language, discussed in the previous chapter. The other two riddles, and many other besides, will emerge in the course of the book. These desiderata are therefore central to what follows.

A satisfactory theory of the growth of language must fulfil at least the following four desiderata:

1. It must show how it is possible for linguistic innovations to improve the expressive capabilities of a language over time.

2. It must identify the limits of innovation in language, and the breakdown that would occur if innovation goes too far.

3. It must identify the force which impels the changes in language, or prevents its stagnation at a certain level of expressive capability.

4. It must lay bare the mechanisms by which changes in languages are brought about, and lay bare the structures of languages upon which the mechanisms can work at different times.

Let us see why these are important for a theory of the growth of language, and what prompts us to consider them.

B. First Desideratum

We know that all languages, with the possible exception of languages that have 'died', are constantly changing.[1] For one thing, we have a historical record of changes in languages as they were spoken and written. For another, we know of new fashions in speech and writing which have occurred in our own lifetimes. That there are changes taking place in our language, especially phonetic changes, is well known. But there is also another kind of change which is constantly occurring in language which is not as easily recognized. This is a process of change in *the expressive power or capability* of the language. Let me first argue for the thesis that languages do have expressive capabilities and limits, and that these change. Thereafter the point of several of the desiderata will become clear.

i. The Growth of Expressive Capabilities in Children

Let me begin with what is nowadays a commonplace: languages are in some sense of the word conventional.[2] One does not speak English or Hindi or Spanish because one is born with the ability to speak that very language and no other. One learns the language of the community in which one is brought up. Any child born of parents from one linguistic community who is brought up in another will learn the language of the latter and not that of his forefathers. Learning linguistic conventions, which starts at a very young age and continues all through life with decreasing intensity, is a necessity if the language is to be spoken. Without the conventions there is nothing like a human language to be spoken. All this is trite, but it points to something of interest. It points to the fact that an individual's language can have some, and lack other, expressive capabilities.

Nothing is clearer to see than the difficulty that a child between the ages of two and four years has when it tries to speak of issues which are beyond it. Other children and adults will often be able to make out what is intended, but not always. In any case the child will not be able to convey shades and subtleties of meaning. A great many expressions which are a commonplace among elders are incomprehensible to a child. The child lacks concepts as well as grammatical and syntactic understanding. Since the concepts and grammar differ from community to community, we can call these items conventions. So what the child lacks is conventions, though this not all that it lacks. Without having learned these conventions there is a *dearth in the expressive capability* of the language of the child. It is only in comparison with the language of adults, of course, that the language lacks expressive capability.

At a certain age a child learns to ask and understand questions of the form 'What is this?' and to understand answers to them. A little later it learns the 'why' of things. Each of these is an example of the changing expressive capability of the child. No doubt, when a child learns to ask and answer questions of the form 'Why is this so?' the child has not only learnt a linguistic convention and improved its ability to express itself; it has also learnt something about the world around it. But these two are not necessarily incompatible. The question may be raised, of course, whether there is a real improvement in expressive skills, even though it seems obvious that there is one. Could it not be solely the child's understanding of the world which is improving?

There are two clues which indicate that definite skills are being learnt. There are the mistakes made in learning which indicate that there are linguistic skills involved, and there is the behaviour during and immediately after the learning which indicates that linguistic skills have been learnt. Children of around two years of age usually learn to ask "why?" long before they full understand the question. Typically they will ask the question in circumstances which make the question inappropriate, or meaningless. At first a question of this form is learnt by imitating the parents or other children, and is used largely for one of two purposes: to evoke a response, any response; or as a stopgap expression to delay some action or to cover up embarrassment or confusion. The question does not make sense from a conventional linguistic point of view. Here is a conversation with my daughter when she was under two years of age which illustrates what I mean: Me: "Why don't you pull it and see?" Daughter: "That one?" (indicating a lead worn by a strange but obviously friendly dog). Me: "Yes, pull the dog's lead." Never having heard the expression "lead" before, and not being sure of the dog's reaction to such an action, daughter: "Why is the dog's lead?"

Soon afterwards when she began to understand a bit more about why-questions she would ask why-questions correctly, but would routinely answer such questions with "because I am tired". This answer was probably picked up from someone's response to her question, and was used as an obvious reply which seemed at least appropriate. Still later, she learnt to reply "because" (without completing the reason). By this time she herself asked the question appropriately, but I was dubious as to whether she wanted the right answer, or just the satisfaction of a response. On at least one occasion when I tested her to see what she wanted, I found her to be impatient with inappropriate answers, or with "because" for an answer. When I made a long statement beginning with "because" in reply, however, she was happy, even though it had no bearing on her question. All these pieces of evidence, which can easily be tested with other children at appropriate stages of development, clearly suggest that the child is involved with learning linguistic skills from its social environment long before it can use them to make any cognitive gains.

A much surer clue to show that a skill has been learnt comes after the initial learning, when the child repeatedly asks questions of the same form. The question at this stage is meaningful, but pointless and inappropriate. Each of us has come across the child which makes a nuisance of itself by asking the why question of everything that it can think of, however irrelevant under the circumstances. This is a form of *funktionslust*, or the love of exercising a skill, especially a newly-learnt one.[3] This need for exercise is a sure sign of a skill not only in children but in all animals and among adult human beings also. A puppy running excitedly back and forth is exercising its newly-combined motor skills. A mathematician who has mastered a new technique feels a great need to find applications for it. How many new students of computer science or computers fail to see the world as full of computers or computable systems? Thus we see that the *funktionslust* exhibited by the child is similarly a clue to its having just learnt a linguistic skill.

These considerations may seem to belabour the point. But once it is granted that children have to improve the expressive capabilities of their language, then there is not much to accepting that the language spoken by an adult, and even a language as such (e.g., English) has expressive capabilities and limits.

The most obvious case of differing expressive capabilities in the language of adults lies in their command of jargon, for example that of an intellectual discipline. Some of us understand the language of economics but not that of geology, while others may find geologists comprehensible but not logicians. The same is also true of nontechnical discourse though it may be harder to spot. Some tell stories better than others; others may evoke pathos best of all; yet others may present their own views succinctly and powerfully. We are also receptive in different degrees to the language used by others—this being one of those factors which determine our 'taste' in literature.

ii. Difference in Expressive Capabilities of Languages and the Conventional Nature of Language

What about a language itself? No doubt each one of us possesses a different range of expressions. We may still speak the same language. What about the expressive capability of this language itself which each of us can only partially command? It is not a straightforward matter to decide on the basis of what we have said that a language itself can be said to possess expressive capabilities and limits. Many would find it an obscurantist claim to say that there may be a great many things which are simply not expressible in English. A language is a flexible instrument. There is a great deal of room for its use in new and ingenious ways to say what might have been thought inexpressible.

Benjamin Lee Whorf found that the precise meaning of Hopi statements can not often be caught in English. But his papers, which are in English, are able to display the usual character of Hopi grammar and syntax from the Indo-European linguistic point of view. This makes us question the very claim which Whorf has so brilliantly illustrated. If Whorf can illustrate in English the very different expressive capability of Hopi, then is there not some hope that with ingenuity we may be able to render it in English after all? We could make use of lengthy paraphrase and use explanations and footnotes, if necessary. It must be said on behalf of Whorf's hypothesis, however, that there is certainly a difference in the degree of difficulty involved in translating from different languages. There are also variations in the degree of difficulty in translating different pieces from the same language. An adequate literal translation and an adequate literary translation may be very different. Translations from Omar Khayyam and from Chinese poetry into English have to be unfaithful to the original if they are also to be as elegant in English as in the original, except in rare instances. Translating Voltaire into English can be managed with considerably greater faithfulness to both literal and literary features of the original.

A rough measure of the difference in the expressive capability of the language of two writings might be the number of lengthy paraphrases and explanations which are necessary to explain the meaning of the original. By this measure we can judge how much further our language is from the Greek of Heraclitus, Parmenides, or Empedocles than it is from the Greek of a post-Aristotelian intellectual.

The question which remains is this: is the difference in expressive capability simply a difference in the difficulty in intertranslation or is the latter only a measure of the former? Are there also definite limits to the expressive powers of languages, and do these differ from language to language? Unfortunately, it is not easy to settle this question by a mere inspection. The best test case to decide this issue by inspection might be a comparison between the Greek before Plato and modern French, English, or German. Is it possible to understand something of Parmenides' meaning from translations? Is there some part of the meaning which is lost, or which must be lost? Here there appears a great difficulty. Even the most careful scholars of Classical Greek, scholars who spend years studying both the language and the text of Parmenides, cannot agree about what exactly Parmenides' view is. For this reason the test is inconclusive, even though every classicist will avow that without understanding the language of the original one could not even appreciate many of the differences of interpretation. What is true in this case would seem to be true of any test case into which enough effort has been spent in the attempt to translate faithfully. If we are to judge the issue about expressive capability we shall have to look elsewhere for a clue.

There is an abstract argument which allows us to decide this issue. This argument does not depend on any actual comparison of languages. It yields the conclusion that a language at any one time must have expressive limits and capabilities but it does not identify what these may be for any language. The argument starts from the commonplace that *every human language presupposes social conventions.*

English, Hindi, and Spanish differ from each other not only in the different sounds used, and in different meanings attached to the sounds, but also in the different manners in which semantically equivalent sounds might be used in combination. Let us overlook the question, for the moment, of what exactly these conventions are which govern a language. Whatever governs the forms and combinations of a language is not determined biologically, or in some other natural manner. It is open to change by us. We could, for example, use the written expression 'pain' to signify bread or what it ordinarily signifies in English. We could also signify bread by an entirely different sound without precedent, like 'thunderstorm', if we made it clear to our audience that we wish to do so. This is why there can be a code language between parties who wish their messages to be kept secret from every one else who might have access to their communications. Slang is often a substitution of new expressions for old ones in this manner. The existence and proliferation of slang is a constant reminder that languages embody social conventions in the sense that concerns us. The simple and equally trite fact that we are lost in an alien linguistic community is also an indication that our languages are social products, whose conventions we need to learn.

We proceed with the argument.

iii. The Improvement of Expressive Capabilities over Time and the Conventional Nature of Language

Any human language embodies social conventions, and is not entirely given to us by a god or determined by our genes. Since we have been on earth only a finite time, our language also must have had a beginning. But what sort of beginning could language have had? It is immediately obvious that it could not have begun with all the complex and difficult conventions which govern the meaning, syntax, and grammar of any language known today. For just imagine: if such a system were to be proposed, no one would be able to understand it. The case is analogous to that of a visitor to a new land: he cannot understand the language naturally. Nor can one learn English by having the conventions recited at once—in English! In the beginning everyone was a foreigner to every language.

A social convention, such as one underlying a language, does not help establish communication between individuals unless all those individuals understand the convention. Therefore language could not have emerged as a whole, like Pallas Athena emerging fully formed from Zeus. Whatever complex and subtle conventional systems ultimately came to stay must have begun as the simplest kind of convention. It is not difficult to imagine that once a certain level of complexity is reached, then one could fall back on existing conventions to establish, or propose, or test a new convention, or even to be aware of the need for a new one. The existing conventions can establish a communication which can act as a springboard for further enrichment of linguistic conventions. Imagine trying to learn an entirely new language for the first time. How helpful it is to have a guide who can speak your own tongue. The pre-existing conventions are like the common tongue which help all of us to understand the new conventions.

Let us continue with the example of second language learning. Anyone who has tried to make his way in a second language feels at first a great disadvantage in not understanding the subtleties of idiom as well as those in the mother tongue. It takes many years to be able to make use of intricacies of a new language, to express shades of thoughts and feelings which come easily to the native speaker. How better can we describe this state of affairs than by saying that one's second language lacks some expressive capabilities? These expressive capabilities will be part of one's language only after certain necessary linguistic conventions are understood. Imagine, then, a time when these necessary conventions did not yet exist. There must surely have been such a time, since every social convention must have a beginning. How better can we describe this earlier language than to say that it lacked certain expressive capabilities?

Each successive stage in the evolution of a language, when compared to a later stage, must be seen as limited in its expressive power. To deny this is to assert that language could have begun all at once. Such an assertion would not be compatible with the fact that language is a complex social conventional institution. But once we accept the gradualism that is forced upon us, we can even make a plausible conjecture about the rate of growth of linguistic complexity: since the existence of conventions helps to establish more conventions which we can all learn, it follows that the rate of growth of linguistic complexity must be on the average (or roughly) a geometrical progression—that is to say, the more it grows, the more it is capable of growing. The more expressive it is, the more quickly it can improve its expressiveness. For example, a language in which one cannot now describe features of languages will certainly not grow as fast as one that is able to express something about itself and about language in general.

We need not ask at this stage whether language is still growing. The presumption is that it is, since one can think of no reason to suppose that it has changed its character recently. But we can postpone this question. It is enough to note for now that any human language must have had a long history of gradual change. In this history there must have been constant innovations until language acquired the complexity that it presently has. Language is so complex that it takes many years to master its rudiments, and it is only partially mastered by any individual.

This argument can be put more tightly, if less simply, in the following manner, which I reproduce for the reader's convenience.[4] We must first satisfy ourselves that when fundamental theories change, meanings do also, and to state precisely in what way.

Let every extant expression of English which may be a predicate expression in some sentence of the language be called an 'atomic predicate' (of English). This is a finite list. We could use the Oxford English Dictionary, for example, as the lexicon. Consider every predicate which is atomic or which can be defined by using atomic predicates (a 'molar' predicate). The class of molar predicates will include at least all the truth–functional definitions of more complex predicates, so that it is at least denumerably infinite. Other methods of definition, which we cannot specify in a natural language, may also generate molar predicates. Let us call the class of molar predicates of English which is closed under all definitional operations at time t, the 'semantic field' of English at t. The semantic field of English at time t, then, is a class of meaningful predicates of the language. But is the class of meaningful predicate expressions in English greater than the semantic field?

Let us call all predicate expressions which fall outside of the semantic field 'problematic expressions'. Then we can study the question of meaning change more precisely by asking if there is any reason to believe that (a) there are problematic expressions which are meaningful and (b) they arise in the context of theorizing. Since the class of molar predicates has not been adequately determined (because we have allowed unspecified definitional operators in the definition of a semantic field), it may be impossible to say of any given concept at time t whether it is a molar predicate or a problematic expression. A discussion of cases is therefore of no value. We can, however, use some abstract considerations to guide us.

Languages presuppose social conventions. If we understand each other to any degree of sophistication, then it is because we share the conventions (e.g., the "idiom") of some linguistic tradition. The argument for believing that social conventions are necessary for language—in some sense of the word "convention"—lies in the existence of a diversity of languages. These languages are not genetically determined in us. A child from one language community can learn to speak the language of another community, with proper exposure. Moreover, learning a new language involves at least learning how others communicate—that is to say, learning the conventions of that community. A great many conventions have to be mastered over a period of years before one acquires that facility in a new language which one has in one's mother tongue. So the semantic field at one's command depends upon the social conventions that one has learnt.

Social conventions, being socially and not genetically determined, must have a beginning in time. The reason is that according to the neo-Darwinian conception of the descent of man, man had a beginning in time, and therefore, so must have had human social conventions. It follows that the semantic field of English has grown gradually to its present proportions. Since this can only happen if the semantic field at time t_i is smaller than the field at time t_{i+n}, for some $_i$, it follows that new expressions are added to the semantic field from time to time.

C. Innovations

The expressive capabilities of our languages must have improved gradually. It must be the case that languages can grow in this fashion. Yet it is incredible that they do so, or even that they can do so. Let us see why.

i. Innovations Contravene Conventions

For a language to grow, or to change in any basic way, some of its conventions must change. But these conventions cannot be put into words. We might at best name a few of the many conventions governing an expression, whether they be old or new. Even this would take years of study. No one can expect all the conventions to be stated explicitly. And even if that were possible, it would still be irrelevant. A concept or a syntactic or grammatical device need not be said to be unknown to a person just because the person cannot recite the rules governing its use. All the conventions governing a language are implicit, in the normal course of events. A person may even recite the wrong rule for an expression while continuing to use it correctly. These facts, together with a plausible hypothesis about meaningfulness, leads to the paradoxical conclusion that it is impossible for languages to grow.

Let us assume for this argument that the following plausible hypothesis about meaningfulness is true: in any language only those expressions have meaning which are given meaning by conventions (implicitly) agreed upon by communicants; and these expressions have only that meaning which the agreed–upon conventions impart to them. It follows that a new expression in a language lacks meaning because it is new. (Or else, if any new expression is meaningful, then sense and nonsense cannot be distinguished.) A new use for an old expression is a misuse of the language. Of course the new word will become meaningful and an old word will acquire a new meaning if the agreed upon conventions are modified. But neither the modifications, nor the old conventions governing the expressions, can be stated. It follows that a new expression or a new use of an old expression must not be used by people who wish to talk sense. If they ignore this rule, then we can conclude that they literally talk nonsense.

Somehow, the very social agreement which makes language possible seems to rule out changes in language. How can there be a changing social agreement? If there is a change, then there must be a lack of agreement. To that extent there must be a breakdown in communication. Let me argue this.

ii. Innovations are Necessary but Impossible

There are two possibilities: either a social change occurs for many, simultaneously, or it starts with one and spreads slowly. First, it is impossible for there to be a simultaneous change in everyone's language. If everyone leaps into the unknown, what coordinates the leap so that there is a new social agreement and not chaos? The innovation must come from one individual, who then gets every one else to adopt the innovation. Second, the new sentences of an individual are literally nonsense in social terms. How can one person persuade a whole community to speak nonsense with him or her when there exists a perfectly good language which each person has not yet even fully mastered? Nor can linguistic innovations by individuals be encouraged. If all of us each made a few innovations, and did not agree to accept some standard or paradigm, then in our effort to innovate we would have destroyed many of the most useful features of the system of communication which is language (namely, conventions). Novelty for the sake of novelty would reduce language to the state of modern art. Communication would be restricted to, at best, small elite groups. If there remained a semblance of communication between them, it would have to be transient and uncertain. The opposite is true of language. This shows that there must be a stable conventional agreement which underlies our language and which we guard by discouraging innovations. It is the individual who is obliged to conform to social norms and not vice versa. So the leap into the unknown which cannot be taken by many of us together also cannot be taken by individuals one by one. Therefore it follows that it can not be taken at all!

There are some similarities between this and a problem in psycholinguistics. A child learns social conventions of a language even though they are never explained. Before the conventions are understood, the respective expressions lack meaning. What is the cognitive process by which expressions acquire meaning? No one would deny the difficulty of this question in psycholinguistics. But our problem of the change of conventional agreements is even more difficult. In the case of the child, there is a social standard which has to be internalised. The standard already exists in the form of successful communication. In the case of the innovator, it is the successful communication which has to be abandoned to accommodate the idiosyncrasies of an individual. Since all of us are, from childhood, learning to master our language, while this mastery is never to be perfected, the situation is curiously like parents learning to babble with the child all their lives, instead of the child learning to speak.

This difficulty is even bleaker than it appears to be. For we must accommodate not only changes in language but *a growth in expressive capability*. We are not concerned with changes in conventions of a superficial kind. There could be, for example, phonetic changes over a period of time, precisely because children do not learn the speech of their parents exactly. Little modifications could well add up to a very new dialect, with new sounds substituting for old ones. But this is not a description of what happens when there is *a growth in expressive capability*. This growth cannot be identified with an aimless and largely incidental phonetic change or "semantic drift", to use Sapir's term.

Yet, as we have seen, the growth must have occurred for language to exist in its present form. This then is why the first desideratum must be satisfied by any theory which attempts to account for the growth of language. *It must show how it is possible that there are linguistic innovations which facilitate a gradual improvement in the expressive capability of a language.*

D. Second Desideratum

i. Limits of Innovations must be Identified

This second desideratum derives its importance from considerations closely related to the ones we have just considered.

The very fact that linguistic conventions are the basis of communication makes them resistant to change. However, change in the conventions must be possible. But if one uses expressions by unilaterally changing the conventions, then this leads not to a change in the agreed–upon conventions, but to a misinterpretation of the message itself. To utter an ordinary sentence with the intention of expressing something quite novel is to run the risk of being taken to mean the ordinary thing. To use entirely new expressions, or new combinations of old ones in an unconventional manner, is to run the risk of being obscure.

Though innovations must occur, these must be chosen by some process which prevents the language from degenerating to the point that communication breaks down. Innovations must therefore have limits and those innovations which go beyond these limits must be irreconcilable with the language. These limits would constitute criteria for meaningfulness. It is necessary to identify these if we are to understand why language grows as it does. This is the second desideratum. An adequate theory *must identify the limits of innovation and the breakdown that would occur if these were exceeded.* It would be a mistake, however, to treat this simply as a criterion of meaningfulness, as this concept has been understood among philosophers.

ii. Russell's Theory of Meaninglessness

The question of the meaningfulness of expressions has been central and crucial to many modern philosophical schools and movements, largely because of Bertrand Russell's influence on professional philosophers in this century.[5] Philosophers in some of these schools have followed Russell, perhaps with a few reservations, while others have opposed him by proposing other criteria of meaningfulness. Russell's special interest in the study of meanings stemmed from his desire to show that mathematics can be grounded in logic, which he took to include a theory of classes. To deal with certain paradoxes generated by the theory of classes, he began entertaining the hypothesis that apparent paradoxes arise in sentences that are literally meaningless. This is one possible way of getting rid of statements whose truth could be proved by assuming their falsity, and whose falsity could also be proved by assuming their truth. If they are meaningless, or ill-formed, then the question of their having logical consequences should not arise. Wittgenstein, in his early writings, was also inspired by the idea of using an analysis of meanings to dissolve many paradoxes which otherwise would have proved troublesome. He sought, in fact, to distinguish legitimate intellectual endeavours, like science and mathematics, from illegitimate activities (a category in which he included philosophy) which seemed to derive their inspiration from insoluble riddles arising from paradoxes of some sort. Russell's work in this area inspired a whole school of philosophy—logical positivism. Logical positivists took seriously the analysis of meanings, using it as a tool to dispel all those theories and theoretical concerns which they believed to be spurious or illegitimate. They took to constructing languages, or preparing for their construction, in such a way that the possibility of illegitimate intellectual activity was ruled out.

The crux of all these theories was a kind of empiricism—the doctrine that words must acquire meanings by virtue of their relation to what is observed or what is observable.[6] However, no theory of meanings in terms of observations and observables has been successful, even by these empiricists' own admission. Many logical positivists and some of their friends were great critics of their own and other empiricists' criteria of meaningfulness, and of meaning. Such an enlightened policy facilitated a quick appreciation of the difficulties inherent in this entire program, and today a great many philosophers who would privately support an empiricist theory of meaning are nevertheless, in practice, severe critics of any existing theory of this kind.

To the extent that the second desideratum requires some criterion of meaningfulness, it will be met by a theory like those made famous by the logical positivists. But there are two respects in which the attempts of the positivists differ from what we require. The first difference concerns the emphasis on the relationship between language and observables. There is no requirement that meaningfulness should have exclusively to do with observation. This freedom in stating the second desideratum becomes necessary if we are to avoid the pitfalls of *radicalism*. This brings me to the second respect in which what the second desideratum asks for differs from the criteria of the logical positivists. The desideratum is *developmental* rather than *radical* in character. These terms will soon become clearer.

The logical positivists were looking for a criterion which would enable them to construct a meaningful language which could not be used for metaphysical purposes—they were looking for a foundation for scientific language, for the roots of a rational language which are absolute. The second desideratum presupposes that the relevant criteria arise from the existing linguistic situation, irrespective of its foundations. In this respect it is more like Wittgenstein's approach to meanings as it appears in his later writings, as indicated below.

iii. Wittgenstein's Later Theory of Meaninglessness

It appears that the difficulties with his earlier theories in the *Tractatus* prompted Wittgenstein to become a severe critic of some of his own earlier views. These critical pieces have been posthumously published. They are inspired by the conviction that (in my words) meanings are to be understood in terms of the existing linguistic tradition in a society. For Wittgenstein, meanings are given by *usage*. This point of view has much in common with functionalism in anthropology. Malinowski and E. E. Evans-Prichard made anthropologists aware of the extent to which apparently senseless behaviour among members of an alien society makes excellent sense when one interprets it in terms of the *function* of this behaviour in the society under observation. Russell's charge that, from a logical point of view, much in English is irrational, can be met by Wittgenstein's linguistic functionalism. Apparently irrational aspects of English do play a valuable role in our saying what we say. Wittgenstein's students and those influenced by him are like functional anthropologists studying English-speaking society who concentrate on the language, giving us a functional rationale for its apparently irrational elements.

The difference between Wittgenstein's two approaches to language can best be understood in terms of political theory. There is a point of view called 'radicalism' according to which a rational society would be one in which all existing institutions and traditions are uprooted and a new society built upon entirely new roots. All the new institutions would have to be fully just and justified. No custom would be allowed to remain merely because it happened to be there. Such for example was the hope which inspired the French Revolution, and many Utopian revolutions before and after. By contrast, the conservative point of view denies that it is possible for any society or institution to be organized in this manner. If we attempt to eradicate all traditions, conservatives maintain, we will only fall back on other ones—worse ones. Society can not be *constructed* by us along any principles, whether rational or not.

Wittgenstein's later view finds itself at the *conservative* end of this theoretical spectrum, while the views of the logical positivists and also of Wittgenstein when he wrote his *Tractatus* are at the *radical* end. Perhaps it is not so surprising that Bertrand Russell, who was a great political radical all his life, felt that Wittgenstein was deserting rationalism in his later writings.

Wittgenstein's conservatism with respect to language is very close to what the second desideratum presupposes. Nevertheless his views, even if properly formulated, will not meet the desideratum. For Wittgenstein's views are too conservative! If the meanings of words are determined by their usage, then a new way of using a word is meaningless.[7] If every word is fixed by its usage in this respect, then language cannot grow. We can also turn this into a refutation of the view which seeks to explain meanings solely in terms of usage: if there was once no human language, (a plausible assumption which I need not defend again) then there was a first time that every word, phrase and grammatical or syntactic device was used. At that time its meaning could not have been determined by usage, since it had no usage. But each expression must have had some meaning the very first time it was used, or it would not have been generally adopted. Hence there must be more to meaning than usage.

Those philosophers who like to think of themselves as analytical often judge meanings in terms of a Wittgensteinian criterion. That is to say, they conclude that a word has been used illegitimately if they are able to show that it is not normally used in quite that way. Wittgenstein seemed to have remained convinced to the end that philosophical problems arise out of the misuse of words. He changed his mind about what constitute the criteria for the use of words, but not about *what they ruled out*. This is another important respect in which Wittgenstein's theory and the second desideratum diverge: if we are to accept evolutionism with respect to language, then we cannot rule out the meaningfulness of an expression in an absolute manner. The criterion of meaning sets limits on how far innovation can go, but it does not rule out innovations, including philosophical or other intellectual innovations which might involve new uses of language.

The second desideratum therefore cannot be fulfilled by a theory which is radical, nor can it be fulfilled by a conservative theory which, like functionalism in anthropology, makes no proper allowance for evolution and growth.[8]

E. Third and Fourth Desiderata

Language is a social phenomenon. Communication is perhaps its main function. To the extent that people wish to communicate, they must conform to each other's ways of using expressions. To the extent that there are deviations from socially understood norms of speech, there is failure in communication. Let us call this feature of language *the conservative principle in language*. Its strength has been fully appreciated by Wittgenstein and those whom he has influenced.

At the same time we must accept the fact that language grows. Precisely because language employs or presupposes complex *social* conventions, it could not have come about suddenly. Its growth must be gradual and sustained. Therefore, corresponding to the conservative principle in language, there must be a countervailing force which impels change. The more convinced we are of the conservative character of language, the more convincing is the case for a *progressive principle* in language. The third desideratum requires us *to identify the force which impels changes in language*.

We are now looking at languages in one sweep—from the moment they began to this moment. When we consider the matter from such a general point of view, we see that developing complexity and increasing expressive capability must be factors of some importance in the evolution of man. Otherwise it would be impossible to understand why an institution such as language survives and even grows in every human society that exists. The progressive principle must be closely related to the adaptation of human beings to their environment.

This Darwinian aspect of the third desideratum makes it both easier and more difficult to study the growth of language. The study is more difficult because the subtle but rigorous logic of the neo-Darwinian theory of evolution makes it difficult to find easy solutions to many of our problems. On the other hand, it does afford us a method with which to study the growth of language. Where there are many possible solutions to our problems, or where our criteria for selecting between candidates is otherwise poor, here the set of criteria which neo-Darwinism provides is a welcome addition. For with these additional criteria it is so much easier to rule out alternatives which might otherwise consume much time and effort.

The progressive principle and the conservative principle should together provide a framework within which it is possible to explain the gradual but sustained growth of language.[9] The conservative principle has already been identified as the necessity to communicate, which is always present wherever there is a human language. It remains to identify the progressive principle with some other feature of language which is equally ubiquitous and which is also of evolutionary significance. But to do so would still not be enough. Our understanding would remain very schematic. Since languages grow, and the growth is necessary to support further growth in the case of expressive capabilities, the manner in which language is acted upon by the ubiquitous principles would be different at different times. It becomes imperative therefore to study the interaction between the two principles in a language.

This is, of course, the fourth desideratum for an adequate theory of the growth of language. It is by far the most difficult one to fulfil, because it is best satisfied after we have learnt a great number of details about a history that we are unable to inspect. This desideratum demands that an adequate theory *exhibit the mechanisms by which languages change and identify the structures of languages upon which the mechanisms can work at different times.*

3
The Structure of Language and the Limits of Innovation

A. The Nature of Meaning

i. Introduction

The evolution of language, which has caught our attention, is such a broad topic that were we not to force ourselves away from its interesting ramifications we would soon get lost in the mist which surrounds it. Unfortunately, much of the mist connected with the evolution of language has to do with the evolution of its semantics. It is extremely difficult to understand how communication is possible between human beings who are innovative. This is especially so if the innovation concerns their language.

The distinctive theory that is being proposed in this and in the following chapter, as a possible solution to some of these problems, is a double theory of meaning: each word or phrase has two semantic items associated with it (quite apart from *reference*) which are often conflated and called 'the meaning of a word or phrase', or 'the sense of a word or phrase'. One of these I shall call the 'total' meaning of a word or phrase. It is something very volatile, changing with each intellectual situation. An aspect of a part of this total meaning will be called the 'restricted' meaning of a word. It is the other entity associated with a word and is not only much more stable than the 'total meaning', but is also an entity that depends more clearly on context and, at times, on explicit convention. Both these meanings can change from speaker to speaker, from time to time. We shall see how having these two semantic tools facilitates an understanding of linguistic innovation which surpasses that provided by any theory previously available to us.

The central problem of this chapter is the somewhat technical task of finding a way of subsuming the theory of reference under the theory of 'total meaning'. To do this we shall have to elaborate the thesis that the meaning (total meaning) of a word or phrase is a set of theories. This will be our first task, and it must be undertaken with some care. Deriving a theory of reference from our theory of meaning has, however, one great accidental benefit. It shows how our theory can satisfy the desideratum which stipulates that we must indicate the limits of innovation in a language. Since this is such an important aim, we may even make this the main point of the chapter and treat the satisfaction of Frege's desideratum (see *iii* below) as a means to that end. Accordingly, the other central problem of this chapter will be: *how far can linguistic innovation go before it breaks down?*

My answer will be as follows: *a new word is acceptable so long as any set of sentences will continue to obey the laws of logic when the new word or phrase is substituted systematically for some appropriate older word or phrase.*

Simple as this answer is, its elaboration nevertheless requires an entire chapter. First of all, it will be necessary to understand the concept of 'total meaning' in some depth. Secondly, in what sense can a new word fail to obey the laws of logic? It is not immediately evident what this possibility amounts to. The main connecting link between the meaning of a word and the logic of a language is Frege's desideratum, namely, that reference is a function of meaning, with the usual provisos. Let us therefore begin with the preliminary task of looking at the details of meanings themselves, so that we can understand how they determine reference, which, in turn, dictates the way in which the meaning of a word is related to logic. We will thus have produced a theory that fulfils two of our desiderata: the desideratum that a good theory must show how far linguistic innovation can go before it breaks down, and Frege's desideratum.

ii. The Meaning of a Word is a Set of Theories

Language is a crystallization of theories. Every word, whose meaning we normally believe to be an 'idea' or a 'sense', is an encapsulated set of theories about the world, about ourselves, about little and large things. If one is ever in doubt about the meaning of a word, there is no point in looking for the idea which is its meaning. Neither is there any point in either hunting for all the objects to which the word applies, for these may be quite inaccessible; or in looking for all the different ways in which a word is used, for difficult words are often used incorrectly. But any one who knows it can explain the meaning of a word to us by telling us the sort of thing that would be true of an object if the word applied to it.

Every word has not one or two but an indefinite number of different theories embedded in its meaning. Especially if we take the most common of concepts—such as, let us say, 'book'—we find that there are a great many things that we expect an object to be if it is to be a book. This includes various items about its production, its appearance, its structure, its contents, its influence on others, etc. If asked, we may not be able to remember all the different things that we mean by the word 'book', but certainly we know that we can say a great deal and not exhaust the topic.

Naturally everyone does not agree with everyone else about the meanings of words or phrases. Since it is very unlikely that two people will agree with respect to everything that they believe, they will almost certainly disagree about what they 'mean' even by words that are commonly used. How, you might ask, do they communicate if their words have different meanings? The answer is not easy. But there are certain devices for establishing contact when one discovers a troublesome misunderstanding. These devices deserve to be carefully studied later on. The problem of communication deserves a chapter of its own.

A word or two about the use of the word 'theory' is appropriate. This word is often used in contrast with 'fact', and is closely associated with science and opposed to 'common sense'. As I use it, both these usual aspects of the word 'theory' must be ignored. The reason is that from a certain point of view, which I adopt, the content of every statement can be looked upon as a theory—as a hypothesis that might conceivably be false, even though we may provisionally accept it unconditionally. This use of the word 'theory' is possible only because I adopt a certain epistemology in which the distinction between scientific and commonsense knowledge, and that between theory and fact is not drawn in the usual way. As I see it, the difference between fact and theory is not an eternal one, but one which depends very much on the intellectual situation at hand. Under appropriate circumstances any statement may conceivably be a conjecture. Hence there are no absolute distinctions of this kind, and how one distinguishes fact from theory depends on one's point of view. From a certain abstract point of view one can ignore the distinction altogether. These issues will be discussed in a separate chapter on epistemology. Suffice it now to state that a theory could be an unconscious expectation (like a child's expectation to be fed regularly); or an 'established commonsense fact' (like 'heavy objects are harder to lift than light ones'); or even an implicit unexpressed attitude (like 'children are like slightly irrational adults'). In the case of expectations and attitudes, the theory would be an explicit statement of what is implicit in an attitude or expectation. Of course, theories also include all the other things one might mean by a word or a phrase.

In most of this chapter we will therefore hold our questions of dynamism in abeyance, so that we may understand the intricacies of language a little better before we go back to its evolution. In dealing with the static structure of language, however, the theories that are trapped in language will have to be treated as if they are believed to be true. Often, of course, they are not. But their not being so believed is of less importance for the structure than for the evolution of language.

Let me briefly explain why. At any stage in the evolution of a language one can find some traces of beliefs which were held in an earlier stage, and then discarded. Children who have learnt the words 'up', 'down', and 'stand' seem regularly to be surprised when they first learn that people on the other side of the earth stand with their feet towards the earth, because this would be 'upside-down'—just see what happens if we were to draw a line straight through the centre of the earth in the direction 'down'. They have to learn the directions of a radial theory at a later stage. The fact that this is a widespread phenomenon suggests that the language by its very structure teaches discarded theories quite unintentionally.

Nevertheless, *one can reorganize one's use of the words in such a way as to suit one's beliefs.* It is possible that someone's language might be badly adjusted to his beliefs. Such a person might encounter very great, or comparatively small, difficulty in expressing himself, depending on how vast a change of language is necessary. The classic case where great change was necessary is that of Heraclitus, whose obscurity is well known, and springs from this very difficulty of expressing the radically new idea that everything is in a *process* of change, within the confines of an old language in which it is difficult to say exactly that.

We may, however, ignore such a problem by pretending that there is someone who finds a perfect coherence between his language and his beliefs. If we assume this for the purposes of this chapter, we will automatically have ruled out many of the problems of dynamics which would otherwise distract our attention. No doubt a modern chemist can still understand the term 'phlogiston' without believing in the fire principle. But that is only because he can *consider* or *suppose* its underlying theories—in other words he can make believe. In what follows, theories in language will be treated as *beliefs*, even though I shall expect the reader to remember that I have in mind a whole host of cognitive attitudes that are to be substituted for beliefs where necessary—cognitive attitudes such as supposition, doubt, consideration, assumption, etc. With that explanation I shall describe, as simply as I can, the nature of meaning as required by the evolution of language.

The view that language is a crystallization of theories has as its central doctrine the thesis that *meanings are encapsulated theories.* But it also has a number of subsidiary theses, some of which are worth noting straightaway though they will be investigated later on. The most important of these is that *the progressive principle in language, which impels the improvement of our expressive capability, is intellectual endeavour.* This indicates the identity of the force which our desiderata required us to locate (cf. Chapter 2).

Because language has grown in such widely different human societies, and has grown so relentlessly in spite of the sluggishness demanded by any stable system of social communication, as we have already noted, *the progressive principle must have adaptive significance in the recent evolution of man.* The progressive principle can be identified now with the expectations of improvement that we have as a result of intellectual endeavour. What is the biological significance of improved expectations? An animal with more realistic expectations of its surroundings is better adapted to its environment than one with less realistic expectations. There can, therefore, be little of more direct evolutionary significance than this. Human beings are able to make use of their intellectual or abstract understanding of their surroundings to better adapt to them. With our better understanding, for example, we can move to climates in which we could not otherwise have lived. Similarly, clothing, or the use of fire, are obtained nowadays with the help of an advanced intellectual knowledge of materials and processes. Hence, if language grows in response to improving human expectations, it is growing directly in response to human adaptation.

But how can language grow in response to theories? The theories that impel changes in language are stated theories, since intellectual endeavour takes place at least partly at the explicit level. How can a theory stated in a language change the very language in which it is stated?

The key to the connection between the growth of language and human adaptation through the use of ideas is the thesis that *the meaning of an expression is a set of theories.* (By 'expression' we mean any word or phrase that is a predicate in any sentence.) If new theories are proposed, they may contradict a theory already existing as part of the meaning of a word. If so, then one is obliged to change one's concepts in order to accommodate and coherently express the new theory. The growth of language is then assured in the following way. The old concept is still available for use even though the new concept may be used in the new manner. Thus, whatever we could once say can remain as an institutional element of our language, while our new speech habits allow us to say something new. Thus grows the expressive capability of a language.

There is a third subthesis of the thesis that language is the crystallization of theories. Its relevance will only become important later in the book. *The grammatical structure of any language at any time is a residue of speech forms of different discarded theoretical points of view which have accumulated over time.* We saw that the process of the growth of language leaves us with expressions which embody points of view at variance with our own. However, if these can express certain useful things, they will be retained. And to the extent that they become redundant they will be given new significance. Thus their peculiar feature will be that they appear to be irrational from the point of view of our accepted and current view of the world. Nevertheless, they will have great importance from a functional or Wittgensteinian point of view. To the extent that they see correctly, our theory subscribes to all of the functionalist's views and Wittgenstein's insights about language. In short, usage does give meaning to expressions;

but it is not only usage which gives meaning to expressions; and furthermore, where usage does give meaning to expressions, the meaning it gives to expressions is a set of theories and not the usage itself.

There is a fourth subthesis of the thesis that language is the crystallization of theories. *This is the view that to learn the devices of a language—its concepts, grammar and syntax—is to understand new theoretical points of view.* The model we must accept for all language learning is that of a student at the university who is studying a new subject. Just as he learns a new 'technical terminology' and new theories at the same time, so, too, is the learning of language at every level closely bound up with a changing conception of the world. Even learning a second language which closely mirrors the cognitive apparatus of the first will involve this feature, though to a much lesser extent at the level of basic learning.

A study of all the subtheses will quickly reveal that the central doctrine about the connection of language and theory is that *meanings are encapsulated theories*, (or, crystallizations out of theories). The foregoing considerations show that this is the key to my view of the growth of language. But in addition to its value within my system of theories, if this view provides an adequate theory of meaning, it will stand in its own right.

Central to any viable theory of meaning must be the attempt to show how our language enables us to talk about the world around us. It must, for example, explain how 'pen' refers to pens, and 'table' to tables. Because our language somehow enables us to identify, isolate, describe, compare, and specify, various things about the world around us, a theory of meaning must show us how language is able to achieve this. To see what this requirement amounts to, we will consider how it is met in some of the prevailing alternative theories of meaning. We will then compare these theories with our own theory. This comparison will allow us to better ascertain what is required of our own theory.

Apart from Wittgenstein's approach, which we need not go into again, there are two other significant approaches to meaning. One is the holist-idealist conception of meaning—for example that of the phenomenologists. Then there are the theories of meaning as reference, and associated theories of sense. The phenomenologists' theories of meaning are not generally about the meanings of words so much as the significance of things (value of things, how we interpret them, etc.). These theories take the meanings of words as but another item in our understanding. Since there is no specific theory about the meaning of words associated with phenomenologists' treatment of meaning and since this is what concerns us here, we can neglect a consideration of the phenomenologists' concern with meanings.

With theories of reference on the other hand, the situation is quite different. Our views must come to terms with these theories, if only to show how language helps us to deal with the objects around us.

iii. Frege's Desideratum

The theory of meanings as reference has been so successful in this century that it has led philosophers to wonder whether we need any other theory of meaning. Frege formulated two simple arguments which demonstrate the need for a theory of *sense* in addition to a theory of *reference*, the idea that in addition to denotation there must be meaning associated with a predicate.

(1) "The nominatum (referent) of a proper name is the object itself which is designated thereby; the image which goes along with it is quite subjective; the sense lies in between, not subjective as is the image, but not objective either."[1]

Sense can be described as epistemologically valuable. That is to say, it is the means by which we know a language and its expressions.

We rarely know (personally) the reference of a universal, and often are not acquainted with even one member of a class associated with a word we know perfectly well. (Take, for example, the nightingale, or the white tiger). If in fact *meaning* is simply *reference*, then there would be serious doubt as to whether one ever understands what one has said. Furthermore, we would have to know the world as it truly is to find out what we are saying. But we do not know this—not only not at first, but perhaps never. The fact that language is a tool for finding out about the world shows that what a word means to us must be more than our familiarity with the objects to which it in fact refers. Meanings must be more approachable than the truth if language is ever to be a tool in our search for any truth. In order to make this possible, sense (as in Frege's quotation) must somehow determine the reference. This was well known to Frege, and so we may call this *Frege's desideratum for sense*. Unfortunately Frege said little more about sense that will be of direct help in our investigation. He did, however, give another related argument which shows why we need the notion of sense in defining meaning. It follows in outline.

(2) Suppose the meaning of a word is given by its reference alone. We have then the following difficulty. The expression 'the morning star' and the expression 'the evening star' refer to the same object (Venus). Hence 'morning star' and 'evening star' must mean the same thing. But the discovery of the orbit of Venus, which connects the sighting of Venus in the East with one of the West, was a great astronomical achievement, and not something that could have been discovered by wondering about the meaning of the expression 'the morning star'. Hence the meaning of the expressions cannot be the same as the reference of the expressions.

This difficulty has been cleverly dispensed with by Jaako Hintikka, who has extended the notion of 'reference' in such a way that senses are definable within it.[2] Suppose we were to assign to each expression a class or classes of objects, so that for every possible assignment of references for the expressions of the language, the expression in question gets an appropriate assignment of a class. Suppose now that 'the morning star' and 'the evening star' were the expressions in question; 'the morning star' and 'the evening star' would be given a reference for each possible world. In some worlds neither might exist (the expressions will refer to the null set) in others only one, in others both. The assignment of objects to these two expressions will coincide in at least a few of the worlds. We call the wider assignment of classes the *sense* of the expression, and the narrower assignment of reference in the actual world the *reference*. In order to see if the morning star is the evening star, we would have to find out which of the possible words is the actual one, and this is exactly what is involved in discovering the orbit of Venus.

Hintikka's solution definitely meets the technical criteria of Frege's desideratum. Reference is certainly determined by sense. But it is achieved at the cost of making the meanings of expressions like their reference, and yet more inaccessible than when they are simply identified with reference. For if I do not know the classes which are the actual reference of most expressions of the language, I cannot know the assignment of reference in all possible worlds for those expressions of the language. On both these theories it is a miracle that we are able to use language at all, given how little we know of the meanings of its expressions.

Thus an accessible theory of sense is necessary for us to be able to explain how we handle a language and understand the world. Reference, whether in the original manner or in the extended definitions used by Hintikka to simulate 'sense' within it, is like truth in that it is too inaccessible to be an epistemological tool. A language is after all a human language, and humans must use it. Any theory which suggests that we cannot know most of what we mean would be hard pressed to explain how we manage to survive as a species—let alone how we manage to make any discoveries with the use of language. (The theories of language developed by Quine and Davidson would seem to fall prey to these difficulties, too.)

The hypothesis that the meaning of a word is a set of theories must help us explain *how learning the meaning of a word helps to determine its reference*. This task is taken up in the next sections. Before we come to that, I must mention that there exists a difficulty for the Fregean theory of meaning which needs to be considered. We can bring it out best by strengthening Frege's desideratum to state that *the reference of a word is a function of its sense*.

The difficulty with this desideratum for a theory of meaning is the existence of perfectly meaningful expressions which have no reference. Consider the expression 'the greatest prime number'. It can be shown to be nonreferring. Suppose there is such a number. Since it is a finite number, there must be a finite number of primes less than it. Let these be n in number, and let the number be called *Pn*. Now if we take all the primes 2, 3, 5, 7, 11, . . . *Pn* which are *Pn* or less and multiply them together, we get a number larger than *Pn*, call it *A*. Now *A* + *1* is larger than *Pn* and it cannot be divided by any of the primes less than or equal to *Pn*. Hence A + 1 is either a prime larger than Pn or a multiple of such a prime.

This elementary proof of the nonexistence of the greatest prime number makes use of the notion of 'the greatest prime number'. So the concept of 'the greatest prime' is meaningful. Hence it must be assigned a reference while it is being denied a reference. How can we solve this problem?

One solution is to expand the reference assigned so that even nonreferring terms are given an arbitrary assignment. This is Frege's approach. Another is to restrict the language to which the theory of meaning properly applies so that there are no peculiar expressions—but making sure, nevertheless, that all we need to say in the natural language can be translated into the 'canonical' language. These are the two classical solutions.[3]

Frege's solution is to assign an object, let us say the null set, or the moon, to the nonreferring terms. Let us suppose we assign the null set to the expression 'unicorn'. Then it follows that the null set is a unicorn. But this does not impede our theory of reference for discussing mathematics. It only means that we get some unnatural statements coming out to be true on our theory of meaning.

We could on the other hand translate statements with nonreferring phrases of English into a smaller set of expressions all of which refer and behave themselves. On this line of thinking Russell proposed his famous theory of definite descriptions according to which 'The Author of *Waverley*' must be translated as 'There is at least one object and at most one object such that it wrote *Waverley*'. 'The greatest prime number is not 11' is false, because it asserts, according to Russell, that there is a greatest prime number and it is not equal to 11. But there is no such number, and hence one conjunct of the statement is false—and so is the statement itself.

Russell's theory is also a consistent one which might be acceptable were it not for some peculiar consequences. On Russell's theory 'the golden mountain is identical with itself' is false, because there is no golden mountain. But this sounds just as peculiar as does the null set being a unicorn. In short, both methods are consistent but unsatisfactory in minor ways.

There are also other ways of getting out of this difficulty, such as more complex ways of assigning reference by allowing that words can be meaningful even though they be nonreferring, and determining truth of sentences to compensate for the lacuna.[4] All these different ways have their uses. Any of these techniques can be used to solve the problem of nonreferring expressions. But the problem precludes the strong version of Frege's desideratum—namely, *that the reference of a word is a function of its sense.* Instead we require something weaker, namely, *that the meaning of a word must help to locate the reference.* This leaves it open which of the many devices we choose to accept for the problem of nonreferring expressions. Our task is to show how my theory of meaning *as sense* can help locate the reference of a word, but we are free to adopt any one of the above devices to deal with the issue of nonreferring expressions.

B. Explanation of Meaning

i. One–Place Predicates

Let me restrict myself at this stage to the study of simple 'one-place predicates', as they are called, rather than relational terms, such as 'is the father of' or 'is between', which are, respectively two-place and three-place relational terms. The extension of what I have to say to these more complex cases is simple and obvious. It follows in the next section. It should also be understood that the words and phrases I speak of are either unambiguous, or, if ambiguous, then made unambiguous by a suitable use of subscripts.

Imagine that an explanation, partial or complete, of the word 'red' is provided. What characteristics will we find in an adequate explanation of the word? Here is a list of four characteristics:

No matter what a meaning is, or is not, the expression of the explanation of a meaning requires the use of language. And presumably when we use language descriptively, we state something. (In this context one could include within 'language' not only diagrams and pictures, but even such protolinguistic devices as gestures. The 'statement' implied by a gesture would have to be *paraphrased* into a spoken language.)

Under what conditions would we allow that a statement describing or expressing the meaning of 'red' is correct? At least part of the answer is trivial: we will allow such a statement provided the expression does not require us to believe that 'red' is true of any non-red object. Let us therefore think of a partial expression of meaning as a sentence of this form: 'Any red x is $\emptyset$', where $\emptyset$ is some simple or complex predicate, with x being the only free variable.

Obviously, we will allow such a statement as a part of what we mean by 'red' only if we believe it (or conjecture, suppose, consider, wonder about it, etc.). Thus the meaning of 'force' would be (partially) described by a Newtonian physicist as follows: 'If anything is a force then it emanates from and is directed to bodies.' It is not at all necessary for the statement to be true, of course, but merely for the person in question to believe (consider, etc.) it.

These conditions, however, are insufficient. Consider the word 'unicorn'. Imagine the following expressions of its meaning: '(x)(x is a unicorn ⊃ x has a horn)' and '(x)(x is a unicorn ⊃ x has no horn)'. We must accept both these statements according to logic, since we do not believe in unicorns. But equally well it is hardly a rendering of the meaning of 'unicorn' that unicorns do and do not have horns. What 'unicorn' means is independent of whether there are unicorns, and whether I believe that there are unicorns. How can we modify the proposed form of statements which express or describe a meaning to cover the case of 'unicorn' and other nonreferring terms? The device is simple: let us rule that the statement be *subjunctive* in form: $(x)(Fx \underset{s}{\supset} \emptyset x)$ where F is the word or expression whose meaning we are trying to capture, and $\emptyset$ is some simple or complex predicate. For example, '$(x)(Fx \supset \emptyset x)$' should be read 'If anything should be F it would be $\emptyset$.' This device is useful even in the case of words like 'red'. For even if we believe that all the red shirts in this room belong to me, it is hardly reasonable to believe that this is part of what one means by 'red'. *Thus the requirement that a statement expressing the meaning of a word must be of universal subjunctive form, as I have described them above, rules out irrelevant information, or beliefs, in the realm of meaning.* Any statement of the appropriate form that we believe, will express or describe this mysterious meaning of F.

(a) 'Expansion Sentences'

We can call sentences which satisfy our requirements 'expansion sentences' of the word in question (as opposed to Carnap's reduction sentences).[5] Here is a summary of those requirements which sentences must satisfy to be expansion sentences:

i. They must be universal subjunctive sentences;

ii. With the predicate to be 'expanded' as the antecedent, and some other simple or complex predicate as a consequent;

iii. They must be believed (considered, supposed, etc.) by someone.

Describing the meaning can be understood simply as 'expanding' the word by means of these 'expansion sentences'. Let us suppose, for a moment, that corresponding to some word like 'red' I have made a list of every expansion sentence of 'red' that there is (i.e., every sentence of the desired form towards which I have a cognitive attitude).

The meaning of the word or expression is identical with what is expressed by the set of all its expansion sentences.

If each sentence can be said to express a *theory*, then meaning can be thought of as being comprised of theories. Each theory expressed by an expansion sentence of a word can be said to be 'embedded' in the meaning of that word; *the meaning of a word is identical with the set of theories embedded in it.*

In order to emphasize certain features of the method of expanding meanings by expansion sentences, let me contrast them with Carnap's reduction sentences. Carnap's reduction sentences are an effort to capture the meaning of dispositional words in terms of empirical, non-dispositional ones. Take, for example, 'soluble'. This is clearly dispositional, for to say that something is soluble is to say something about what would happen to it, given certain conditions. 'Dissolves', on the other hand, was taken by Carnap to be fairly straightforward in this respect, since we can normally tell whether something is dissolved or not, just by looking. For that reason, Carnap saw the empirical part of the meaning 'soluble' as the statement that if it were put in water it would dissolve. But this is a subjunctive conditional. If we translate it into form simple-mindedly we get a bad translation: (x)(Soluble x ≡ (x is put in water ⊃ x dissolves)) in words, "for all x, x is soluble if and only if either x is not put in water or x dissolves or both". This might seem the natural way to go about it, but unfortunately this would make any object not actually put in water soluble. The sun, for example, would be soluble, and so would the centre of the earth. In order to deal with this difficulty Carnap proposed his theory of reduction sentences, which are of the form (x)(x is put in water ⊃ (Soluble x ≡ x dissolves)). In words, "for all x, either x is not put in water, or x is soluble if and only if x dissolves, or both." In this way if x is ever put in water then solubility is attributable if and only if it dissolves. But if something is not put in water, then the sentence comes out vacuously true, but no harm is done since nothing is said about solubility. Thus no counterexample to this sentence can be found, for every empirical instance of solubility would be precisely that instance in which the antecedent is realized. On the other hand, in the vacuous cases we would be left in doubt about the solubility. And this is actually a *merit* of this theory from the point of view which Carnap held.

But if we turn to the proposed theory, the first difference to notice is that expansion sentences do not try to 'reduce' any meaning that is there to be captured. This is reflected in two ways: first, there is no preferred set of concepts in terms of which the expansion is made; second, there is no restriction of any kind about what is or is not observable. Because of these two features, the meaning of a term cannot be expanded into a few sentences—one has to give an expansion to express every theory that is embedded in the term, if this is at all possible.

Furthermore, it necessitates a use of subjunctive conditionals precisely because the cases that come out *vacuously* true using the 'material implication' (⊃) might still be a relevant part of the meaning. And accidental truths may be irrelevant. To put that more simply and bluntly, when one says that one's finger is not soluble, one asserts nothing about whether or not one has dipped one's finger in water, one merely implies that dipping it in water *would not* cause it to dissolve.

The fundamental insight behind expansion sentences should be now be clear: it is that *even to have a language, or a part of it, is to have theories*; that every word has many theories embedded in it, many of which we may not always or even ever be aware of; that every statement no matter how simple it seems carries unsuspected theoretical force.

Before turning to some concrete examples we should note that *one is never conscious of all the individual members of the set of expansion sentences of a word*. Certainly one could not state them *all*. One can and often does discover expansion sentences that one did not even realize one believed. Usually, of course, we find out that we expect something when we turn out to be wrong in expecting it. This again involves us in preconscious and unconscious expectations. But the reader who has pursued my thought thus far must have resigned himself to expect it of this view. For this reason, though we can find many expansion sentences of words fairly easily, and some with difficulty, I do not see how the possibility of knowing all the expansion sentences of any word can ever be realized. There may be too many of them to be ever realized; in any case they are much too hard to discover.

(b) Examples of and Conditions for 'Expansion Sentences'

Let us now turn to some examples. Consider the word 'red' again. Let us just look at the following sample of expansion sentences where R = 'is red'. All of the following up to and including vi., A and B are expansion sentences of "red".

i. $(x)(Rx \supset_s x$ is not blue)

ii. $(x)(Rx \supset_s x$ is not green)

iii. $(x)(Rx \supset_s x$ appears orange when viewed through yellow sunglasses)

iv. $(x)(Rx \supset_s$ if (bull y and y saw x) then y would charge at x)

v. $(x)(Rx \supset_s$ the light reflected from x has predominantly wavelength w)

vi. $(x)(Rx \supset_s x$ is neither blue nor green)

A. $(x)(Rx \supset_s \emptyset\, x)$

B. $(x)(Rx \supset_s -\emptyset\, x)$

The following are NOT expansion sentences:

vii. $(x)(x$ is a unicorn Rx)

viii. $(x)(Rx \supset_s x$ is not blue) or John loves Mary

ix. $(x)(Rx \underset{s}{\supset} x$ is not blue) and (x) $(Rx \underset{s}{\supset} x$ is not green)

x. $(x)(Rx \underset{s}{\supset} x$ is not greener than y)

C. $(x)(Rx \underset{s}{\supset} \emptyset x \ \& \ -\emptyset x)$

The list of sentences from the first, up to and including the sixth sentence, is a straightforward list of expansion sentences, and can be expanded at will by the reader simply by applying the three conditions laid down earlier. A and B illustrate an interesting point. At any one time we may discover that a word we have been using has an incoherent meaning. Naturally, this is not a satisfactory state of affairs (since the theory expressed by the list of sentences will be inconsistent, and therefore unsatisfactory). When such a possibility occurs, we mark out two meanings of the word 'red' by a *verbal distinction*. As this subject has to be dealt with in some detail when we come to the skeptical possibility that no two persons can understand each other, let me only make note of this sort of situation as the case of *apparently incoherent meaning*.

Examples seven to ten are not expansion sentences, and each for a different reason. Seven is not an expansion sentence because it is not a subjunctive conditional. Eight and nine illustrate an important point. Not every consequence of a set of expansion sentences is an expansion sentence. The set of expansion sentences do not, in other words, form a deductive system. By thus sticking close to the form of an expansion sentence we lose nothing, *since the meaning of a word is not the set of expansion sentences themselves but of theories expressed by them.* Hence, even if nine is not allowed, it is quite redundant, since we may still allow the first and second cases, which produce the same effect. Ten is not a statement, only a predicate, unless the variable y is bound.

The last example, C, is similar in some respects, but not in others, to A and B. Obviously we cannot have it occurring in our language. If we could prove that it must be an expansion sentence of some meaning, then that would indicate that the 'meaning' is incoherent—i.e., that it is not satisfactory to express anything of a descriptive sort. (It may, of course, still have emotional impact, and therefore be of some value for some purposes.) Notice that if A and B occur in a list and one knows that they do, then C must also occur in it. Let us therefore treat the occurrence of a sentence such as C on a list as an indication of *a real incoherence in the meaning* concerned, as opposed to the occurrence in A and B, where it becomes an apparent incoherence only when one discovers that they both occur in it. Then the requirement that *there should be no incoherence in the meaning of any word* will be a general rule for the descriptive or theoretical use of language. This will not rule out the possibility of undiscovered incoherence, but it will rule out any discovered incoherence. The incoherence of meanings must be left until later when it can be examined in more detail.

To summarize what we have said about the structure of meanings thus far:

1. A meaning is a set of theories expressible with the help of the rest of language.

2. The set of theories embedded in meanings are expressible as expansion sentences, whose form is (a) universal, (b) subjunctive, (c) such that the word in question is the antecedent, with some simple or complex predicate as consequent and (d) is believed by us, considered by us, is part of our expectations, etc.

3. No acceptable meanings are really incoherent though some are apparently so. This question of incoherence, which will be taken up later, is of the greatest significance for solving a difficult problem for this theory—namely, the problem of setting the limits of innovation.

(c) Meaning and Reference: Frege's Desideratum

Let us now turn away from the details of expanding meanings to a more general overview of the structure of language. The most important desideratum which any theory of the structure of meaning must satisfy is that *the reference must be a function of the meaning*, with some provisos. This desideratum, which we call Frege's desideratum, is, as we have seen earlier, the pillar upon which an entire army of logicians rest their theory of language and meaning. The very least we can do is to see how the structure of language reflects Frege's desideratum. Frege recognized the special epistemological character of meanings (sense). Meanings lie in an *intermediate* position between our subjective world of consciousness and the objective world around us. One of the central features of this intermediate position is its *accessibility*. The subjective is immediately accessible to one to a much greater extent than either of the other two categories. The objective world, on the other hand, is remarkably inaccessible to us. Our acquaintance with it is limited to a very small finite part of it and further limited to those features whose signals our very weak receptors, the senses, can discriminate. The intermediate character of sense, or meaning, is also shared by theories, insofar as they are both means to understanding a partially accessible world. The equation of meaning or sense and theory that is proposed is therefore in character with the general Fregean approach to language in this respect. Since we use a language to theorize about, and perhaps thereby gain an understanding of, the world, this very similar intermediate status of meaning can be called 'the *epistemological basis* of language'. In this sense the theory suggested in this essay is about the epistemological basis of language, where meanings are also tools for the learning of a language which is in turn a tool used to deal with the world. A large part of the learning of language consists of the learning of meanings of words, which simultaneously consists of the learning of theories.

Although there are differences between Frege's ideas on meanings and the ones set forth here, there is a measure of agreement at least on the value of *Frege's desideratum*.

Let us suppose that we are interested in the reference of the word Fx. We do, naturally, know the meaning of Fx. Let us imagine that a list of all the expansion sentences were available. We may also suppose that the reference of other words in our language is also given. *The New Fregean Rule: 'Fx' refers to the set of objects which is the set–theoretical intersection of (or the set consisting of elements common to) all those sets which are denoted by every '0x' which occurs in every expansion sentence of 'Fx'.*

A very important feature of the new Fregean rule is that although the reference of the word is a function of its meaning (or sense) and the reference of other words, *the reference of all the words in our language together cannot be understood in terms of the meanings alone.* Knowledge by acquaintance is an ineradicable part of referential knowledge. This is not surprising, since we chose subjunctive conditionals to express meanings precisely because we wanted to rule out accidental information about words, and allow only what we can call its 'meaning'. We wanted to rule out 'John is wearing red socks' from the meaning of 'red'. Naturally, now we cannot know if 'red' refers to a class of objects which includes John's socks or not, merely by looking at the meaning of 'red' or of 'socks'.

It is also possible to understand the 'intended reference' of a word by following this account of how references are determined by theories. Let us understand by 'intended reference' that which would be the reference if someone's point of view about the world were true. Thus, the atomist's view of the world may be false, and hence there may be no atoms. Yet we want to know what it is that the atomist thought he was referring to when he talked of the hydrogen atom. There may well be something in the world which can be interpreted atomistically and which can be identified (incorrectly, as we assume) as hydrogen atoms. If so, then this is the intended reference of an expression. The intended reference of a word is determined by the sense of the word and the (coherent) intended assignment of reference to the other words of a language (in exactly the same way that reference is made a function of sense, and the reference of the other words). This idea of 'intended reference' is useful in certain epistemic matters which will come up in the next chapter, but is of little use here.

(d) Limits of Innovation: New Meanings and Logic

With the new Fregean rule we can go on to answer the fundamental question regarding the limits of innovation—how innovative can one get? What is the limit of innovativeness? E.g., one can invent a word with only one expansion sentence, or with only two, or with none, etc. But are these words with such weak meanings acceptable? If we keep increasing the expansion sentences, we are obviously going to keep increasing the *richness of the meaning*, and we are going to keep increasing the *interpretability* of the meaning in terms of the rest of language. But at what point does a new word become acceptable, or understandable, in terms of its expansion sentences? This, then, will be the limit to which innovation can be taken: no word introduced must be essentially poorer than that allowed by a certain standard of richness which we have yet to specify.

We can state this criterion as a modification of the new Fregean rule: *A new word can be satisfactorily understood in our language if and only if its expansion sentences, together with the reference of the other words in our language, yield a satisfactory reference for it.* All we need now is to know under what conditions a word can be satisfactorily assigned a reference. There is a rule which suffices. It is simple: (but will nevertheless require some explanation) *a word has a meaning which satisfactorily assigns a reference to it if, and only if, all well-formed sentences which include that word obey the laws of logic.* What, for example, is a 'satisfactory assignment'? Where does logic come in? In order to explain this, I have to say a little bit more about the structure of meaning. If we are given the meaning of a word, then we can immediately know the meaning of the *negation* of that word. Similarly, knowing the meaning of the conjuncts (or disjuncts) of a conjunction (disjunction) of words yields the meaning of the conjunction (disjunction) itself. But what is the rule by which, given the expansion sentences, we can produce expansion sentences of words defined by means of the logical connectives: 'not', 'or', 'some', 'all', etc.?

Given the meaning of a word, the meaning of its negation is automatically determined. Now its negation can give us a meaning in two ways: one can put the negated word down and ask for its expansion sentences; or one can transform the expansion sentences of the unnegated expression to give us the expansion sentences of the negation as follows: change every '$\emptyset$' to '$-\emptyset$' and admit as an expansion sentence if and only if it is believed. It is essential that *the transformations by the second method must yield all and only those referents from expansion sentences we would get by the first method.*

If the reference assigned to a word and the reference assigned to the negation of the word are mutually exclusive sets and jointly constitute the whole universe of all objects, then (and only then) are the meanings assigned satisfactory. For imagine that a word F and its negation do not determine mutually exclusive referents. Then there is some object such that 'Fa' is true and ' – Fa' is true! But this our logic will not allow. On the other hand, if there is an object which falls outside of either of the references then 'Fa' and ' – Fa' are both false, which again we do not wish to allow.

Thus we see that logic plays a regulative role not only in our arguments and beliefs, but also in the introduction of new words and in the structure of language generally.

ii. Relational Terms and Proper Names

We must see how this theory of expressions which can stand as predicates can be extended to relations (predicates with more than one variable) and to proper names. In the case of relations the modification of expansion sentences is this: the consequent of the subjunctive conditional may contain only the free variables in the antecedent, and at least one of them. For the relation 'mother of' the following are expansion sentences:

1) $(x)(y)(x$ is the mother of $y \supset_s x$ is female)
2) $(x)(y)(x$ is the mother of $y \supset_s y$ was born)
3) $(x)(y)(x$ is the mother of $y \supset_s x$ is older than $y)$
4) $(x)(y)(x$ is the mother of $y \supset_s (\exists z) (z$ is a male adult and impregnated $x)$

These show how only one variable, or two, can occur freely in the consequent (the variable z in (4) being quantified, or bound).

In the standard theory of reference, the reference of a relation is an ordered n-tuple of sets. For example, in the case of the relation 'mother of', it is the set of all pairs such that the first is the mother of the second. We can determine such a reference of a relation from the expansion sentences as follows: wherever there is only one variable, as in (1), construct an artificial set of ordered pairs $<x, y>$ in which x takes each of the values for Ø and y takes every possible value, in every possible combination. (Similarly for y.) Then we have associated with every Ø a set of ordered pairs. Now the set–theoretical intersection of all these sets will be the reference of 'mother of'. Note, however, that if the original expression was 'Whistler's mother' then we must treat as a predicate 'x is the mother of Whistler' and not as the relation 'mother of' with two terms we have been considering. There are interesting relations between relations and the predicates formed by filling in a value (or binding) one of the variables. While the relationship between the meanings is very complex, the reference of such a predicate will be simply a subset of one set of the ordered pairs to which the relation refers. Let us note also, finally, that some expressions are not to be taken as predicates produced by replacing a variable in a relation merely because of some accidental similarity of construction: 'mother of pearl' is not in this respect like 'the mother of Pearl'.

Proper names, however, pose a different sort of problem. They have long provided a battleground for intense debate between various logicians regarding what a name *means* and what it *refers to*. The classical theory of Mill is that proper names have primarily a reference, and that they may or may not have a meaning. Frege, Russell and most modern logicians could not accept this view because of the new theory of number. Thus '2' is the name of a number. This numeral is clearly a proper name because there is only one number corresponding to it, and we could easily have another numeral stand for it, such as '10' in the binary system of notation. But the great revolution in the foundations of mathematics was the reduction of the entity, the number 2, to a class of classes (pairs). But if '2' primarily *names* the number 2, and it lacks a meaning, then the analysis of numbers is pointless. In order to make a genuine analysis possible, numbers must have meanings, and each number must have a reference which can be determined in terms of its meanings.

For this reason, Russell and, following his lead, many modern logicians believe that names have meanings, which are given by definite descriptions. (Thus '2' means 'the classes of all classes which are pairs', 'Everest' means 'the highest mountain in the world' and so on.) As a result, definite descriptions became a central part of their theory of language. The difficulty with this view is that what is obviously a question of fact becomes a question which is analytic, since these philosophers also believe that what is true by virtue of meaning is also true analytically. Quine avoids this consequence by denying that the concept of analyticity has any value.

Recently, Saul Kripke has proposed that we must return to the analysis of proper names as terms which primarily attach to their referents. The reference is determined, according to him, not by a definite description, but by an extralinguistic device which is a history or a tradition of communication.[6]

(a) The Counter-Fregean Rule

Actually, both Mill and Frege (and for that matter Russell) are right about proper names. A word which is used as a proper name does act primarily as a reference. But it also has a meaning which is derived. When I named my daughter 'Anandi', for example, the word 'Anandi' had no meaning (though one in the Indian culture context would probably be able to tell that an object so named is a female). As soon as she was given the name, however, the name acquired not only a reference but also a meaning. *All the subjunctive conditionals that are believed of Anandi became part of what I meant by the word 'Anandi'.* Thus we see that not only does sense determine reference, but reference also determines sense. We can call this the *Counter-Fregean Rule.* It is generally true of any sufficiently rich language. There is no circularity in these two rules, because neither meaning nor reference is primary, but theory and a few references are, and they give us the intended reference of an entire language. As we have seen, the few references which are primary differ from person to person and still give the same intended reference if they believe all of the same theories.

The fact that some objects must be identified extralinguistically follows simply from the fact that the reference of each predicate is determined by every other predicate to form a system, but one which has no intended reference unless some appropriate objects are picked out to form a basis for the system. Knowledge by acquaintance is in this sense prior to knowledge by description. But it is not necessary at all to identify every object or even the same set of objects to build up a particular intended reference. The fact that reference forms an interrelated system is sufficient to guarantee that if we believe the same theories, then we will have the same intended reference for every word in the language (even if our referential 'basis' is virtually exclusive).

C. Subjunctive Conditionals and Extensional Logic

One difficulty with everything said so far is that it relies upon subjunctive conditionals, and there is as yet no satisfactory way to express them in logic. Subjunctive conditionals cannot be given a truth functional, or any purely extensional analysis. Many unsuccessful attempts have been made to find a more complex analysis. Let me briefly indicate two approaches.

One of these is in terms of possible worlds.[7] A subjunctive conditional is said to be true if it is true in the nearest possible world(s) to our own in which the antecedent is fulfilled. Now the trouble with this is that not only do we have no way of knowing if there is such a nearest possible world, but we have no way of checking whether some statement is true in it. These problems are bad enough. But it is also true that any two worlds which differ maximally with respect to the antecedent must differ with respect to exactly a denumerably infinite number of statements. The reason is that any statement has a denumerable number of nontrivial consequences, and the two worlds must differ with respect to them if they differ about anything. If the nearest world is necessarily so far away, then even if it exists, in some logical heaven, and even if we can divine somehow that the consequent is true in it, it seems irrelevant to the truths of *our* world. What does nearness prove if the nearness is always so far away? What consolation that other worlds are supposedly even farther away?

Another difficulty is the holistic character of a possible world. A possible world is an integrated system of reference. If we translate a subjunctive conditional into terms of a 'possible world' we are immediately thrown into abstract questions of what a world would be like if the antecedent were true, which have no relevance whatsoever to the subjunctive conditional. Thus: 'If there were an elephant in the room it would be crowded' is said to be true of a world which is the nearest possible world in which there is an elephant in this room. But what our world would be like if an elephant were to find its way here is very complex. Would it be an elephant from the circus, and what would happen when they discovered it missing? What means of transporting it here? How would it get in through the narrow doorway? The point is that all these are irrelevant to the truth of the sub-junctive conditional. Insofar as possible-world talk brings in these red her-rings, the whole approach is suspect. We may restrict features of the possible world to those of significance, of course, but even if this can be done with some measure of accuracy, the point of invoking possible worlds when the world-like character is then subtracted seems to be going the long way around. Finally the ideal of 'nearness' of possible worlds, or that of maximal similarity between worlds is peculiar. Normally when two things are said to be similar, they are so in some respect. If no such clause seems necessary, it is because a contextually clear point of view is presupposed. It is hard enough to say whether Galileo is more similar to Plato than to Archimedes. Yet this approach requires us to judge similarities between two worlds which are separated by a denumerably infinite number of statements. Having done so, there are, of course, different 'intuitions' about what similarity consists in, and what may count as 'plausible.' But if this is all that we are left with in our theory of subjunctives, it seems that we are far better off without the theory.

Another much more promising line is taken by Quine. Quine notices a close relation between dispositions and subjunctive conditionals. "To say that an object *a* is (water-) *soluble* at time *t* is to say that if *a* were in water at *t*, *a* would dissolve at *t*."[8] But having noticed this relationship between the predicate 'soluble' and the subjunctive conditional above, Quine goes on to use the subjunctive conditional to paraphrase 'solubility' into state-ments about what dissolves. But since subjunctive conditionals cannot be translated by using the horse-shoe of material implication, Quine looks for another way of dealing with subjunctives.

Solubility, he notices, seems to come with a theory of subvisible struc-ture. The solubility of something is due to some structure which makes it liable to dissolve. "What we have seen dissolve in water had, according to the theory, a structure suited to dissolving; and when we speak of some new dry sugar lump as soluble, we may be considered merely to be saying that it, whether destined for water or not, is similarly structured."[9] Using this insight of similarity in structure, Quine invokes a relative term M corresponding to the word 'alike in molecule structure' in some appropriate sense. Thus 'x is soluble' is paraphrased as '(∃ y) [M (x,y) and y dissolves]'. (This may be written ambiguously as '(∃ y) [M (x,y) and y is put in water and y dissolves]'.)

Let us now see if we can find a general method of treating subjunctive conditionals this way. Consider Elmer, a giant whale, and the largest mammal that ever lived. Now we may discover a new hormone which, if injected, increases the size of any mammal by a percentage above its actual weight. I could say 'If Elmer had been injected with this serum he would have been even larger', a perfectly plausible statement. But translated by Quine's method of paraphrasing it, we invoke a relation M of similarity, and it becomes '(∃ y) [M (Elmer,y), and y is injected, and y is larger than Elmer]' which is false for trivial reasons, since Elmer is the largest mammal ever. This shows us that using the existential quantifier and hunting for another object of similar structure cannot be a general way of proceeding with the paraphrase of subjunctive conditionals. Quine himself makes it clear, of course, that his method is not a general one. But Quine believes that for the purposes of science it will do. Let us consider an example from science. We can proceed with a Newtonian analysis of the motion of Mars as follows: 'If there were no force on Mars at time t it would move in a straight line. But there is a gravitational force on it, so it takes on the following direction . . .' and so on. Now the first sentence 'If there were no force on Mars at time t it would move in a straight line' invoking a relation M, would have to be translated as follows:

(∃y) [M (Mars,y), and y has no force acting
upon it and y travels in a straight line]

But this statement is trivially false in Newton's theory of the solar system, in which there can be no body without some gravitational force upon it, however small. Even for the restricted case of science, it seems, Quine's approach breaks down. But there is an insight in Quine's approach which we can disentangle from his attempted solution, and transform into a general theory about subjunctive conditionals.

Quine's theory of subjunctive conditionals has two requirements. First, he requires that dispositional predicates be eliminated in favor of manifest predicates. Thus, 'soluble' should be translated into terms of what does and does not dissolve. Secondly, Quine requires that a subjunctive be translated by invoking a new predicate which is hinted at. Thus, 'soluble' should be understood in terms of a subvisible structure M. Let us call the first of these the principle of predicate-elimination and the second the principle of predicate-construction. If we accept a generalized form of the principle of predicate-construction only, we shall have as general and complete a theory of subjunctive conditionals as possible.

Let me begin by arguing against predicate elimination. Quine wants to eliminate dispositional predicates in favor of manifest ones. His reasons are not germane to the issue, so we need not go into them here. But it is worth noting that this is a reasonable procedure only if the predicates of English are at least partially ordered with respect to their dispositional and non-manifest character. If we have a set of predicates A then there must be a subset B of A, the elements of which are uniformly less dispositional, if we are to eliminate some of the predicates in favour of others. Suppose this were not so, and each predicate F is reduced to another, and the other to a third and so on, and in the end one of the reduced predicates is reduced back to F. We can then see that Quine's programme of elimination becomes pointless, since no predicate will be eliminated or 'reduced'.

This, however, is exactly what happens. Let us take the case of the predicate 'soluble.'[10] There are many dispositions true of a soluble substance: one of these is that it dissolves when put in water. Another perhaps, is that it has the subvisible structure imagined by Quine. A third would be that it does not form a compound when in contact with water. And so on. Let us take the most obvious subjunctive conditional. 'If x is soluble, then if x were put in water it would dissolve'. Let us now take the apparently manifest predicate, 'dissolve'. Many things can be said of any dissolved substance. It can be said that it has not formed a chemical compound with water. How do we check to see what it has not? By resolving it, of course, by distillation perhaps. 'If x is dissolved in water, then if the solution should be distilled, x would resolve'. Thus, we can find that 'dissolves' is a disposition that involves the 'manifest' predicate 'resolves'. Now we can ask what is true of x being resolved. Obviously, x must be the same substance which was originally dissolved. For example, if I put salt in water stir it, then distilled the solution, and grew a new salt, this would not be a resolution, but another chemical process. But how do I check to see that the same substance is produced by distillation? Clearly by finding out if the precipitate has the same properties as the original substance x. Among these properties is the solubility of the substance. We could hardly call something a resolution if what is produced is an insoluble substance. Thus we see that solubility is a manifestation of resolution.

Now we have seen that solubility is manifested in dissolution, dissolution in resolution, and resolution in solubility. In general, 'what would be true' for each word, when fully stated, shows our language to be unordered in terms of manifestation. In a very obvious way, this is what the very notion of 'expansion sentences' implies.

Quine's second principle, however, can be generalized. Let me state it most generally: A subjunctive conditional is a (possibly incomplete) directive for the construction of a predicate. We can obtain a complete theory of subjunctive conditionals from this principle. Let us consider the subjunctive conditional 'If Mars were to occupy positions p_1, p_2, p_3, not in a straight line at time t_1, t_2, and t_3, then for any t_n it would occupy position p_x at t_n.'. This states that given three points of the orbit of Mars we can predict its orbit completely. Since this is satisfied only in the case where Mars moves in a circle, the above subjunctive conditional has the meaning: 'Mars moves in a circular orbit', which has the form 'Fa'.

Now the subjunctive conditional does not mention circles. It is just that with our knowledge of geometry we can construct the predicate "moves in a circular orbit" to capture the conditional completely. We might say that the subjunctive conditional has given a recipe for constructing the predicate. In this case, of course, the predicate to be constructed was completely specified by the subjunctive conditional. This is usually not the case. Usually, a subjunctive conditional gives us an incomplete directive, a partial recipe for a predicate. Thus 'If this match were struck it would light' might be a partial recipe for a property which we might call 'friction-flammable'. This property is ascribed to this match in a sentence whose logical form is 'Fa'.

Since a subjunctive conditional only gives an incomplete recipe for a predicate, it follows that the meaning of the conditional is not entirely determined by its form. This is a well-known phenomenon which has been noted in the literature regarding subjunctive conditionals.[11] It should be obvious that this hypothesis about subjunctive conditionals is the converse of my theory of meaning. Meanings were earlier cashed out in expansion sentences. Now I suggest that subjunctive conditionals be regarded as expansion sentences of some unspecified predicate.

The main novelty of this suggestion is that it reverses a general trend in the search for the logical form of expressions. Generally, such things as numbers, operators, definite descriptions, and so on have been given an adequate logical form by specifying more structure than was first apparent. In the case of subjunctive conditionals, however, the attempt to specify a greater structure has led nowhere because of their nonextensional character. Well, subjunctive conditionals are not extensional, they are the stuff of pure intension. The correct translation into logic is therefore not to look for more structure, but to look for less. In general, a subjunctive conditional is itself a more elaborate way of saying something which is logically speaking much simpler. Why, it might be asked, do we use a more complex form of expression when we could be speaking more simply? Most of the time when we use subjunctive conditionals it is because we cannot find a predicate that applies simply. It is in the absence of a predicate F, which we could use to say 'Fa' that we resort to the circumlocution 'If a were G it would be H'. In order for this to be adequate, the unspecified 'F' must have as its expansion sentence '$(x) (Fx \supset (-GxVHx))$'. But this by itself does not determine the reference of 'F' unless $-GVH$ happens to be co-extensive with F. Hence it is that a subjunctive conditional has an indeterminate character.

A subjunctive conditional hints at a predicate which is dispositional, which manifests itself as the consequent if the antecedent obtains. The predicate hinted at, however, is ambiguous. 'Had Muskie been nominated by the Democratic Party for the Presidential Election of 1972, Nixon would still have won a landslide victory'. What does this assert? Its message is ambiguous. It could mean that no matter who was put up by the Democratic Party, Nixon would have won as he did. Or else it could mean that Muskie in particular could not have done anything about it. In a given context, one may not be able to judge what is meant. And if one cannot judge what is meant, one could ask 'Do you mean that there was nothing the Democratic Party could have done to stop Nixon?' And if the answer is 'Yes, incumbent Presidents who have just terminated a war cannot be beaten', then it is obvious that the import was universal. If on the other hand the reply is 'No, what I was getting at is the fact that McGovern's and Muskie's policies were not that far apart', then we see that the subjunctive ascribes some property to Muskie as a politician. In the latter case we could translate the subjunctive as 'Muskie held unpopular policies in 1972', and in the former case, 'Nixon was invincible in 1972'. Note the great difference in the two messages. In each case, however, some object is described in terms of a predicate, which is only hinted at in the subjunctive. The logical form is: 'Gm' and 'Hn' respectively, where 'G' = 'held unpopular policies in 1972' and 'H' = 'was invincible in 1972', and m stands for Muskie, n for Nixon.

There is another kind of ambiguity that is worth noting, namely between subjunctive conditionals of particular or universal import. For example. 'If Hitler had not invaded Russia he would not have lost the war' could either mean 'Hitler had a winning strategy', or it could mean 'No European power can invade Russia and win a European war'. In the first case, the logical form is 'Fa', in the second case '$(x)(Gx \supset Hx)$'.

If we compare this treatment of subjunctive conditionals with, let us say, Russell's theory of definite descriptions, we find one striking difference. Russell's theory gives a simple algorithm for translating definite descriptions. There is no algorithm in this analysis of logical form. This might be thought to be a defect in my view. But is it? The fact is that subjunctive conditionals are ambiguous; their meanings depend upon context. This is a fact we have to face, and no analysis can be successful which does not take into account this ambiguity. Yet, the logical form of any interpreted sentence cannot be ambiguous, since in classical logic we wish to preserve the principle that every statement is either true or false but not both.

More philosophically speaking, a subjunctive conditional is used precisely because the predicate being invoked cannot be formulated (does not exist). It is the very paucity of language that compels us to resort to them. Their use is a constant reminder that our lexicon is inadequate for the expression of even very ordinary things that we would like to say in our everyday life. Of course such conditionals may also be used when a perfectly good predicate is available, for emphasis, or to be polite, or as a joke.

　While there is no algorithm for reducing subjunctive conditionals to logical form, there are a few guidelines we can lay down.

　Given any subjunctive of the form A⊃C, the logical form is either Fa, or (x)(Hx⊃Gx) (or some more complex form which I need not elaborate) where F has as one of its expansion sentences (x)(Fx⊃($-$AxVCx)) and H has as one of its expansion sentences (x)(Hx⊃(Gx⊃($-$AxVCx))). Beyond this, we have to use the context, and possibly further questions, to elicit what is being suggested by a subjunctive conditional.

4
Communicability and Communication

A. Differences in Meaning

What if our language is not a system of communication after all? Each of us who speaks one language makes sounds not dissimilar to those made by others. But the sense or meaning of these words is different for each of us, so, we must be systematically misunderstanding each other. It would seem that we would always be talking at cross purposes. But if we examine what we learn when we say we 'misunderstand each other', we discover that we must understand each other well enough to learn to recognize misunderstanding. Were we simply to pass each other by as ships in the night, then we would not have any problem with the thesis that we never understand each other. It is on those occasions when we do recognize that we misunderstand each other that we clearly demonstrate to ourselves that we must have an understanding of sorts. We must therefore ask how it is that, if each of us has such different meanings for words, we nevertheless manage to have a modicum of understanding of what others are saying. Is it possible that we cannot ever really understand anyone else, that we have different languages? This criticism presents a very strong case against the theory that the meanings of words are theories, and unless we can find a way of getting around it, the whole approach must be abandoned.

This question must be distinguished from a related question, which will have to be considered later, namely the question of why the children of one linguistic community speak one language. The answer to this question would be in terms of common biological factors, and common cultural factors. But since our views of the world are hardly likely to be the same—and in fact are not—the similarity in speech in a gross sense does not solve the problem of communication. For that, we must do more.

It is useful to begin by stating the problem crisply. Let us begin with an argument whose conclusion is that *no communication between any two people is possible*. Because the conclusion is obviously false, we will have to pinpoint what it is that we must do to the premises in order to avoid such a conclusion.

Let F and F' be two words. Normally, one would assert as a principle of semantics that if these words have the same meaning, then Fa and $-$F'a are contradictories. If not, then they cannot be contradictories. Let us assume that this principle is true of meanings as I have described them. Suppose I say that an object (say a ball) is round, and you deny it. If the above principle is correct, there is no contradiction, because what you mean by 'round' and what I mean by it are different. You may have different theories embedded in the meaning of 'round', and hence you have a different concept. But if this is so, then no linguistic communication is possible, because no two words from any two people's repertoire are likely to have exactly the same meanings. Even if, by chance, there were a few, they would not be enough to constitute a basis for communication.

One way out of this difficulty might be to say that two words which are sufficiently similar in meaning afford contradictions. But a difficulty with this formulation is its vagueness. An even greater difficulty is that sometimes disagreements are merely verbal, such as when people disagree as to whether or not a particular country is democratic. Two people may hold largely similar theories as part of the meaning of the word, and yet their disagreement may not depend on any disagreement over what is the actual character of the political system in question. They may mean different things by the word 'democracy', which, in this instance, leads to a misunderstanding. So long as we wish to acknowledge that such misunderstandings do occur, we cannot treat differences in meaning lightly.

i. 'Restricted Meaning'

The solution to our problem is to give up the view that if meanings differ from person to person, then we cannot communicate. We must show how, if F and F' have different meanings, they may sometimes still yield contradictions of the form Fa and − F'a. In order to achieve this, let us distinguish two kinds of meaning, 'total meanings' and 'restricted meanings'. This distinction is, in addition, of course, to the distinction between 'sense' and 'reference'. Neither of these meanings is to be confused with reference.

The 'total meaning' of a word is exactly what I have been describing so far—an encapsulation of theories. But this meaning yields another meaning which I call a 'restricted meaning' of the word. Out of the total meaning, we can pick certain predicates which, when restricted in a certain way, give us this new kind of meaning. A restricted meaning of a word can be understood as a feature of the meaning of a word, which is chosen because it is by itself sufficient to characterize the intended reference of the word. 'Restricted meaning' is a phrase which can be regarded as an abbreviation of 'a feature of meaning that has been chosen to act as a criterion for determining the reference of the word'. In the more rigorous account set out below, restricted meanings are not themselves expansion sentences, but rather features of what is expressed by expansion sentences. They are *some of the predicates* which occur in expansion sentences.

A restricted meaning of a word, F, is G if, and only if, all the three conditions below are satisfied:

a) One believes some expansion sentence of F with G occurring in it as the other predicate.

b) One believes '(x)(Fx ≡ Gx)'.

c) It is not the case that '(x)(Fx⊃Gx)' or '(x)(Gx⊃Fx)' is a theorem of the predicate calculus (is not a logical truth, a trivial truth).

Condition a) makes restricted meaning an integral part of total meaning, since a ∅ that is the restricted meaning of F must be part of at least one expansion sentence of F. But on the other hand b) restricts it in such a way that not every ∅ can by itself be satisfactory as the restricted meaning of F while c), the last clause, rules out trivial cases like––F in '(x)(Fx) ≡ ––Fx)' which does satisfy a) and b). Condition c) is necessary because one would hesitate to allow something like ––F as an adequate rendering of the restricted meaning of F because of the circularity that F should be defined in terms of a phrase which itself contains the expression F. To make my meaning plain, let us imagine that I wanted a criterion to determine which triangles are isosceles. Two clear definitions can be given, both of which satisfy requirements a) and b) above.

1) 'An isosceles triangle is a triangle, two of whose sides are equal to one another'.

2) 'A triangle is isosceles if, and only if, it is not nonisosceles'.

Now the first is certainly a satisfactory criterion and the second certainly unsatisfactory. It is to rule out such cases as the latter that one wants to introduce clause c). This clause rules out the second definition and all other such definitions which involve trivial manipulation of logical symbols and therefore provide no real criterion of meaning.

Now we can state in a much more satisfactory way what the condition is that it is necessary for Fa and − F'a to be contradictory from the intuitive standpoint that we have been considering. *Fa and − F'a are contradictories if and only if there is a G which is a restricted meaning of F and also a restricted meaning of F.'*

Thus Fa and − Fa are contradictories because F has the same restricted meaning as itself (whatever it is). This notion can also be introduced by defining synonyms: F and F are (loosely) synonymous if and only if there is a G which is a restricted meaning of both F and F'.

ii. 'Restricted Meaning' and Communication

There is often a considerable amount of choice regarding what one takes to be the restricted meaning of a word. This idea of the possibility of several adequate restricted meanings of a word is one of the central features of my thesis, and shall therefore be illustrated. Let us consider Euclidean geometry and the concept of 'parallel lines'. They could be defined thus:

1) *a//b if and only if a, b, are straight lines on a plane, and a, b, do not intersect. (// = parallel); or*

2) *a//b if and only if a, b, are straight lines on a plane and a, b, keep a constant distance from each other.*

Let us imagine that the second is taken as the restricted meaning and someone discovers for the first time that a transversal, or any line that cuts the two parallel lines, always has equal alternate angles. This discovery may change the *meaning* of the concept, if a Euclidean or other geometry is not already part of the concepts of the language. In that case, a new theory is associated with parallel lines. Yet it leaves the two *restricted meanings* intact. A third definition of parallel lines could now be constructed out of the discovery:

3) *a//b if and only if a, b, are straight lines on a plane and every straight line c which cuts a, b, makes equal alternate angles with a, b.*

All of these are obviously satisfactory as restricted meanings of 'parallel lines' in Euclidean geometry; if the two of us use 'parallel lines' in such a way that *one* of these restricted meanings is agreed upon, then we can communicate about parallel lines using this restricted meaning as a criterion.

We have seen that restricted meaning is only one feature of the meaning of a word. Words may have different restricted meanings for different groups of people. For example, 'light' for the physicist and artist may not only have different meanings, but, even if they agreed on the meaning, it could have different restricted meanings. Moreover, light may have different restricted meanings for the same person in *different contexts*.

What we take to be the restricted meanings of words is very largely dependent on *the purposes* for which we are using the words and *with whom* we are speaking. Thus, in a theoretical context, when we are doing intellectual work, for example, it is convenient to include in the restricted meanings of words a great many predicates that we would hesitate to include in less esoteric contexts.

In any particular argument one might in that context use a restricted meaning of a word or phrase that would not be suitable for some other argument. Suppose we wanted to know whether space is Euclidean or not, and we went out to check empirically whether in fact parallel lines exist in our world. We could not, in such a project, define parallel lines in such a way that by this definition two rays of light must necessarily be parallel if at some point they look very similar to parallel lines of Euclidean geometry (for example, if in a certain region the lines had equal alternate angles). Defined thus, there are certain geometries which have nonparallel lines which do not meet, and parallel lines which do meet. If we take *parallel lines as lines which do not meet*, then in certain geometries they do not have the same equal alternate angles. So if we are given the nature of the argument about our own space, we can let 'parallel lines' mean 'lines which do not meet', and then ascertain if indeed such lines exist in the actual world and whether they do or do not have equal alternate angles (or 'normal' triangles with angles adding up to two right angles). Thus, in a dispute between a man who believes in *Euclidean* space and one who believes in *non-Euclidean* space, one need only agree on some one restricted meaning for key words, each definition of which must be internally satisfactory to each of the opposed positions. The disagreement is then over a matter of fact.

Choose a predicate as a restricted meaning of a word and then conjoin more predicates with it, provided these other predicates occur in the meaning of the predicate to be defined by restriction. The resulting predicate is still a restricted meaning. Thus, there are two dangers in any argument: one is to choose an inappropriate restricted meaning; for to debate properly, contestants must at least agree about the meanings of key words in the debate. The other is to have too comprehensive a restricted meaning, which makes argument equally difficult.

The packing of predicates (and therefore theories) into the restricted meanings of words can be called 'semantic density'. Generally speaking, the more semantically dense one's words are, the more succinctly one can express oneself. On the other hand, this manner of expression, of course, will be somewhat less transparent to one who is not entirely familiar with the precise semantic content of the concept. But most intellectual disciplines are learned not only by grasping the theories of the subject and their associated problems, but also by learning how to 'speak the language' of the subject. The latter is simply a device that enables one to say a great deal in a very few words.

While the achievement of semantic density is valuable in some respects (e.g., quick communication), it also poses some grave dangers. One of these dangers is that once theories are packed into the restricted meanings of words they are not discussed openly, and hence if they are wrong they will not be easy to correct. A second danger threatens some people more than others. That danger is to pack so much into the restricted meanings of one's words that one becomes too obscure, or too technical, or too involved to be understood by anyone. The greatest danger is that of mistaking semantic density for depth of thought. While semantic density might in some situations aid in communication, and while it does indicate considerable familiarity with a theoretical view, it is no sign of either great understanding of its objects or lack of it.

The highest level of semantic density is achieved when restricted meaning is equated with meaning proper (or rather, the most comprehensive $\emptyset$ which occurs in meaning). In that case, all the most crucial theories will be part of the restricted meaning of words and will thereby become uncriticizable. When stated, they will come out as trivial, or analytic, or as statements with little or no empirical content.

B. Analyticity

i. Synonyms

I have mentioned the word 'analytic' twice earlier in this chapter. And twice must my contemporary philosophical readers have pricked up their ears. What are these analytic statements? How are they distinguished from synthetic ones? Other such questions, which are considered topics of burning interest, might be raised. A corollary of the view that there are two kinds of meaning is the idea that there are two kinds of synonymy. Corresponding to the (total) meaning of a word, we have:

1.   F and F' are strictly synonymous if, and only if F and F' have the same expansion sentences. (In other words, F = F'.)

     (Following from this, one can say that a statement is strictly analytic if and only if it is a theorem in an expanded predicate calculus with the equality sign. One may, of course, take any number of such strict synonyms as axioms, provided that they are true. If we stipulate that F is equal to F' if, and only if F and F' are the same unambiguous word, then the class of analytic statements will be restricted to theorems of the predicate calculus with equality.)

2(a).   F and F are loosely synonymous if and only if there is some restricted meaning which is common to them both.

2(b).   F and F' are loosely synonymous with respect to a debate or an argument, if and only if some restricted meanings can be agreed upon by the different parties in the debate for the purposes of the debate.

     (A statement S is *loosely analytic with respect to a certain choice of restricted meanings* of F and F' if and only if the statement F = F' together with the usual axioms of the predicate calculus, yields S as a theorem.)

The difference between these two notions of synonymy (1 and 2) are quite radical. Take, for one thing, their logical character. *Strict synonymy is a transitive relation:* if F is strictly synonymous with G, and G with H, then F is strictly synonymous with H. *Loose synonymy, however, is not transitive:* F' may have a common restricted meaning with G', and G' with H', but F' may not have a common restricted meaning with H'.

In both kinds of meaning, facts are involved. But there is an additional element of conventionality in restricted meanings. (We have to choose one if many are available.) But in this also the two meanings differ from the sorts of meaning associated with everyday discourse as well as from each other.

Our intuitions about analyticity and synonymy and meaning are somewhat at variance with this theory of meaning. Ordinarily, one understands by meaning something purely linguistic, something which is not made factual by virtue of some feature of the world we live in. In my view, such an intuition is misleading and must be given up. Precisely because our language is theory-impregnated, what a language presupposes cannot be taken as an *a priori* given, never subject to revision in the light of the facts. Rather, our meanings are epistemic and conjectural, they are to be tested like hypotheses. That they have this character can be substantiated by studying all those writings which discuss *concepts* rather than *statements*. The concept of mind, or of value are not only linguistic entities but are also hypothetical points of view about the world. Furthermore, we cannot find the total meaning of concepts in dictionaries—a dictionary can at best give an indication of meaning, never the meaning itself, for this is too comprehensive to be included in a dictionary. What a dictionary can do is to indicate various different cases of meaning and give us analogous expressions and possibly paradigms of good usage. But no one could hope to learn to understand the jargon of physics, for example, simply by consulting a dictionary.

ii. 'Matters of Fact' and 'Matters of Meaning'

That feature of our everyday conception of meanings, and even of some sophisticated conceptions, which is not shared by either of the two meanings that I have described, concerns the distinction between matters of meaning and matters of fact. There seem to be excellent reasons for questioning the distinction, and for holding on to some sort of distinction of that kind.[1] On my approach one can, so to speak, have one's cake and eat it too. Meanings are theories and therefore inextricably linked with matters of fact. But restricted meanings involve some theories and not others. If one takes a certain restricted meaning of a word as given or agreed upon (perhaps for an argument or a treatise), then all those facts not involved in the restricted meaning will be 'matters of fact', rather than 'matters of meaning' (to assume a vulgar manner of speaking), even though they are also matters of total meaning (more strictly speaking). For example, we could write a textbook of mathematics defining 'parallel lines' either in terms of *invariant distance*, or in terms of the *equality of alternate angles*, and prove the other as a theorem. Then one is a 'matter of fact' (in the sense that it requires to be argued, or proved), and the other a 'matter of meaning' depending only on one's choice of axiom system. Nevertheless, one must not forget that given the total meaning of 'parallel lines' the choice of alternative restricted meanings is severely limited.

Another example, perhaps a better one, is the case of a word like 'force'. One could for the sake of some arguments take it to be defined by the predicate 'mass × acceleration'. But surely this is not what one would do if one were questioning Newton's second law—if, for example, one believed, following Descartes, that force is the quantity of motion or 'mass × velocity'. In this case one will have to accept as the restricted meaning of force, something like this: 'the cause of all change of motion'. We would have to leave it open whether it is 'm × a' or 'm × v', to put it in symbols. But for someone who does not wish to question Newtonian mechanics, there is no need for this procedure. He can regard the laws of motion as a set of "implicit definitions" as they have been called, and proceed from there.[2] Then, indeed, 'F = ma' becomes analytic (loosely, as we have defined it)— but not in any essentially troublesome way: one always allows, or always should allow, for the possibility of questioning a theory when the need arises, showing a willingness to fall back on other restricted meanings (whether they are adequate or not).[3]

Notice, however, that if $(x)(Fx \equiv Gx)$ is a theorem of the predicate calculus, then F and G are analytically equivalent or synonymous, regardless of one's choice of restricted meaning.

In a slightly more rigorous vein one could say that 'loosely analytic' can be defined only with respect to an *argument*. With respect to an argument, then, a sentence is analytic if it is deducible in the predicate calculus from the axioms and those sentences which express the equivalence of words *due to the corresponding restricted meanings as assumed in the argument*.

Where the restricted meanings are inadequate, or where one is ambivalent or ambiguous regarding the choice of restricted meanings, their analyticity is to that extent harder to discern. As for the idea that for some language, L, there are some such things as statements which are analytic-in-L, these must reduce to the theorems of the predicate calculus.[4] Any extension would be possible only by an *assignment* (arbitrary, or conventional) of restricted meanings which must be chosen *ad hoc* ('from a logical point of view'), which makes argument or debate on anything interesting also a matter of definition (or, a 'manner of speaking'). This is the price that some have to pay for trying to rid language of metaphysics.

We have laid down that any proposed restricted meaning must be capable by itself of being a defining characteristic of the reference of the word. This requirement is entirely natural, for surely we would not accept as the restricted or definitional meaning of 'swan' something that allowed even a slightly ugly duckling. Nor would one be satisfied with a definition of 'man' which would restrict the reference to individuals who lived in the years of the Peloponnesian War.

iii. Choice of 'Restricted Meanings'

Now we can see how restricted meanings can be conventional in one sense and not in another. They are but features of subsets of meanings, and since meanings are determined by our beliefs, we are not free to choose them, except insofar as we choose our beliefs. But there may be, however, more than one appropriate subset within the set of subsets of the predicates associated with the theories which constitute meaning. *This* choice can still be a matter of convention. It may still be worthwhile to indicate how much latitude we do have in choosing restricted meanings. Here is a summary of the conditions:

1) $\emptyset$ is not a restricted meaning of F unless $\emptyset$ is the only other predicate which occurs in a sentence which is: a) universal; b) subjunctive conditional; c) believed (entertained, supposed, etc.) by us.

2) Every restricted meaning $\emptyset$ must serve to define a class that is identical with the class of objects which constitutes the intended reference of the word F. (The class is defined by the same assignment of objects to expressions, of course, as that which assigns the intended reference to F.)

3) The conditional $(x)(Fx \supset \emptyset x)$ or $(x)(\emptyset x \supset Fx)$ must not be a theorem of the predicate calculus.

There is no rule which tells us how to look for restricted meanings. For that reason, and also because of the restrictive conditions that such meanings must satisfy, the vast majority of our words lack adequate restricted meanings. 'Pots', 'pans', 'colds' and, to take a celebrated example, 'games', fall in this latter category.[5] We might find adequate characterizations of some words, of course, given only a little ingenuity, but there is no algorithm for doing so. One very unsatisfactory way to find restricted meanings would be to pack as many $\emptyset$'s in as possible. But even this is difficult since we can, in actual practice, state so few expansion sentences. Besides, as we have seen, this may be quite useless for the particular argument at hand, and in any case leads to semantic density.

The *discovery* of an equivalence relation is an empirical matter, not one calling for 'analysis' of meanings. Even if an expansion sentence is believed (or considered), the corresponding biconditional may be rejected. And since the truth of the biconditional is a matter of conjecture, to be tested and evaluated, to that extent choice of restricted meanings is not arbitrary. This shows us that the restrictions on restricted meanings are severe indeed. The adequacy of any characterization of a word is often closely connected with highly testable empirical theses, and a restricted meaning is in this respect much like a theory—we accept it until a better one comes our way, and when we find the old one to be wrong.

The clue to an understanding of *inadequate restricted meanings* lies in our readiness to use *ad hoc* modifications to save our characterizations. In other words, we can add a *ceteris paribus* clause to the characterization, with words like 'normally' or 'usually'. In this way we can at least associate one restricted meaning with each word or concept, even though we know that sometimes they will need to be replaced by improved ones, and also that usually they are inadequate, or are in need of constant readjustment, to be made to work. Yet the association of a restricted meaning with every word in principle, though not in practice, is a fruitful event, for now we can see once again that the logical relations of contradiction, equivalence, etc., remain extensional in nature. One can say generally that Fa and −F'a are contradictories if and only if F and F' have some common restrictive meaning (irrespective of what meaning they have). If two of us look at the sea and I say 'The sea is blue' and you say 'No, it is not blue', then I can take for granted that our statements are incompatible no matter *what* your optical theories or theories of vision are, provided only that the identity of the sea and the reference class of blue things can be agreed upon (and to the extent that we can trust the rest of our language to help us do so).

C. Misunderstandings

There is no guarantee that we do refer to the same things with our words, any more than there is a guarantee that the theories which we believe are true. How can there be one? There is the possibility that we misunderstand each other no matter how carefully we proceed.

Accepting such a possibility and learning to live with it does not mean that we despair of communicating with others, but merely that we should not be surprised to find misunderstanding, and should be ready to eliminate it when it arises. There is a great difference between the person who accepts the possibility of misunderstanding and tries to eliminate it when it does occur, and the man who does not wish to accept the possibility, and so typically takes great pains to define his own terms when he speaks or writes. Such a person always finds everyone else's writing imprecise or vague. The difference between these two is that one of them, the one who accepts the skeptical possibility, will eliminate misunderstanding piecemeal as it turns up, whereas the other will try to eliminate every possibility of misunderstanding completely before the case is stated. And this is invariably unsuccessful.

Once one has accepted the possibility that misunderstanding may arise, even if one is quite sure that there isn't any, there is less surprise in finding it. But how can one know that there is a misunderstanding when in fact there is one? The test is a simple one: if someone utters a statement which, to another, seems to have an incoherent meaning, then this is a clue that there is a misunderstanding. In other words, if accepting some statement would lead one to discover that one of our words has a set of expansion sentences which is inconsistent, then there is a misunderstanding.

i. The Use of Distinctions to Settle Misunderstandings

The way to resolve misunderstanding is simply to reduce it to questions of fact. The method is to find words which have neutral restricted meanings in terms of which to settle the dispute as a question of fact or theory. 'Neutral' restricted meanings are of course, only neutral in a particular context, and the restricted meanings may be made adequate by a *ceteris paribus* clause. But the most common way of settling disputes does not involve an appeal to restricted meanings at all. Disputes about meanings are often settled by *a distinction*. I shall illustrate this method below.

The use of distinctions to settle misunderstandings is very well known and very widespread. The claim that we can reduce disputes involving meanings to disputes involving matters of fact may seem a little startling, but it is really quite a commonplace method of settling disputes. Sometimes we might think we disagree but we may in fact only be using words differently. To find this out is to resolve the dispute. To resolve a practical dispute in this way is most satisfying. On the other hand, after making all the distinctions and clarifying verbal issues we may find that there is a real problem or dispute left to be settled. This is unfortunate in the case of practical affairs, but most welcome in any intellectual matters.

When we reduce the confusions of a debate to disagreements about factual issues, we do not use *definitions*, but only *distinctions*. There is a most important fact about distinctions. *Distinctions can be drawn with and for words which have no adequate restricted meanings.* Therefore, in order to resolve misunderstandings we need no more than the inadequate critical meanings which are possessed by almost all the words of any natural language.

Drawing a distinction consists in pointing out that the total meaning of a word includes two expansion sentences which are inconsistent, and *dividing* the original word into two alternative cases, each of which contains one of the two expansion sentences but not the others. In this method, restricted meaning and definition are not involved at all.

ii. An Example: The Evolution of the Concept of Reason from Plato to Aristotle

The method of drawing distinctions is illustrated by a famous distinction made by Aristotle in a debate about the nature of reasoning.

Plato believed that knowledge differed from opinion insofar as the former was 'tethered' by Reason. All knowledge, for Plato, had to be proved. Plato was convinced that there are certain innate ideas that we can recollect, and from which we prove whatever else we can know. All that we *can* know, however, are Ideas, and reality was therefore understood to be the world of Ideas. The world of perception was not an object of knowledge, but only of opinion, which was unreasoned, or even irrational.

Aristotle could not agree with Plato that the reality underlying the changing world around us was a separate Ideal unchanging reality. Reality, said Aristotle, must be in the changing world; and he thereby banished Ideas from his world and replaced them with *essences*. But one consequence of this view is that reasoning is also banished from Aristotle's methods. For if Reason deals only with Ideas, and there are no Ideas, then there is no Reason.

Aristotle, however, drew a distinction which transformed the theory of reasoning and of knowledge. He distinguished two kinds of reasoning— demonstration and derivation—which were not sufficiently demarcated by Plato. Demonstration, or proof, yields truth, but a valid derivation does not necessarily yield a true conclusion. Aristotle introduced the distinction between *soundness* and *validity* in an argument. *An argument is valid* if the conclusion is so related to the premises that it is not possible for the premises to be true and the conclusion false. *An argument is sound* if it is valid, with premises that are true. Finally, an argument constitutes *a proof* if it is valid, and if its premises are demonstrated. One can only find proofs within the realm of Ideas, but one can use derivations even regarding things belonging to the changing world.

With this distinction he was able to show that Reason can be applied to anything—for even if we cannot prove the truth of some things, we can assume things about them and *reason correctly on those assumptions*. Thus we can derive *some* conclusions from the statements that the moon is made of green cheese, and that green cheese is inedible. But we have only *derived* this, not *demonstrated* it. If Reason is thought to include both demonstration and derivation, then even if demonstration is only possible with regard to Platonic Ideas, it is still possible to make correct derivations from hypotheses. Reason, therefore, is not banished when Ideas are banished from our world.

In this manner, Aristotle's distinction between demonstration and derivation, without offering a definition of Reason, led to the elimination of a misunderstanding that was present in Plato's thought. Since then, Reason includes both proof or justification, and also derivation or valid inference.

A proof or demonstration is that derivation which has premises whose truth is demonstrated. These are in turn derived from premises whose truth is in turn derived from premises whose truth . . . and so on. Aristotle's distinction led to his own discovery of *logic* and the *problem of induction*. Since derivation does not depend on what the argument is about, or on the truth of the premises, Aristotle was led to discover the *formal character* of argument (or, to discover that the validity of an argument depends on the structure, not on the content or veracity of its sentences). The problem of induction arose when Aristotle discovered the argument which shows that the demand for proof involves a vicious infinite regress. How, then, can we attain knowledge?

Had the distinction between demonstration and derivation not been made, there could only have arisen a bitter debate over whether or not one can reason about the changing perceptual world. Notice, however, that no definition or adequate restricted meaning of 'reasoning', 'derivation', or 'proof' has been given here. Nor is this necessary. We can always make more distinctions if the need arises when we try to communicate.

Once one has accepted that the skeptical possibility cannot be eradicated, then one knows that no matter how careful one is, misunderstanding is still possible, and does not look for definitions, or methods of avoiding *possible* misunderstanding. One concentrates only on those misunderstandings which have *actually* arisen. To try to do more is to try to do the impossible.

If one feels threatened by the possibility of misunderstanding, and if one does not accept that its *possibility* is inescapable, then one begins to take precision and definitions too seriously. This makes every trivial point so difficult to express, and once expressed, so difficult to understand, that to spot real misunderstanding becomes almost impossible. Lists of definitions before any statement is made, or long qualifications about what one is not about to say, and why, are syndromes of this malady. It is ironic that this obsession with the elimination of misunderstanding should, in the end, harbour misunderstandings, but even this is not as sad as the futile digression from the original point to be expressed to the wrangle regarding the adequacy of the definitions which besets so many pieces of writing.

D. Incommensurability between Theoretical Systems

While that is all that need be said about the skeptical possibility of misunderstanding, I should nevertheless add a few words about a version of this skepticism that has exercised a great many philosophers recently. This is the problem of so-called *incommensurability* between theoretical systems, which first attracted my attention to the group of problems discussed in this essay.

The thesis regarding incommensurability is this: When really large-scale revolutions take place in the history of ideas, such as the Copernican Revolution in the history of the physical sciences, or the Darwinian in the history of biology, the new theories are so radically different from the ones they replace that the meanings of many words change radically. This precludes the possibility of a neutral evaluation between the theoretical systems by empirical means. If these revolutions are the pinnacle of rationality, then all of rationality is called into question.

It is claimed, then, that not only are there no observation statements, or statements neutral to all theoretical disputes, but furthermore, that there are not even neutral statements for some *given dispute*, such as that between the Newtonian and Einsteinian points of view.

One of the mistakes in this account of the history of ideas is that it fails to take into account the rich interconnectedness of our picture of the world. In particular, insufficient attention is paid to the use of auxiliary hypotheses. By using a great many auxiliary hypotheses, it is possible to deduce as consequences from a theoretical system (together with the auxiliary hypotheses) statements whose terms have not the remotest connection with the theoretical system in question.

This fact is of considerable importance, though it is quite a trivial fact of logic. It is almost always true that premises involve terms that do not occur in conclusions. For example—'All swans are white', and 'all white things are easily seen' yields the conclusion that all swans are easily seen. The conclusion does not include the term 'white'. When one thinks of a complex system of theories with enormous numbers of hypotheses auxiliary to it, the derivations allow us to escape entirely from any terms that we wish to avoid. If we take two theories in conflict, we can use auxiliary hypotheses with each to drive incompatible conclusions in terms which have nothing to do with the original theories. In this way, each consequence of each theory will be freed from the danger of a surreptitious change of meaning. And if by chance we can check which one of these is mistaken, we have a valuable test to discriminate between the two original conflicting hypotheses, which show every other sign of being 'incommensurable'.

Of course, the rejoinder may be made: What if the change of meaning is so vast that it affects every word in our language? For we have already seen that the slightest changes in belief can make an enormous difference to the meanings of words; we have seen that a change of belief affects meanings in somewhat the same way that a change of belief affects a system of ideas. A radically new theory or even a not so radically new theory might well lead to enormous changes in the structure of our world picture. Furthermore, if one word changes its meaning, then all the expansion sentences in which the word occurs also change meaning and in this way the change of meaning of one word will soon affect an entire language. The answer to the rejoinder is this: *A restricted meaning, which is only one of the hundreds of kinds of predicates one might find among expansion sentences, need not change merely because some of the expansion sentences have changed.* In other words, they are much more stable than meanings. Secondly, even if one of them has to be changed, there are still other restricted meanings one can fall back upon. But it is true that even these might be changed. So, thirdly, for any radical change of ideas, the number of words that so change in meaning that even their restricted meanings must change, can be counted on one's fingers. Besides, the test statements can always be expressed in entirely different words. Thus we see that the possibility of incommensurability is very remote indeed.

There is still, of course, the skeptical doubt that meanings may have to be changed because of a new theory, and that we have not yet spotted these changes. Therefore, two theories that we think are commensurable might in the end turn out not to be so. Certainly such a possibility cannot be ruled out. But it is not necessary to rule out a skeptical possibility. Rather, we accept it, and therefore always remain on the lookout for signs of *actual* misunderstanding.

To understand how it is that restricted meanings save us from misunderstandings of the sort envisaged in the thesis of incommensurability, we must recognize that when a restricted meaning is offered, *it thereby picks out the reference without regard to meaning.* This function of picking out reference without regard to meaning has been brilliantly analyzed by Kripke, though he calls it 'rigid designation.'[6] But Kripke uses this idea to suggest that some words *are* rigid designators, where the thrust of my view has been to *use* words to designate rigidly to avoid a discovered misunderstanding. The difference between these two is vast.

E. Kripke's Analysis of Proper Names

In a celebrated paper, 'Naming and Necessity', Kripke shows that the sort of view that I have proposed is false.[7] His paper is a fascinating one, though it is rather rambling and somewhat obscure in places, being a transcription of a talk given in 1970 at Princeton.

The paper is extraordinary in many respects, but what I find most extraordinary seems to escape most philosophers who consider themselves analysts or logicians. I find it astonishing that in this paper Kripke purports to establish by analysis alone a certain metaphysical aspect of reality. He proposes a metaphysical doctrine of essentialism by analysing proper names. Not since Hegel established with the aid of Reason, that there can be only so many planets, in the year that a poor deluded astronomer discovered one more, has there been such a triumph of reason over mere empiricism. Kripke's timing is perhaps less perfect than Hegel's for his corollary that cats have an essence was demonstrated some time after Darwin had convinced us otherwise on mere empirical grounds, but his thesis is no less remarkable for all of that.

The reader may think this unfair. Does Kripke not have a right to propose a philosophical theory without being ridiculed in this manner? I let Kripke speak for himself on this point. "Let me state what the cluster concept theory of names is. (It really is a nice theory. The only defect I think it has is probably common to all philosophical theories. It's wrong. You may suspect me of proposing another theory in its place; but I hope not because I'm sure its wrong too if it is a theory.)"[8] He goes on to describe the cluster concept theory. If my theory fits in his schema, it would be as a cluster concept theory.

Nevertheless, Kripke goes on to offer not just a metaphysical theory, but a false one. What is puzzling, however, is to work out what Kripke hopes he is presenting if it is not a theory. It is not hard to work out that an analysis of language, which is not a theory, is a metaphysics (this is *his* description) which we suppose must be based on Reason alone. One searches through Kripke's writings for a defence of this conception of what he hopes (or thinks) he is doing.

I suppose that Kripke would not be worried the least bit by any results from any empirical science, because they could not *in principle* affect his enterprise. An argument may be made for him thus: The logical analysis of language gives us what must logically be the case. If an empirical science discovers anything, and this discovery contradicts what must be the case, then it cannot be the case. So no empirical science can contravene what the logician discovers regarding metaphysics. Plausible though this sounds, it is quite erroneous. For the logical analysis of language is based on a great variety of assumptions, about logic and about language. Kripke willy-nilly proposes a theory, and a false one at that.

Kripke's theory of necessity, based on his analysis of naming, depends upon a distinction between two ways in which a phrase in our language can refer to an object, namely, as a proper name, or as a definite description. The former, is in some sense 'simply' a name, because it is attached to an object in a way not dependent upon the structure of the name. 'Wittgenstein' and 'the inventor of the idea of the linguistic structure of the world' are two ways in which one man is picked out. Of these two, 'Wittgenstein' is an expression commonly regarded as a proper name, and the latter a description—the reason being that the latter phrase describes features of the man (Wittgenstein) whereas the name 'Wittgenstein' picks out no identifiable features of him, according to Kripke. Now an astute observer of European custom may infer a great deal about Wittgenstein from his name—which would cast doubt on the notion of a difference between proper names and descriptions. But Kripke quotes Mill on this very issue, who points out that Dartmouth might have been so named at one time because it was at the mouth of the river Dart, but should the river change its course, it could with propriety be continued to be called Dartmouth. Thus, 'Dartmouth' is a proper name and not a definite description. If a new town were to spring up where the river Dart met the sea, it might be called 'the town at Dart's mouth,' which would be a correct description, while Dartmouth would not any longer be a correct *description* of the original locality so called, but it would still be the right *name* for it.

In modern logic, there has been a strong tendency to deny that there is a fundamental difference between names and definite descriptions, and proper names have been treated as shorthand for definite descriptions. Thus, Dartmouth may not describe 'the town at the mouth of Dart', but there may well be another definite description—in fact there must be a countless number—which truly describe it now. (For example: the town at such and such latitude and such and such longitude on the Earth). It has been suggested that all proper names in a natural language be treated in this way as shorthand for definite descriptions. There are several reasons for this, the main one being that in order to use a proper name we need a definite description to identify the referent. To speak of 'Napoleon' or 'Robespierre' cannot convey anything to a present-day hearer unless we could follow up by explaining that the bearer of the name was 'the such-and-so.' In a limited number of cases, one might think, definite descriptions are not necessary, for example when we can point to the object named. But, as Wittgenstein has noted, to understand the convention of pointing is to know that the named object is the one in the direction being indicated—an implied or mute definite description. Imagine we pointed with both hands, in two directions at two different objects. . . . For these and other more technical reasons modern logicians—until Kripke—have treated proper names as descriptions.

But Kripke thinks "it's pretty certain that the view of Frege and Russell is false."[9] If 'Scott is the author of *Waverley*' were taken to be the definition of Scott, then we could not ask the factual question 'Is Scott the author of *Waverley?*' as we well might, because this would be equivalent to asking 'Is Scott, Scott?', which is not what one wants to know. Another way of putting the same thing is that in this view, the statement 'Scott is the author of *Waverley*' becomes analytic, when in fact it is not, because *Waverley* might have been written by another person (if the reader will excuse an old joke, of the same name.)

The doctrine of Frege and Russell is often criticized by the followers of the later Wittgenstein, who subscribe to the doctrine that a name is given its meaning not by a description, but by a cluster of descriptions. This, however, does not solve the problem, because the disjunction of all the clustered descriptions would be synonymous with the name, and hence the statement that that object is F_1 or F_2 or . . . Fn (where Fi are the descriptions in question) becomes analytic. This, says Kripke, just is not so. If we take a whole bunch of definite descriptions of Aristotle, each of which is true, and contingently true, it is not the case that Aristotle could not but be the disjunction of these definite descriptions. He might have been different, not satisfying any of the definite descriptions, and still be himself.

Kripke calls proper names and definite descriptions 'designators'. When an expression is used to simply pick out an object, he calls this rigid designation, and when it merely describes a property which picks out one object, he calls it non-rigid designation. Then, in this terminology, Kripke argues that proper names simply *are* rigid dsignators. 'Nixon' rigidly designates the man (Nixon). Along the same lines, Kripke concludes that 'cat' rigidly designates the kind (cats) and 'gold' the kind of matter (gold). All these are names, says Kripke, and they designate rigidly. There is a test for this involving identity. One cannot imagine 'if cats were not cats' or 'if Nixon were not Nixon' without presupposing what is impossible. But one could imagine that any contingent definite description as false: 'if Nixon were not the president of the United States of America at one time' is a perfectly possible supposition, as opposed to 'if Nixon were not Nixon'.

Finally, Kripke argues that 'Tigers are cats' is a necessary truth if it is a truth at all, (the *knowledge* is empirical). All identity statements, if true, are *necessary* truths. I have read through several of Kripke's writings to find out what is picked out by some things being *necessary* as opposed to being contingent. Apart from a certain obscure analysis of subjunctive conditionals in terms of 'necessity', there seems no other way to distinguish necessity from contingency. We turn now to the relation between his view and mine.

To begin with a parallel between Kripke's analyses and my theories, one can see that restricted meanings act as *rigid designators* which locate the extension of reference of an expression. Every predicate-like expression, and every designator, has a meaning, a reference, and consequently the possibility of a device to restrict its meaning in such a way that the expression functions in some context as a rigid designator. Exactly the same analysis attaches to what is called a 'proper name', even though it is true that when a proper name is first attached to a referent it may be attached not because it is appropriate, but only as a means of identifying the object. It is tempting to think that a name has only a reference, or that it designates rigidly and has no meaning.

"One of the intuitive theses I will maintain in these talks is that *names* are rigid designators. Certainly they seem to satisfy the intuitive test stated above. Although someone other than the U.S. President in 1970 might have been the U.S. President in 1970, (e.g. Humphrey might have), no one other than Nixon might have been Nixon. In the same way, a designator rigidly designates a certain object if it designates that object wherever it exists; if, in addition, the object is a necessary existent, the designator can be called *strongly rigid. . . .*

"In these lectures, I will argue, intuitively, that proper names are rigid designators, for although the man (Nixon) might not have been the President, it is not the case that he might not have been Nixon (though he might not have been *called* 'Nixon')."[10]

On this, the central issue of his paper, Kripke is just plain wrong. For when someone acquires a name, the name acquires a meaning. In general, when an expression acquires a reference, it becomes a part of the system of reference, and so means each of the theories in the expansion sentences which come to be part of its meaning. An expression with a meaning, as we have seen, can also acquire a reference, under certain conditions. So the difference between proper names and predicates is only a matter of history, and not of function and even less of their *nature* as Kripke seems to think. But even regarding history, exceptions abound.

'Vulcan' was the name given to the planet closest to the Sun which caused the orbit of Mercury to lag. Well, there is no planet 'Vulcan', because we learnt in this century that the perihelion of Mercury can be explained without recourse to postulating the existence of a planet, by the General Theory of Relativity. Some sightings of 'Vulcan' were reported in the nineteenth century, but in any case this proper name seems to have reduced itself to a definite description in a Russellian manner, ('the planet that was postulated to explain, etc.'). 'Dartmouth', on the other hand, seems to have been a definite description which has become a proper name at a time which one cannot pinpoint, which creates some difficulty for Kripke's thesis that naming is an historical event of some sort, a thesis that I have not explored.

Proper names can also be given restricted meanings, in the form of *definite descriptions*. Thus restricted meaning as described earlier in this chapter is a more general form of what is also exemplified in the relation between names and definite descriptions. A definite description does not define or delimit the meaning of a proper name. Nor does the entire class of definite descriptions believed by an individual exhaust its meaning. A proper name may also have as part of its meaning properties which do not uniquely identify it, e.g. 'Venus is a heavenly body'. But in a given context, a proper name can be used to designate rigidly whatever is referred to by a definite description. In a similar vein, a physicist in the nineteenth century could treat 'force' as (implicitly) defined by 'proportionate to mass times acceleration'. If there were a debate in Newton's time between a Cartesian and a Newtonian then this could not be taken as a restricted meaning, even though in many nineteenth century physical discussions it was adequate.

In general, Kripke's mistake lies in failing to see that *whether a name or a predicate designates rigidly or not is not a characteristic of it, but just its function within a context*. While a proper name can be used to designate its reference, it can also be used descriptively, just like a predicate. An expression like 'Nixon' can function non-rigidly, for example: (1) 'If Nixon were not Nixon, the Watergate Scandal would not have grown to such proportions'. In the first instance, 'Nixon' designates rigidly, but in the second instance it is a shortened form of an implied definite description; (2) 'Carter is no Nixon, so we expected more civil rights legislation'; (3) 'And this is Professor Quine'. In each of these cases a proper name designates non-rigidly.

Rigid designation is *a use* made of expressions, which is useful to dispel certain kinds of misunderstanding, but it is worth noting that it is only because expressions have referents (intended referents, actually) that we can use them to designate rigidly. An interesting use of language, largely neglected among logicians, is the use of expressions to *rigidly-not-designate*. Interpreted descriptively, for example, Tennyson's lines are nonsense: "His honour rooted in dishonour stood, and faith unfaithful kept him falsely true." But these lines do capture the conflicting loyalties of a medieval knight in an unusual situation. This is possible only because we can use words deliberately to not indicate their reference, but only a part of their meaning, as in most 'figures of speech'. In a pun, or a play on words, a word rigidly indicates its own sound (or shape) rather than its referent or its meaning.

I have criticised so far only Kripke's view that names are rigid designators. His paper 'Naming and Necessity' also deals with necessity, and what he says about necessity has had great influence on contemporary logical analysts of language.

'A tiger is a cat' and 'Nixon is Nixon' are necessary truths, says Kripke. Some of these truths which are necessary may be empirically difficult to establish, and hence, of these we would say that *if true* they are necessarily true. What does 'necessity' describe in this context?

'All tigers are feline' may in fact be empirically false, though we believe that it is true. But since 'tiger' and 'cat' denote natural kinds, a statement saying 'A cat is a cat', or 'A striped cat is a cat', or 'a tiger-cat is a cat' is (if true) necessarily true. Let us for a moment assume that all tigers are feline, as we may know empirically. Then in what way would tigers being *necessarily* feline differ from their being only *contingently* feline? Since all tigers in any case are (we assume) feline, is their felineness somehow more exalted in case it is necessary? The necessity seems somehow not to affect *tigers*.

Consider another sort of case, the celebrated issue of 'physical necessity'. A group of planets identified in the solar system have elliptical orbits. "All planets of the solar system" announces Kepler "move in elliptical orbits." 'Necessarily' intones the philosopher. We assume now that Kepler is right as far as planets go. How does the philosopher's additional blessing alter the path of these planets? Do they now travel in the same orbits, only more emphatically? The emphasis, if any, is purely unempirical, because the 'necessity' of an orbit has no influence on mass, kinetic energy, potential energy, or on the price of beans.

What distinguishes the necessity of one orbit from the contingency of another is not empirical at all, but *logical. A statement describing a necessary state of affairs supports subjunctive conditionals.* Necessity is therefore the projection into the world of a grammatical form of our language. It is no wonder that the biologist cannot investigate the necessity of the tiger's being a cat, for only the logician can do this. Only the logician can conclude that since 'A tiger is a cat' is a necessary truth (we assume that it is true) therefore a tiger has an 'essence' which includes being a cat. Poor Darwin can only struggle with the empirical fact of the mutability of species, while Kripke can establish their essences with a simple analysis of proper names.

This view of Kripke's is often called 'Aristotelian essentialism', which is most unfair to Aristotle, whose essences were meant to be empirically evident. Kripke's essences are a mystery, for they make no difference to the world, except perhaps to make some room for God, (with the concept 'strongly rigid designation').

The difference between regarding subjunctive conditionals as features of our language pointing to itself, (as I have suggested) and of regarding them as cosmic signs of necessity, (as Kripke suggests) is a difference in approach to language and to philosophy that cannot be settled by logical analysis alone—whether of subjunctive conditionals or of proper names. It is, in the end, a question of an entire approach to science and metaphysics, as I indicate in the Introduction to this book.

5
Empiricist Theories of Meaning

A. Introduction

The theory that meanings are theories is a little surprising at first, especially to most of us who accept some form of the standard view of how meanings have come about. It can be called 'the empiricist theory of meaning' and corresponds to the empiricist theory of knowledge. This theory of knowledge divides knowledge into *that which is known directly by observation*, and *that which is inferred therefrom* (that which is confirmed or supported by our direct observations). Similarly, the empiricist theory of meaning divides meanings into *those that are learned ostensively* (i.e., from pointing), and *those that are learned later by a process called 'generalization'*.

Both of these theories, the theory of learning (and scientific method) and the theory of meaning, can be characterized as *two-tier* theories. One of these tiers is the theory-free empirical tier, that is, observation statements or observation terms. The other tier consists of everything else, from observation with a theoretical bias to theories with little or no connection with observation. The two-tier conception of knowledge and the two-tier conception of meaning are combined in the theory of observation terms and of statements. I believe that there is no such distinction to be drawn, that there are no tiers. This 'no-tier' theory can be sustained by distinguishing the *character* and the *function* of 'observation statements' in science.

The pivotal point of the no-tier thesis is this distinction. One does not want to deny that at any one time there may be numerous statements that *function* as 'data', to be left unchallenged at that time. One denies only that this function of such a statement is due to any intrinsic character of the statement itself. One would say, rather, that the same statement which today functions as an observation statement, may on another day be challenged on account of its theoretical bias. In short, as far as *character* is concerned, there is only one category of statements—although there may well be more than one tier of statements at any time if we use as their distinguishing feature their *function* in our scheme of ideas.

Thus, the thesis that meanings are theories is closely related to the no-tier conception of meaning. In fact, the former is a generalization of the latter. It therefore becomes imperative to defend my theory against the two-tier conception of knowledge. But if the thesis that meanings are theories is to have a chance I must first evaluate the two-tier conception of science and language to see if the true insights of the latter refute the alternative that I propose to support. I shall conclude, of course, that the two-tier conception is mistaken, because *every word and phrase and statement is theory-laden.*[1] This does not mean that ostension plays no part in the teaching and learning of languages. But even the very ostension of objects and especially our ability to discern which objects are being pointed out are also theory-laden.

Let me now study the two-tier conception of knowledge and language. I shall first study its strength, which I shall try to state as forcefully as possible, to show that there is no insight that is contained therein which cannot be accounted for later on. Only then shall we be in a position to evaluate its difficulties fairly.

B. Four Insights of Empiricist Theories

i. First Insight: Observations Alone Enable Us to Evaluate Our Expectations of the World

If we reflect upon ourselves as organisms that inhabit a complex and sometimes hostile universe we can hardly help noticing how limited our sense organs are in giving us information about the world. Not only are we restricted spatially and temporally by being separated from most of the events in the universe, but even within our spatio-temporal vicinity the range of information that we can assimilate is severely limited. Not only are our senses very few, but our sense-organs have limited receptivity. Yet we behave, as do all life forms, with supreme assurance. We may be cautious, now and again, about this or that minor detail, but on the whole we breeze through life taking all kinds of things for granted. When we walk we expect the ground to hold firm, when we breathe, the air to sustain us, and when we eat, to find ourselves nourished rather than poisoned. Clearly this assurance takes us beyond 'observations' or the information given to our sense organs.

These natural anticipations or expectations about the world around us can also be consciously made. For example, the first men who went to conquer the South Pole took a great deal of warm clothing, even though no direct information about the temperature was channelled through their senses in advance of their trip. Thus every morning we expect the sun to rise, and we plan our lives around such a regularity. We expect a tennis ball to bounce on the ground, and the hare to run faster than the tortoise. In this motley bunch, those expectations that are consciously made or stated we call 'theories' or 'hypotheses' or 'conjectures'. Otherwise, we call them 'expectations' or 'anticipations' or sometimes even 'reflexes'. I would like to stretch the meaning a little and call all of these 'theories', since the difference between those that are written or uttered on the one hand, and those that are merely lived by, on the other, is not of particular significance in this discussion.

If we consider any theory, it is clear that it may one day let us down. In fact, we are let down much more often than we tend to remember. Every time we are puzzled, surprised, shocked, thrilled, and so on, some expectation has not been borne out. But belied expectations can sometimes be disastrous, and often decidedly awkward. One wants to do the right thing. This desire is closely related to the wish to improve one's chances in life. This is where observation, or the information channelled through our senses, comes in. We learn that our anticipations are borne out, or let down, through observation alone. This is a truly important insight of the two-tier conception of knowledge and language, and may be restated as follows: it is only through our sense organs that we can discover whether what we had expected has come about.

ii. Second Insight: The Difference Between Observational Statements and Theoretical Statements is Evident

A second insight of the two-tier conception concerns language. Some statements that we make are very remote from anything that could be called observational. Other statements are much closer to information that is channelled into us. This distance from observation to statement can be compared intuitively, for example, in the following contrasted pairs. 'Every electron is negatively charged' and 'that star is shining brightly today'; or 'I have hurt my hand' and 'the average manual labourer hurts his hand two and four-fifths times per year'.

The whole class of statements that are so closely geared to observations are, of course, 'observational statements', all the others are 'theoretical statements'. There are logical relationships that hold between statements of these two types. We hope to find in them some basis for theoretical knowledge.

iii. Third Insight: Observational Statements are Felt to be More Certain

Thirdly there is an insight regarding our *feelings* towards statements that express channelled information: we trust them. It is universally accepted that a trust or feeling of certainty guarantees very little for we often feel certain about the most ridiculous of our theories and these may turn out to be quite mistaken. But we do trust our senses. This is what is so appealing, of course, when someone holds his hand up and says 'I am certain that there are five fingers on my hand'.

If we want to rely on our theories also, and yet do not want to be let down, then we must learn not to trust our theories except insofar as they are themselves in some way guaranteed or at least supported by our observation statements. What precisely this relation is that will lend trustworthiness or acceptability to theories is, of course, a difficult question. But logic or probability theory might help us here, and it is the study of this relationship that is undertaken by those who formulate theories of confirmation.

iv. Fourth Insight: The Success of Science Shows that there is a Firm Basis for Knowledge

So far, I have tried to formulate as convincing a picture as possible of the two-tier conception of knowledge in general. It views science as a particular instance, but introduces a special twist in this case, for it argues that since the success of natural science is so dazzling to modern eyes, since it is, intuitively speaking, superior to any other method of obtaining knowledge, clearly natural scientists have somewhere along the line discovered how to find theories that are more reliable than others. Natural scientists must implicitly use methods that give their theories this trustworthiness. Scientists have learned, in other words, how to transmit the trustworthiness of observational information to their theories. An explicit statement of this method, of course, has yet to be given. Such a statement would be a great help both for understanding knowledge in general, and also for the less successful social sciences that seem to have such a hard time of it.

These, then, are the insights, whether correct or mistaken. Taken together they form a very convincing argument, and are immensely popular, especially among scientists. But we must be on our guard, if only because we are ourselves asserting the conviction that trustworthiness should be reserved for observation statements, or theories clearly 'based on' (in some sense) observation statements. On what fact is our theory based? How can we show that our conviction does not have the spurious kind of reliability that magic or superstition might have? How can we demonstrate this conviction?

C. Objections to the First Insight

i. Observations are Theory-laden

The first tentative objection, of course, has already been made. We cannot rely on this argument judging by its own standards. This is a rather weak objection since it may be that if we were to formulate it correctly or know how to argue well in its defence, we might show that it is not mistaken. We must go into more detail.

The two-tier conception of science and language is itself based on a certain view of the human being and his relationship to the physical world. Most empiricist theories seem to refer to a view that is closely related to what I have stated very nontechnically (in order that it may be seen more as an insight than as a sharply defined theory)—namely, that we have theories, and we also have, besides, information channelled into us that is reliable or trustworthy. This second idea is already a little peculiar: how can we rely on our theory that information from our senses is reliable? If indeed all our facts come from sensory information channels there can be no independent fact on which the theory is based, since, according to this conception, we have no way of going beyond our sensations to check on our channels of information.

Yet, the remarkable fact is that we *correct* information even as we receive it through our senses! Often we say 'I thought I saw but I was mistaken'; we describe things as 'illusions', 'mirages', or we describe them as 'deceptive' and so on. Quite apart from that, we have ample evidence that our senses, and hence, what we see may be controlled to some extent by what we expect, that is, by our own theories. Thus, theories can lend their untrustworthiness to observation. But how could we ever decide that *our senses are deceiving us?*

The answer, sometimes, is that the information received may clash. Two people may 'see' differently while observing the same things or for some other reason contradict each other's observation statement. In either case we cannot use observation itself to mediate between observational discrepancies. The criteria we use to mediate are theories. And thus we see that far from always relying on observations, we are sometimes forced to rely on theories!

The immediate temptation is to look for kinds of observations that are reliable. For example, things are more deceptive in the dark than in the light, or at a distance than close at hand. And so on. But this will not do. For our theory about what to rely on is itself not channelled in through our information channels, that is, through our senses.

Perhaps I can illustrate this theory–dependence more clearly through an example, so that this purely abstract discussion, which looks a trifle suspicious, can be argued, if necessary, in concrete terms. Let us take the example of mirages.

Mirages are often seen in deserts, and though they are isolated phenomena, they seem to be quite well attested. Typically, a traveller sees a blue stretch of water in the distance, but walking towards it he never seems to be able to come close enough to drink out of it. If he walks long enough, he realizes that his eyes have deceived him, for there is no water where he saw it earlier. The explanation that is normally given is roughly like this. Light from the sky is refracted through the air off the desert in a strange way, so that some of it finally comes to the eye from an unexpected direction, a direction whose continuation hits the desert in the distance. Since the sky is blue, this accounts for the distant blue patch that is mistaken for a patch of water, on account of its position in the desert. Of course, this explanation is very sketchy, but enough has been said to show how a sophisticated theory can be invoked to explain a 'mistaken observation'.

In all such examples our illusions are explained by evoking rather elaborate theories. All such illusions are explained along the same lines: we show that our piece of interpreted information is mistaken by showing how we misinterpreted otherwise reliable information. It is tempting to take this further and state that in general there is pure uninterpreted information given to the senses, and this is what is always reliable. But in order for such a theory of so-called sense data to work, we must have a *general* theory of isolating interpretations from the given, for it to be of any use. To know that there is something that is reliable is not very helpful, unless we know how to locate it each time we want it.

This in fact constitutes a very general argument against the theory of sense data as put forward, for example, by Bertrand Russell.[2] The argument consists in showing that the sense data theory is false if taken literally, for nothing is purely 'given'; one can find no givens of the senses that are incorrigible. But if sense data are defined or understood in such a way that though they are incorrigible we can never actually recognize them when we have them, then the theory is untestable, and furthermore *of no use in the critical evaluation of observations;* so that, whether or not there are sense data, we need to think again about which observations to trust, which not to trust, and *why,* in terms of (corrigible) theories.

Contrary to what we initially assumed, it seems likely, or at any rate not unreasonable to believe that our senses are actually systematically deceptive in conveying what is truly out there. Sometime we catch this deception, for example, when there are discrepancies between observation reports; or when our theories lead us to expect something else, and we are so committed to the theory, that we do not take information channelled in through our senses at face value, but question it. The motion of the sun, for example, was assumed so emphatically to be a given by many people, that the theory that it was stationary was thereby considered refuted. Take two other cases of an imaginary sort. How do we know that a patch of sky that we see is not really in the direction in which we seem to see it, but in a different one and being refracted? If the sky is uniformly blue, we will not pay much attention to it. And how do I know that the itch in my foot while I was lecturing had anything to do with the nerve endings of my foot, but not of my abdomen, which the brain misinterpreted? Of course in each special case such as this we can investigate the issue in the light of our theories of physics, chemistry, physiology, etc., to decide between various explanations. But in general one cannot decide between veridical and non-veridical impressions simply because one has to discover them either accidentally or from a special investigation into the matter which is prompted by a (theoretical) doubt.

Thus, at the level of observation itself a whole host of theoretical problems arise that we clear up, if we can, only piecemeal as they turn up. It is not, then, the unanimity of what people find through observation that is such a blessing to us, but the occasional disparity. If everyone were always to have the same information under similar circumstances, the task of finding where our interpretations are mistaken would become so much more difficult. There is, of course, much knowledge contained in the unexamined observation, but the analysis of what it is that is reliable in it will have to be postponed to a later chapter.

Another important sense in which our observations are themselves theory-laden is the extent to which the physiology and psychology of perception can limit and even misinform the most careful observer. The best way in which to understand this is perhaps from the Darwinian point of view.

The human organism is a product of several billion years of natural selection. If it has the particular structure it does, then one can expect that this structure would be a suitable one for this sort of organism to survive in its normal surroundings from the evolutionary point of view. Man's sense organs, in particular, are well adapted to allow him to do the sorts of things that he would have to do as a more or less successful primate.

Thus, for example, our eyes are best suited for middle-range sight, and fail for most longer-range tests as well as for very close ranges. For a fruit-picker who converted rather late to hunting, this is natural. An insectivore would have to have much better vision at close quarters, a high-flying predator much better vision from a distance. Our eyes are also adapted to see only certain ranges of colours. Thus a bee can see ultra-violet, which we can only see as white. We are insensitive to the difference between white and ultraviolet. Furthermore, our eyes are not as good for catching fast movements as they are for locating still medium-sized objects . . . and so on and so forth.

So much for limitations. The Gestalt psychologists have also shown how our perceptions can err by providing dozens of examples of situations where we 'naturally' see something which is not there. These illusions are clues to the *structure of perception*. A very bold recent attempt to do without the 'objective' layer of sensation altogether in the psychology and physiology of perception is that of J. J. Gibson.[3]

ii. Critical Evaluation of Observations, not Observations Themselves, Form the Basis for Science

All these developments in psychology and biology can be seen to fit in very well with the idea that it is not our observations themselves, but rather our critical evaluation of them which form the basis of science—if there is such a basis. To take the classic case, let us consider the motion of the sun across the sky. An organism can distinguish its own motion from that of another because in the one case the entire visual field moves, while in the other only an element in the field does so. Now going by the general rule 'whenever an object moves across a stationary screen, it is really in motion', one may conclude that the sun actually does move across the sky. That this information cannot be trusted is of no biological value to the primate because none of its adaptive behaviour depends upon the difference between the Ptolemaic and Copernican systems. Hence, it is not at all surprising that we discovered fairly late in our history that it is the sun and not the earth which remains motionless. (Our kinaesthetic and other perceptions supported the Ptolemaic hypotheses.) But *after* the Copernican system was proposed, we could reevaluate our perceptual experience, and argue that the observations that we should trust are not these at all, because they are interpretive, but others. . . . Not that we would ever doubt that when an individual star moves across the background of the other stars we will once again say that it is the star that moves, and not the rest of the universe!

In short, what we have gained from our evolutionary past are sensors which are better at detecting some things than others. The closer our interests are to the normal interests of a fruit-gathering primate who has recently turned hunter, the more we can trust the evidence of our senses. Since intellectual curiosity has taken us far beyond this original adaptive range, we have to rely more and more on critically evaluated and theoretically informed observation. A geiger counter linked to a computer might, then, make an excellent observational tool for a scientist—and this is no less observational in spite of the use made of theoretically interesting equipment.

The least that biologists have taught us is that our own organs of perception are no less complex and no less theoretically interesting. Indeed, to understand empiricism in its proper light, we must consider it from a biological perspective.[4]

D. Objections to the Second Insight

Another set of difficulties arises when we consider the theory that some statements are 'observation statements' in that they *express* only information from the senses. These difficulties can be brought out by considering various different distinctions between theory and observation and showing that they break down. Such a task, however, would have no end.

i. All Statements are Theory-laden

Let me instead turn to more general considerations, to show why any theory that tries to draw the distinction would be inadequte. I shall make this claim most pointedly (though hardly for the first time) by asserting that *language itself is theory,* thereby ruling out any possibility that there are 'observation statements'. This is intended to be equivalent to saying that all statements are of a theoretical character. But theoretical as opposed to what? How can statements be theoretical if there are no observational statements with which to contrast them? As this question has been dealt with before I shall state somewhat cryptically what the answer to it should be. There are indeed observation statements in the sense that there are statements which function as observation statements. But there are no statements which have a character that makes them observation statements. Thus any statement whatever might function as an observation statement or as a theoretical statement in some conceivable context. So my theory that language itself is a theory should be interpreted to mean that any statement whatsoever can function as a theory in the appropriate intellectual context.

To see that any unit of language is theory-laden is to have two basic insights. The first is that there is always a chasm between any statement and the observations that it might sometimes seem to do no more than express; and the second is a related insight into language, which can be expressed by saying that there are no nondispositional descriptive concepts. Though these views are familiar, they are controversial. I shall deal with each in some detail.

(a) The Gap between Observation Statements and the Observations Expressed

This first point is really quite commonplace, and all I need to do is to point out that whereas a statement is true or false, and can stand in all kinds of simple and complicated logical relationships with other statements in the language, a sensation just *is*. To bring out the force of this cryptic remark, let us consider the following question: can a statement stand in such a relation to a sensation that the truth of the statement is guaranteed by that sensation? My claim is that every statement is corrigible or possibly misleading, and this shows that a gap between the sensation and the statement exists. This is counterintuitive. How can one doubt that one sees five fingers on one hand? If a ball is seen to be thrown up in the air how can the expression 'the ball is thrown up in the air' turn out to be misleading or mistaken? I think that this intuition about the truth of the statements is mistaken, but there is still something in it. What I am now invoking is not the skeptical doubt that I may be dreaming or having an illusion. Our critical evaluation of sensations places us in such a situation but rarely. What I am trying to get at is that although a statement may not be grossly mistaken, it may be subtly mistaken. That is, it may be a good first approximation, or even a second, or a third, without being true. And usually these subtle ways in which a statement can be mistaken cannot be discovered easily. In order to explain this better let me take three celebrated examples of intuitions that had to be reordered, and let me show how some statements were subtly wrong though they could only have been taken as plain and simple observation statements before the reordering became necessary.

'I threw the ball straight up in the air' when uttered a few minutes after one has thrown a ball up in the air would seem to be an example of a straightforward observation statement. (This is Feyerabend's argument, in a nutshell). Let us suppose that someone said this 3,000 years ago. It would still make no difference provided the conditions were more or less the same as described. But a closer examination of the word 'upwards' in 'throwing upwards' would show that the historical speaker might have said something subtly mistaken. For when he uttered the sentence he would have meant by 'up' a great many things that we do not normally mean today. Part of the meaning of the word 'up' to him would be that (a) all 'up' directions are perpendicular to the surface of the earth (barring local irregularities), (b) that they are parallel. *Together these would yield a statement that the earth is flat!* Of course I am not claiming that he must be aware of all this. No one need ever actually have uttered the general theory. Nevertheless he would expect all 'up' directions to be parallel, etc. Thus the word 'up' could be subtly misleading, and his statement 'I threw the ball up in the air' when conjoined with other appropriate statements might lead to false conclusions. For example, the statement 'he threw the ball straight up in the air' would seem to him reason to believe that the distances between the two lines of flight would always be equal. But he would be wrong.

That this kind of unconscious expectation is due to a part of our language (it is my guess that it is embedded in the concept 'is an upward direction' and other related words) can be seen from the fact that our language still incorporates this theory.[5] This is why children who have learnt these concepts can easily be puzzled by the question: 'How is it that the people on the other side of the earth do not fall down?' It seems that this is puzzling only because the radial theory of 'up' and 'down' is still not fully incorporated into our language. Other pieces of evidence in our language which point to this embedded theory are phrases like 'the ends of the earth' or '*the* horizon', phrases which seem to have embedded in them a theory that the earth is flat and finite in size though very large.

As we look at this example, we see how, when we use the word 'up' we can implicitly assert all kinds of beliefs even though the statement 'I threw the ball up' is clearly not blatantly mistaken. It is mistaken only if it is taken to mean, for example, that I threw the ball parallel to someone else's ball, when in fact I did not.

It is of course possible to say with hindsight that the idea of 'throwing the ball up' was perfectly all right, and to deny that it had this other, mistaken theory embedded in it. But that is only because with hindsight we can always disinfect the concept. If someone succeeds in showing, for example, how to disinfect the concept 'between' he would have simultaneously discovered many theories of the universe that are embedded in it. There may easily be a geometrical theory in it, and perhaps other theories, too. But such a task could not be thoroughly and successfully carried out. For we can find out that we believe in a theory only when we learn how to challenge it.

As a second example, consider someone looking up at the sky in the seventeenth century and saying 'I see that the sun has moved up quite a bit'. Once more, the statement might seem to be a perfectly innocuous observation statement. But the sun cannot have moved! This example is once again easy to deal with by saying that the word 'moved' was understood as a relation between the sun and, let us say, the ground or a nearby mountain. But because we can do this today is not to say that this is how the speaker understood it. To see that this is not an altogether spurious example, we only have to reflect on the way the church once interpreted 'stopped the sun' as proof that it moved, not relatively, but absolutely. Our relativization can only be done with hindsight. Now in this case the Bible certainly has no astronomical theory explicitly stated. But the church was quite correct in reading the theory embedded in the words.

The third and last example is from the theory of matter. If someone were to say 'the fire was quenched' this might seem quite straightforward. But in the ancient world of Greece this would have been understood as 'the thing fire, was overcome or annihilated by the thing water'. When the Greeks spoke of fire they did not distinguish between the flame and the process of burning. They called it all by one name 'fire'; and the meaning of this word had embedded within it the theory that it was a substance. For evidence that this theory and other such theories are embedded in language one has only to consider how hard it is to translate early Greek into modern English or even into modern Greek. Not all statements about fire, when translated literally, would be intelligible in English. And this shows how concepts can be strange, or different from our own, and how when we use them even as straightforward observation statements we may be unconsciously subscribing to many of their embedded theories.

(b) All Descriptive Statements are Dispositional

To return to the second way of looking at observation statements let us once again concentrate on the words that are used in them. It is clear to us that a word like 'brittle' cannot be used in an observation statement, and neither can the word 'soluble'. Why this is so can be expressed by saying that these terms are dispositional. What this means is that when one says that something is brittle, one asserts that it is disposed to behave in certain ways, in this case, to break very easily. A statement of the form 'x is brittle' cannot be observational no matter what value x takes, because what an object would do under various circumstances cannot be observed *now*, or in any moment of time. If we had an implicitly held or explicitly stated belief that something is brittle if and only if it has a certain (let us say) phenomenal quality, then 'x is brittle' might seem to be an observation statement for in this case we could identify the brittleness of an object just by looking. But the theory *could* be wrong. And this is why no matter how good a theory of brittleness one has, and no matter how simple it is in this theory to decide whether an object is brittle or not (by looking), the word 'brittle' remains dispositional. In fact even if we hit upon a true theory that satisfies the other condition, we still have a disposition on our hands. Once this is accepted, it is simple to show that all predicates have a dispositional character. Expressions that have been mistaken for observational phrases (like 'is yellow') really refer to complex dispositions, one of them being that a certain phenomenal mark would indicate the presence of that disposition.[6]

To say that a book is red implies that it would look orange through yellow sunglasses and that the wavelengths of the light that would be reflected off it would be predominantly lower than those which would be reflected off a blue object. The fact that we operate with an implicitly held theory which makes a sensation define the existence of this property is neither here nor there. The concept remains dispositional. There are two reasons for holding this position: (1) we are ready to say 'I thought it was red' if in fact it can be shown that the embedded theory was mistaken. For example if I look into the bright sky for a while, and then turn to a piece of white paper it looks red, but it is not red. So even the sensation is not a *simple* mark that what we see is red. (2) Statements containing the word 'red' can be used in all kinds of situations where the phenomenal quality or sensation cannot be observed. For example, one can say that there was a dim red light in a room in which the eyes could detect no light at all; or that stars which have their light shifted to the 'red side of the spectrum' are moving away from us at an enormous rate. (The spectrum may have no red in it at all.)

Notice that once we have resolved some difficulty in the theories embedded in the concept of 'red' we can also find something *post hoc* to which 'red' can be attributed on the basis of sensation. This is hardly surprising. But there is no way in which we can rule out the possibility that our sensation may turn out to be misleading in many unsuspected ways, which may yet have to be discovered. On the contrary, when we hope for progress in optics and in the physiology of vision, we hope that we will find a better theory of colours among other things. I might add in this connection that words which describe happenings might seem to be nondispositional. Some examples are 'broke' or 'fell' or 'turned'. But when we reflect on how a doctor tests a patient's arm to see if it is broken, or how we would test in the dark to find out whether we broke our glasses, we realize that there is no descriptive concept that is not dispositional.

ii. Theories are Embedded in Language

It might be said that I am confusing theories that are held by people with theories that are embedded in language. Thus, Russell's theory of descriptions shows theories embedded in definite descriptions. Am I not really talking about what people believe? To this objection I make the following reply:

(a) The difficulty that is encountered in the translation from one language (for example, ancient Greek) into another (for example, modern English), especially with concepts that are closely related to changed theories in science, is one excellent clue to show that different languages do indeed have different theories embedded in them. A classicist, when he looks at the different uses of a word and all its grammatical ramifications, does manage to get some insight into the thoughts of the ancients precisely because he learns gradually which beliefs are implicit in the language and what world view they must have been given by the language.

(b) Notice that implicitly held beliefs are not common to all mankind. Different societies seem to have different sets of implicitly held beliefs. On the other hand, one's belief system is not an accidental or even an individual affair. While individuals do possess different beliefs, there is generally speaking much agreement within a sufficiently isolated society about implicitly held beliefs. These beliefs are what one might call the culture, or civilization, of the people. These beliefs underpin the existence of social institutions, like money (belief in the value of gold), or community prayer (belief in the supernatural). This does not mean, of course, that individuals may not, expecially after critical reflection, learn a radically new way of looking at the world, or that such a new way may not transform a society's world view. My point is, rather, that by and large, individuals in a society show little difference in the most widely held beliefs, many of which may be implicit. But if implicitly held beliefs, for example cultural ones, are *common* and *peculiar* to a society, and, moreover, if there is some measure of *continuity* to these beliefs within a society through time, which social institution is it that transmits these theories to the whole society through time? I can think of no other institution but language.

E. Objection to the Third Insight

i. Familiarity Breeds Certainty

There remains one intuition of the two-tier conception that has to be dealt with, namely, how do we explain the certainty that we feel with regard to observation statements? This can be simply and easily explained. The feeling of certainty that is generated in us is in no way connected with the truth of the beliefs of which we are certain. The feeling may be connected to many different properties and relations of these statements; for example, to our familiarity with these statements and the words used in them. But when a new word is used, statements employing this new word invariably appear to be highly doubtful. Once we get used to the word and once we have assimilated its embedded theories in our stock of beliefs, we learn to trust it, and in some cases to feel sure about some of the statements using this word. Newton's theory of gravity initially met with hostility because it was 'occult', a great letdown for the *New Science*. This reaction was soon replaced by a feeling of such confidence in the theory that it seems hard to appreciate, in later times, what Newton's contemporaries could have found objectionable in 'the force of gravity'. Early in the nineteenth century this confidence in the theory of gravity went so far as to induce some scientists to try and model all theories on the theory of gravity, for it was thought to be such an easy concept to understand and deal with.

Finally, of course, Newton's theory of 'occult' action was replaced by the concept of a field, but not without much soul-searching on the part of scientists who found statements using this new concept highly dubious and theoretically uncertain. The certainty with which the theory of gravity was regarded, as opposed to the theory of fields of force, is rivalled only by the incredulity with which the theory of gravity was first greeted. And statements about gravitational forces which, in 1700 A.D., would have been considered theoretical were considered quite trustworthy by 1800 A.D., and could even be used to test alternative theories. This clearly indicates how familiarity breeds certainty, and unfamiliarity doubt.

The certainty which comes with familiarity is not without its value. For when we have a well-based skill, we can rely upon it more the more we have practised it. In a certain sense, the certainty does betray something important, though *not that what appears to be certain must be true*. For the relationship between the certainty felt in a familiar setting and what we can use as a fact for the purposes of argument, we must examine the relationship between *knowledge* and *skills*, which shows that empiricism properly construed is closely related to pragmatism.[7]

F. Two Open Problems

There is no need to attempt to show the falsity of the fourth premiss, because it would take us too far away from the issues of this book. The reader is urged to read Duhem's classic *The Aim and Structure of Physical Theory* and Popper's recent *Postscript to the Logic of Scientific Discovery*, expecially Volume I.[8]

We have objected to empiricist theories of meaning, and of learning, from a no-tier point of view. It is not intended that the no-tier point of view is not, in its turn, empiricist. The point of the critique of the old theory of meaning and learning is to see exactly what difficulties we face us when we try to make sense of meaning and learning.

'Knowledge' is a word which, in its everyday use, does not necessarily imply certainty. Hence, to be told that we cannot find certain knowledge in observations, and still less in observation statements, does not entirely exhaust the issue regarding knowledge.

In the ordinary sense of the word 'to know' there is a great deal that we do know in the world, and we rely upon it for our survival, even though it does not constitute certain knowledge, because it is capable of being changed when scientiest tell us that it should be.

Two questions arise, however, that are puzzling and need to be studied in this connection. First of all, regarding science, if it takes it upon itself not to accept what is commonly regarded as fact, (whether sometimes or always) then what does it take to be a fact, and for what reason?

The preliminary answer to this preliminary question is that those statements which confirm one theory and disconfirm its rival in a debate will be regarded as factual. Of course not any such statement will do, for any consequence of one theory which is not compatible with the other will satisfy this criterion.

Nevertheless, what two people with different theories seek when they debate is some statement that is independently established, and which contradicts the rival hypothesis. Naturally, the word 'independent' is most important in this statement, because any purported fact whose establishment presupposes the rival theory will be repudiated as a viciously circular argument. A full treatment of 'discriminating' tests is found in the chapter following this one.

But a second and subsequent difficulty arises if we examine even such facts from our empiricist's point of view, for we said that observations provide us with all the knowledge we have of the world. The 'facts' to which we make appeal when wishing to choose between rival hypotheses may or may not be empirical. Consider for instance, a debate from medieval times, when rival views are judged by facts independently established by divine revelation. Now if everyone accepts that there is a revelation and that it is accurate, because divine, (as was once the case regarding the Bible) then we can decide on scientific matters by appealing to the theological fact.

This does not mean, of course, that the 'facts' alluded to are *empirical* facts. But what *is* the difference? We saw that there is always a gap between any statement and the observation that it may be thought to report. If so, what distinguishes them from the theological statements which might equally well function as facts in a debate? This question, which calls for a new analysis of empiricism is taken up later.[9]

6
Psychological and Biological Ramifications

A. The Problem of Linguistic Holism and Gradual Learning

i. If Meaning and Theories are Interconnected, How is the Gradual Learning of Language Possible?

There is an apparently damaging objection to the statement that meanings are theories. The objection is this. There is a circular relationship between theories and meanings which could make the gradual learning of a language impossible. Let us study this curious point more fully.

The meaning of a word or a phrase is a set of ideas or theories. A theory can be understood only if it is expressed in the form of a statement which must, of course, have words in it. But the words themselves have meanings which as theories involve other words, and so on. If one wants to learn one word then one first has to learn other words which are part of its meaning and, before that, words involved in the meanings of those words, and so on. But to avoid an infinite regress language learning must by cyclical. All words in a language must be learnt all at once if any word is to be understood. But, the most superficial look at language learning shows that language is not learnt in one step. Most learning is very gradual, and even relatively fast learning is always much more gradual than this suggests. This seems to refute my claim that the meaning of a word is a set of theories.

Let us identify straightaway what it is that this objection brings out most clearly about the nature of meaning according to my view. *The meaning of a word is what can be relevantly expressed in the rest of the language.* Meanings are captured in the interrelationship of the words in the rest of language. The unsavoury consequence of this 'holistic' feature of meaning is that it then seems that we cannot understand how meanings can be learnt gradually.

Let us set this feature of my thesis against more traditional theories of meanings, which regard meaning as a sort of Platonic idea, like an abstract picture or an image. According to traditional theory, one can learn the meaning of any word in isolation merely by matching it with its meaning which our intuition can identify. In this view, the learning of a langue is not very gradual either, because words are learnt discretely, one at a time.

The learning of a language, far from being gradual, is atomistic. Thus with such an approach we could actually *count* how well a child knows a language. A measure of a child's linguistic progress would be a vocabulary count. Or we could simply see how many words he could understand out of a sample of a hundred random cases. But although it is not completely continuous, this view of language does explain why there is an appearance of continuity in the learning of vocabulary. Given the hundreds of words, thousands of phrases, and millions of possible combinations that a child learns to recognize we imagine that they are learnt in a steady stream. Thus, we have a fairly good approximation of gradual learning.

One need not believe that meanings or vocabulary are learnt in 'a stream' to see that in any case all the words of language are not learnt all at once, in one *gestalt,* as it were. On the contrary, most of us can hope to improve our understanding of concepts long after we have reached adulthood. The problem, then, is to take account of a comparatively slow learning process involved with meanings, given that the meanings of words are so integrally interrelated to each other.

The clue to understanding the learning of a language is simply that one can learn the meaning of the same word at different levels of complexity. So long as we demand that all words should be learnt perfectly, language is like an indivisible unit to be learnt all at once, or not at all. But that, of course, is not a reasonable demand to make. Degrees of understanding can be clearly discerned in the learning of a language.

ii. Model for Language Learning

(a) The Learning of Language is Interconnected with the Learning of the World

The model for learning that must accompany my thesis is this. Groups of interconnected words are learnt in relative isolation; their interconnection is later studied for better understanding. One always learns the meaning of several words together, or of one word in terms of existing theories. *Learning the meaning of a word in isolation from all theories is therefore strictly an illusion.* The interconnections between one word and another are of course statements. So when a child learns the meanings of words it learns to believe, or at any rate to conisder, certain statements. The learning of a language, and the learning of beliefs are thus closely intertwined. One cannot proceed without the other. Not only is our understanding of the world tinted by our language but our understanding of our language is tinted by our understanding of reality.

This becomes quite apparent in the case of learning the language of an intellectual discipline, let us say physics, or physiology, or psychology, or logic. By the time a student has learned the difference between the pairs of terms 'valid/invalid', 'true/false', 'proof/derivation', he has understood a great many theories about inference. In much the same way, a first-year college course in physics, which gives lists of uninteresting facts in simple mathematical form, can serve no useful purpose other than to teach students the language in which more interesting questions may later be asked. Such a method is not the best but it is a method of teaching just that. There may be some question whether it is not the worst way of teaching students a discipline, since one could go straight away to the most interesting questions, which should serve just as well to introduce students to the subject as well as its language. The other facts, the dull ones, cannot of course be ignored. But do they not cease to be dull when one sees their place in the search for that understanding to which the interesting questions and theories can lead us?

Learning a language, however, is a *revolutionary* process, that is to say, each portion that is learnt transforms the semantic 'field'. Each new theory and concept changes what many of the old words mean, just as some of the old words help determine what the new word means. Although this is quite a plain consequence of the holistic nature of the language, it has a further consequence regarding the nature of 'linguistic competence' which is worth noting.

(b) The Notion of Competence

Although learning a language involves learning at more and more complex levels until one reaches *approximately* a level of 'competence', it would be a mistake to operate with anything more than an approximate notion of competence. The reason is simply that once one understands a language with a *fair* degree of competence, one begins to learn theories whose truth is actively being disputed. Thus, when as a young student of physics, Thomas Young started to learn what the word 'wave' means, his achievements could be judged against a general background of linguistic competence. As his views developed, he learnt more and more theories until gradually he came up against the prevailing physical theories of waves. At this point it would have been a grave mistake to judge Thomas Young's words by existing standards of competence, or in terms of how physicists in his day understood waves. The reason is, simply, that judged by such standards, the theory of transverse waves, which could bend into shadows, would simply not have been understood at the time. Much the same can be said for the early ideas on differential calculus, forces, fields of force, atoms, infinity, the unconscious, etc.

It might seem to be altogether banal to press the point that the use of competence as a regulative concept where the growth of ideas is concerned is a seriously damaging affair. But if we look at the actual reception of Faraday's conceptions of lines of force, or of Freud's notion of the unconscious, it is a point worth making. In fact it is hard to think of important ideas which have been received otherwise.

Even if we were to regard language as a development towards some lofty or ideal goal, each stage in the development (or learning) of a language would have to be regarded as a language in its own right. Each stage that a child achieves in learning a language must be a language, and nothing else. There is no lack of system to it, and no lack of linguistic character. The only arrow pointing towards the goal-language would be the *cognitive problems which can best be solved, presumably, within the goal-language.*

One might wish for everyday examples to illustrate these theses about language learning, but such examples are hard to come by. In general, the learning of language is so complex an affair, and occurs so fast and on so many different fronts, that one can hardly distinguish the stages, the underlying theories or the languages as systems. (One reason for this, of course, is the existence of previous standards of normal speech.) There is, however, a method of studying all these theses of mine about language learning in detail, if we shift our attention from the swift and undocumented learning of languages by children to *the development of concepts and the history of ideas.* There we can see the learning of the language as an elongated process, very well documented, and often supplemented with comments about the utility and difficulty of words with new meanings. One such example, to illustrate one of my theses, should be enough. I have argued that each stage in the learning of a language is itself a language, if one is willing to accept the beliefs of this stage of the language. Thus 'force' was introduced into physics in the seventeenth century, and since then the words 'force' and 'momentum' have been so closely interrelated that anyone who does not know this interrelation cannot understand modern physics. Today they are understood partially in terms of each other. Insofar as Descartes identified forces with 'quantities of motion', we could accuse him of not quite knowing what 'force' and 'momentum' mean. But this is just a mistake, since to do so is to assume the truth of Newtonian physics, which Descartes did not even consider. If one insists on regarding any language as a stage in the evolution towards a goal which alone is language, and whose mastery alone signifies competence, then one would have to say simply that no one really understands the meaning of any word, if our ideas have yet far to go.

All these remarks about the historical growth of language are partially mirrored in the psychology of language learning. The main difference, as has already been noted, is that language learning is guided by the pre–existence of standards and conventions, and is therefore quite swift, whereas the growth of language is necessarily confusing, frustrating, and slow. Learning a language is only partly like the growth of language. It is also partly a process of 'socialization', or learning the rules and conventions of a linguistic community. But the function of rules in language learning has been generally misunderstood.

(c) The Function of Rules in Language Learning

Usually, when one thinks of learning a language in terms of learning the rules of its usage, one imagines that there are rules which constitute the usage in a language, and that the learner makes progressively better guesses about these rules. This view of the matter is far too simple, and mistaken.

For one thing, the rules which govern language are far from uniform. Different people use a language differently, and language is changing even as we are trying to master it—though not so fast that there is no stability to it. Which rules is the child going to learn? How will a child react to the problem of the perpetual falsification of every rule it tries to formulate—or implicitly to follow? Even grammarians who spend their lives studying one language—and who build upon the work of centuries of study—do not fail to discover new and surprising rules, and also exceptions to them, in the languages of their specialization. How can a child hope to learn rules well enough to communicate if the rules are in such a mess?

For another thing, children's languages do not typically develop as partial or incomplete adult languages. A child's language is very much a system, and seems to have an internal organic cohesion of its own. Even a casual look at parent-child relations shows that it is much nearer to the truth to say that it is the parents who learn baby talk in order to communicate with the child—at each stage of linguistic development—rather than the other way round.

The use of linguistic rules by children is, in fact, much more complicated. Children do use hypotheses about how adults speak in guiding their own efforts. But the use is overridden by another important consideration. *The resulting language must make sense to the child.* There are, therefore, two independent factors governing the growth of expressive capability among children. One of these is the internal cognitive growth which limits what the child can understand. The other is the external society-oriented growth in which the child tries to guess the rules of communication used by others. A child imitates adult language only within the limits of its own semantic field.

A remarkable piece of evidence to support this is the phenomenon of 'babbling'. It is not unusual for some children to fail to go through a babbling stage. But if a child does go through such a stage, then more often than not the babbling is not a precursor to language, but is simultaneous with it. A two-year-old child with a normal vocabulary will sometimes babble in accents, intonation, and manner that exactly imitates adult speech. But when it speaks 'properly', it will drop all these mannerisms, and resort to typical child's talk. It is as if the effort to imitate adults is too difficult *within* its language, and so the child must resort to babbling.

The difference between babblng and speech is yet more remarkable. The order in which vowels and consonants are learnt in babbling are exactly the reverse of the order in which these sounds are learnt in speech. Thus, even in the majority of cases, where a great deal of babbling precedes proper speech, it does not seem to be correct to think of speech as babbling-with-a-few-rules imposed upon it.

Language in the child no less than in the adult is integrally interwoven with cognitive knowledge. While the child learns a great many things about the language around it without understanding the theoretical ramifications which the expressive devices had in its history, it learns these devices in its own cognitive terms, and it can only improve upon its language to the extent that cognitive development takes place.

A final point to note is that the interaction between a child and an adult language involves the use of rules in some most peculiar manner. For one thing, a child will play with rules of usage to 'test' its impact. A new phrase or sentence is often used with bright eyes and an expectant smile, just for a response. Often a whole group of similar phrases will be so used, to demonstrate cleverness. Children will also use hypothetical rules of adult language to test their own linguistic competence, as when a child who has learnt a certain group of phrases tries to use the rules (often incorrectly) to apply the phrases to something which it understands. Then again, a child will apply a rule to a word quite unconsciously—as in finding a tensed form of a verb. It is this last activity which resembles most closely the general picture of learning the rules of adult language. But even here, the rules that are considered are adopted even if the child is corrected, and recognizes that adults regard the rule as mistaken. In such cases it seems clear that what limits the child's language are the internal categories of its cognitive-linguistic field (its expressive capability).

The learning of language among children can therefore be described as 'programmed discovery'. The child is hurried along a certain cognitive route by the dual demand of understanding the world, and understanding adult language (and to that extent adult categories and world views). In describing it as 'programmed' I do not of course intend the learning of language to be described as *unvarying*. Rather, I mean that the continuous demand of interacting with pre–existing standards or conventions of language and, particularly the need to understand what is said by others, leads to the development of a language in children which is not so much at variance with the linguistic tradition of the society.

B. The Problem of Novelty

i. The Learning of Novel Meanings

The learning of a language, then, is holistic. But that can only be part of the story. We have excellent reasons to wonder if there may not be other difficulties connected with learning a language regardless of whether or not it is holistic. We argued earlier that insofar as a novel word can be satisfactorily defined or partially explained, it is unnecessary; and insofar as it is necessary, it is novel and therefore impossible to define or even explain satisfactorily. Yet, as we noted, the learning of language is a common enough fact, so there must be some way that meanings are in fact learnt.

This problem of learning is easily solved in my theory, *unfortunately, much too easily*. A word is learnt, in my approach, not by learning its definition. Nor is it prudent to ask for an explanation of the meaning of a word if our difficulty in understanding it is the sort of conceptual difficulty that we are considering—namely if the word is indeed novel. In fact, the best way *to find out if there is a conceptual problem* is to ask for an explanation of its meaning. If, when the explanation is honestly given, it mystifies us even further, then there is a conceptual difficulty—the worst possible strategy now is to badger the speaker to be clear, if the speaker finds it hard to explain any farther. When there is a point of view expressed whose language seems to be incoherent, it is usually because the views presupposed in that point of view are at variance with what we presuppose by the words used. To accept the proffered position would lead to contradictory theories in our meaning, an incoherence in our language. To locate such a circumstance is already to be on the way toward a better understanding.

Having located a misunderstanding in this way, the next step is to ask what underlies it. Whence the need to speak so perversely? Why not speak as others do? Here it may be found that there are traditions in language other than our own, in which case we can learn them as we can learn the technical jargon of a new intellectual discipline. But the language may be idiosyncratic.

Whether or not there is a tradition of speaking in an idiosyncratic manner, the method to follow at this point is *to look for the intellectual problem which prompts the strange utterances*. Once we appreciate the problem, we can find out why the speaker, rightly or wrongly, finds ordinary theories inadequate to solve it. Once we begin to appreciate what would count as an adequate solution to such a problem, we can see how the actual views offered can do the trick.

In short, the answer to 'How can I learn what a novel meaning is intended to be?' is *be creative, and try to solve the problem for a speaker in the manner the speaker might follow herself*. Understanding what a person is trying to say in such circumstances is trying to see the world as he or she does. Naturally such a method cannot guarantee success. The advice 'be creative' is certainly not a formula. Hence the solution to this problem can be said to be *much too easy*, because, to follow it could be much too hard!

ii. The Learning of Correct Meanings: Konrad Lorenz's Theory of Animal Behaviour Extended to Language

There is another problem with the thesis that meanings are theories. The problem is this. The learning of a language is *a 'creative' process* which involves the appreciation *of problems*, of the *inadequacy of alternative solutions*, and of startling consequences. Naturally a child is a problem solver insofar as it does learn a language. *But how does it locate the correct problem, and present alternative solutions which it can see do not work?* Once we have a sufficiently developed language, then we can use this language to arrive at an understanding of common problems and their various solutions. What can the child use to find out these things?

This question is a very difficult one, and the answer will lead me immediately into controversial questions of psychology, anthropology and biology. Luckily a solution to this problem can be constructed out of an extension of the ideas of Konrad Lorenz on animal behaviour.[1] The solution is as follows. *Every human being comes preprogrammed with the same theories, problems, and solutions to these problems.* He also comes preprogrammed to recognize the inadequacy of some solutions.

Konrad Lorenz's theory is quite simple in its basic form. According to him, what is innate in a person is not a capacity or a potentiality, but rather some very specific things which can be isolated and studied. Lorenz sees the instinctive act as a *fixed or stereotyped motor pattern* which the organism performs like a robot. These motor patterns are specific to species, being a factor in their genome. The patterns themselves are enormously complex motor actions. Members of a species will be successful in performing them only because of certain complex features of the environment to which the species is adapted. The example of the predatory attack of the raven, quoted from Lorenz (below) is a typical description of such a motor pattern, beautifully intricate, depending on superb timing and coordination, and yet rarely missing its objective in its complex natural surroundings.

These motor patterns require excellent physical coordination. The coordinator is situated in the central nervous system of the organism. Studies of such patterns in the greylag goose convinced Lorenz that when one repeatedly elicits a motor pattern of this sort, it soon ceases to be elicited after becoming weaker and weaker, as if the bird had exhausted its energy. Yet its muscular energy is at this point quite undiminished. Lorenz concludes that at the coordinating point of the central nervous system there is a continuous build-up of energy, which must reach a certain critical level before the motor pattern can be set off. This energy is act-specific—that is to say, it can only be spent by performing that particular act.

If this were all, then each organism would keep erupting with its fixed motor patterns of behaviour at regular intervals, as the energy builds up. Thus a fledgling would keep opening its beak every few minutes. Its mother would keep pushing worms at it every few minutes. But since the motor patterns are elicited by independent variables—namely the build-up of energy in the two central nervous systems of fledgling and mother bird—the worm would almost never reach the fledgling's beak, with sad consequences.

Lorenz's solution to this problem is that motor patterns are *released*, in the manner of a switch being turned on by a *signal* which activates a *release mechanism*. Thus the fledgling's cry releases the feeding pattern of behaviour from the mother bird, while the shape of the mother's flying form will release the motor pattern of the fledgling's beak opening to receive the food (a sort of pre–established harmony).

Perhaps the most startling feature of Lorenz's ideas is that they have led a host of naturalists to actually isolate motor patterns and the releasing signals, so much so that one can create artificial objects which act as dummy release signals and these signals elicit motor patterns predictably. This is possible, of course, only because of the great simplicity of the release mechanism as opposed to the intricate complexity of the motor pattern elicited.[2]

Observing the function of releasing mechanisms under natural conditions, one is tempted to over-assess the amount and the specificity of innate information contained in them. If one observes a tame hand-reared young raven, which up to that moment has never paid any attention to living prey, make a determined dash at the one sick jackdaw among dozens of healthy ones and kill it skillfully with one well-aimed blow at the back of its skull, one is amazed at the amount of innate knowledge underlying this behaviour. The bird seems to know that it could not prey on healthy jackdaws; it seems to recognize the symptoms of illness, to conclude that they promise success to an attack, and to know exactly how and where to launch the attack. On close examination, the innate information underlying all this complicated sequence of behaviour boils down to very few and simple, if important, data. The raven, like many birds of prey and also many carnivores, possesses a mechanism that releases motor patterns of prey-catching and responds to irregularity in the prey's motor actions. A slight stumbling, an irregularity of wing-beat, or the like elicits a predatory attack with the mechanical predictability of a reflex, as trainers of the big carnivores have learnt to their cost. An analogous response in hawks and falcons is used by falconers in the construction of the "lure". Furthermore, the raven's fixed motor pattern of grasping with both feet and delivering a fearful blow of the bill exactly between them is supplemented by a built-in oriented mechanism that directs it at the back of the prey's head. It is characteristic of all releasing mechanisms that the innate information contained in them is coded in a surprisingly simple, and at the same time, most effective way. For example, the stinging response of the common tick, *Ixodes rhizinus,* is released by any object having a temperature of roughly 37 degrees C and smelling of butyric acid. Simple though these key stimuli are, it is difficult to visualize a natural situation in which the response could be elicited by anything except the animal's most adequate host, a mammal. Similarly, the baby apistogramma will follow any object that shows black and yellow markings roughly corresponding to that of the mother and that performs jerking movements of a certain frequency and amplitude; the male stickleback will fight any simple dummy that has a red undersurface; the jackdaw will attack any living creature carrying something black and dangling; and so on.

There are two kinds of learning that any organism can undergo. There is, on the one hand, genetic or evolutionary learning. This is the Darwinian, or neo-Darwinian, process by which a species adapts to its surroundings. There is however, another kind of learning, which is more important to us, namely, individual learning. In this learning what happens is that the innate patterns of behaviour are combined in new ways, or are modified. Thus in *both cases,* that is the Darwinian as well as actual individual learning, *motor patterns are modified.* The difference, however, is that the modification in the one case is a strictly genetic or hereditary process, while in the other it is strictly a matter of the individual (rather than the species) learning.

Individual learning is possible only if an organism is not completely dominated by fixed patterns. So we could say that individual learning frees us from instincts. But this is misleading. If we merely have an evolution from an adapted structure to one whose adaptive patterns of behaviour no longer hold, then we would simply have an organism which is less adaptive. Such a change in the genome would quickly be eliminated. If there is to be a useful improvement by individual learning, then it cannot be merely the process of liberation from our instincts. What is necessary is a *system of control* over our motor patterns, with feedback, and an *innate base* for this mechanism or system of control.

Since this innate base of learning, or system of control, cannot itself be a stereotyped motor pattern, I shall call it a *stereotyped thought pattern;* I mean by this whatever patterns are involved in the appreciation of the environment and the application of this to the modification of one's behavioural patterns. These may also be described as conscious (or preconscious) expectations. That these patterns are also somewhat stereotyped, or at any rate very limited in their range of variation, is supported by two arguments: first, there would be too many nonadaptive changes possible to allow for survival if it were otherwise. The second is an empirical argument, namely, that animals are certainly characteristic in what they can and cannot learn: e.g., toilet-training even a domesticated bird or reptile is doomed to failure. Innumerable illustrations of such limits can be given—for example, the well known and widely reported study of the wasp Ammophila by G. P.

Baerends, in which he shows that when the wasp visits its many nests to *inspect* them, it can learn what the state of the nest is; but later when it goes to *feed* larvae in the same nests, it is unable to learn about the state of the nest.[3]

Konrad Lorenz in his study concentrates on fixed *motor* patterns. This is not surprising, since *motor* patterns of behaviour are overt and easy to test. It is only a slight extension of this idea which takes us to steroetyped patterns more generally, motor or otherwise, and for our purposes, *stereotyped thought patterns,* especially.[4] These would be patterns internal to the central coordinating system. With this slight extension we can understand the innate basis of human language. Learning, in this slightly extended view, will consist of recombining and modifying one's innate patterns, motor or otherwise, so that other more appropriate ones may be substituted for them.

What an organism can or cannot learn must plainly depend to a considerable extent on what patterns it has started out with. A swan in the company of ducklings will not only be ugly, which may be excused, but will also have very poor manners indeed. No matter how versatile an 'ugly duckling' is, it cannot learn all that a duck can learn, for example in mating or feeding habits. The reason, of course, is that since learning is really a transformation of an already existing innate pattern, a swan cannot learn what a duck can—though it might do other more interesting things on its own—because it does not have the duck's innate patterns to transform. One can only modify what one already has.

In much the same way, a chimpanzee in a human social environment cannot readily pick up the human language because it does not have the basic innate patterns which can be transformed into such a language. The innate patterns which can be fashioned into language are 'prelinguistic' patterns of understanding (or theories), and patterns of problem solving. Here it is interesting to ask what exactly is the difference between a chimpanzee and a human. They both have systems of communication or 'language'. They both have 'exploratory behviour', or curiosity and problem-solving behaviour. They both have expectations, as all animals do. Yet the chimpanzee can barely be interpreted as describing anything. It is the *fusion* of expectation and communication in a special way that is crucial. A chimpanzee can communicate an expectation; for example when it warns its group by cries of distress that there is a danger at hand. But what it cannot do is convey its expectation of a cry of distress at a later date, or expect the expectation of a cry of distress, etc. In short, the special character of our language as a reflexive system is what chimpanzee communication lacks.

Let us now make use of Lorenz's theory of learning. Since language has a holistic character, it must always be learnt creatively, by studying problems for which the language will provide solutions. Children who learn the same language are therefore solving the same problems in roughly the same way. And these *creative* acts can be *stereotyped* (but only up to a point) because the children are born with innate thought patterns which are common to members of the species. These thought patterns are problem-solving patterns, with the problems being determined by the confrontation of innate theories with the world, the family, or society. Thus problem-solving patterns and theories are common to all children, and so are most of the earliest problems. But differences in social and physical conditions as they affect the child will certainly result in different intellectual and, therefore, different linguistic careers for different infants. In particular, children born and bred in different communities will learn different languages for just this reason.

Some may wonder whether common problems, common cultural backgrounds, and social communication are able to *explain how two people can creatively come up with the same idea in a statistically large number of cases.* To allay these doubts, let me point out a phenomenon in the most creative of problem-solving efforts, namely, at the frontiers of knowledge. In science, where there is much *less* similarity in relevant background and influences than among children, and where the problems, while vaguely similar, are often quite different for each scientist, there is a constantly recurring phenomenon called 'simultaneous discovery'. So remarkably common is this phenomenon, that it is hard to find a major intellectual tradition in which any discovery was not made by more than one person, or at least foreshadowed by more than one person.

C. The Problem of Prelinguistic Theories

i. Protolanguage

I turn now to another serious difficulty involved in my theory of meaning. Theories are expressed in a languge. New theories may demand improved languages. *But what are theories* (i.e., expectations) *expressed in no language at all?* For this is what we demand when we say that language arises from a bed of theory. There must be prelinguistic theories, and problems. But how can there be a statement with no words in it, a theory with no language-stuff?

There are two possible and entirely different ways out of this problem. One of these is to insist there can be theories that do not need to be caught in or stated in a language. One could call them 'attitudes', following Kant. But what such a theory is like we could never tell! On the other hand, we could say that there is, prior to human language, another language, a protolanguage, out of which the human language developed. This is a slightly better solution since one can hope to say what this protolanguage is like and discover its properties. I propose to adopt the latter solution to this problem for that reason, and because the other seems to dismiss a serious problem by a linguistic sleight of hand.

Let us call the language in which our 'prelinguistic' theories are found the 'protolanguage'. Then, we can ask, what is the character of this protolanguage, and what sort of properties must it have? What we require is that the protolanguage must have the capacity to capture theories in its network, and to allow change of theory, and to respond to new theories as our human languages do; there must also be some conservative principle, like the need to communicate in human languages, which eliminates changes of theory and language that are too radical. In short, it must be governed by a progressive and a conservative principle, as are languages.

ii. The Genetic Structure of an Organism Understood as a Protolanguage

It is remarkable, and hardly a coincidence, that *we can interpret the genetic structure of an organism*—or that structure which determines the morphogenesis of the organism—*as instructions in this protolanguage*. To do so we need look but superficially at what is known to us today. The analogy is, I believe, a suggestive one; but I shall do little more than suggest, even though the value of such a suggestion would depend very much on how it can be developed.

The 'prelinguistic theories'—the theories that are prior to human language—include all those expectations, attitudes, and patterns of behaviour that have developed in the organism by the slow processes of biological evolution. These include not only such things as the 'knowledge' which enables one member of a species to recognize a fellow member from a nonmember, but all the other complex abilities which it must possess in order to survive—abilities such as locomotion, feeding, social adaptability, etc. But in what language can one say these expectations are expressed?

The very simplest of cells which must have evolved to their present state a little more than a billion years ago, exhibit a structure which they have in common with all the most complex organisms that we know. In this one respect the entire biosphere has but one structure. Every cell has within it a nucleus which contains two long chains of four nucleic acids arranged in the form of a 'double helix', called DNA, one like a negative (as of a photograph) of the other. A replicating mechanism called 'messenger RNA' facilitates the production of a similar long chain with almost the same structural sequence of nucleic acids, which is despatched in the cell to a complex called a 'ribosome' which produces enzymes and proteins. These enzymes and proteins make up the composition of the cell. Indeed the entire mechanism of the repair of cells and of DNA, of replication, and of regulation, are found to involve 'instructions' which are written 'in code' in the arrangement of nucleic acids in the DNA.

These nucleic acids are arranged in groups of three (or six if you count both helices) and a segment of these serves to instruct the cell to produce, to slow down, speed up or stop producing a particular protein.

These proteins have a most singular feature which we most note. Jacques Monod calls it their 'cognitive' and sometimes their 'cybernetic' structure. Proteins are formed out of amino acids, about twenty odd, which are synthesized in ribosomes. When synthesized they become long chains of amino acids, or polypeptides. These polypeptides fold into shapes (for example, almost globular shapes, which are most common) and it is these shapes which determine their function within the cell. Let us look at both stages of this process.

When the 'messenger RNA' goes over to the ribosome, its twin helix, called 'transfer RNA' is fed like machine tape through the ribosome, and the large molecules of the ribosome synthesize amino acids as specified by the triplets of nucleic acids in the sequence of transfer RNA. The relevant proteins in the ribosomes, one might say, 'recognize' the triplets of the nucleic acids, and 'translate' them into amino acids. Moreover, the exact sequence of amino acids is specified in the DNA, transcribed to the transfer RNA and synthesized in that order by the ribosomes. This gives us the polypeptides which fold 'autonomously' into their functional shape.

The chemical structure which allows for this extraordinary ability of proteins to find their own shape, and which allows the extraordinarily specific action of the chemicals of the living cell is now known. To illustrate this 'cognitive' structure, we can take a globular protein, and divide its thousands of atoms into identical units called 'protomers'.[5] Sometimes these protomers can be split easily into their component units (monomers) by the use of mild dissociating agents (chemicals). "In this state" says Monod, "the protein will in general have lost all its functional properties, catalytic or regulatory. However—and this is the important point—if the "normal" conditions are restored (by eliminating the dissociating agent), the subunits will ordinarily reassemble spontaneously, re-forming the original "native" state of the aggregate: the same number of protomers in the same geometrical arrangement, accompanied by the same functional properties as before."[6]

It is also interesting that in order to translate from the transfer RNA into a polypeptide sequence to form protein, *we need proteins in the ribosome*. The DNA, without the translation mechanism, is powerless. The translation mechanism, on the other hand, is synthesized according to instructions from the DNA!

Here, at the level at which all living systems now in existence are similar, we have a relationship between an alphabet (the DNA sequences) and its 'expression', the functioning cell. What, we may ask, is the relationship between them? It is an astonishing thing to note that though the 'code' which specifies which amino acid is specified by any triplet of nucleic acids in DNA is almost universal in our biosphere, it is not quite universal. It is, in fact, 'conventional', or to put it in a non-anthropomorphic way 'arbitrary'.

A particular triplet of DNA might have specified any one of several amino acids, but does in fact specify a particular amino acid. Moreover, there are 64 possible combination marks (4 nucleic acids raised to three, as triplets are notes) and only twenty-odd amino acids, allowing for both 'meaningless' sequences and redundancies. The former are fundamental for the genetic equivalent of punctuation, and the latter for purposes which will only be appreciated in Chapter 11 below.

Why, we might ask, does the code not change through reproduction? It is clear that changes would lead instantly to lethal effects in the cell. If the protein synthesizers were to start producing actively new polypeptides, the cell, which is a functioning unit, would soon be destroyed, due to lack of an appropriate function. This strong conservative principle, which is neo-Darwinian, applies equally well to the most macroscopic features of complex organisms.

But if we turn our attention away from the code itself and study the production of proteins, we find something rather interesting. Any complex structure of cells, or 'organism', which has specialized cells must support not just the internal regulation that all cells have, but also modifications of the internal regulations of each individual cell, by the overall shape and function of the organism as an aggregate.

Thus one cell may produce insulin and another bile, but the DNA in each of these is exactly the same, as are the code–translating mechanisms. Yet, the cells which constitute a mouse and those which constitute an elephant make it impossible for one organism to bear the other as offspring. Between close relatives, however, it is possible: a type A mouse could yield a type B mouse, by a change in DNA called a mutation. Most mutations are lethal, but those that are successful lead to changes in the extant DNA sequences. Thus we see that mutation acts as a progressive principle.

We could regard organisms as simply expressions of a linguistic tradition which became universal about a billion years ago on earth. Instead of regarding the last statement as just a fanciful analogy, let us treat it as an attempt to literally describe what we know of living systems. Then the 'coincidence' to be explained is not how it is that our conception of human language fits the phenomena of life, which seem so far removed, but rather the converse: why is human language such an accurate manifestation of genetic processes? Human languages may be regarded as *a socially objective manifestation of a fundamental process in all living systems*. Why this should be so must await some neo-Darwinian considerations regarding languages which will be taken up in the chapters to follow.

The philosopher who finds that theories presuppose language and language presupposes theories will not be satisfied with an origin one or two or three billion years ago if this in turn faces the same riddle. In the end we have to ask: What specific character of matter itself is it that evolves into the linguistic structure of life? The answer to this is far from clear. How did proteins initially come to be regulated by nucleic acid sequences? How did these sequences come to even be associated with amino acids? How did one such language colonize all the other forms that might have existed, or was there only one dominant form from the beginning, in which case why were there not more?

This question regarding the origins, or evolution of the first living systems with a 'language', from mere molecules capable of replication (the jump from proteins, however large and complex, to the complex whole which is the cell) is perhaps the major question that remains unanswered in evolutionary molecular biology.

From a philosophical point of view, however, it is heartening to note that the origin of life in the chemistry of the earth has a regress of only a finite duration.

7
The Structure of Problems and the Growth of Knowledge and Language

A. The Riddle of Conceptual and Linguistic Innovation

i. The Riddle

The fact that we have useful and well-formed linguistic structures of great complexity shows that linguistic innovation has had a long history. Languages must grow in their expressive capability. But the very idea of linguistic innovation which leads to the growth of expressive capabilities is beset with difficulties. These difficulties must now be faced.

The expressive capability of a language which we use depends on at least two factors. First of all, the meanings of words must incorporate theories or expectations or beliefs which are widely enough known among those who use the words. Such a background of fairly common knowledge is absolutely necessary for any communication. A second factor is the evolutionary residue of past habits of speech. These may no longer be associated with their earlier theoretical content, but only with the flexible and diverse uses to which they can be put in the context of the later linguistic tradition. Syntax and grammar will make use of linguistic patterns which are cognitively redundant by investing them with new uses, somewhat like the conversion of a church hall into a bingo parlour, or the use of the width of the lapel on one's jacket to signify one's social, economic, or political associations.

An important thesis which is maintained here is that linguistic innovations which lead to the growth of expressive capability arise out of intellectual revolutions. Since innovations must occur if language is to grow—and grow it must—uses of language must be possible where, to express a new point of view, a break is made with linguistic conventions. But this leads to a difficulty. A new word or a very new use of a word can hardly be defined in the language if it is to lead to expressive growth. A simple argument shows why this is so. Let us call the words and colloquial phrases that are used 'atomic expressions'. Naturally, using these expressions, others may be defined. Consider all the expressions which may be defined in terms of the atomic expressions. Let us call this the existing 'conceptual field' of the language. (We need not assume that this field is logically coherent, let alone a deductive system, if each concept is spelt out in terms of the theories out of which it has crystallized.) Then the kind of linguistic innovation we are studying is one which goes beyond the conceptual field. Only then does expressive capability improve. But if novel expressions cannot be caught in the conceptual field, how can their meaning be known?

We might suppose that by understanding the new point of view, the novel theory which necessitates changes in the conceptual field, we can understand the new expression. But this can hardly be so: the new point of view can be understood only with the help of new expressions. If not, where is the need for the new expressions? Here, then, is the full puzzle. Since the point of view (which gives the new words some of their meanings) is new, we cannot understand it without first understanding the new words. But the new words require us to first understand the new point of view. Neither can be understood before the other. How can such a situation be resolved? Yet we know that such situations are far from isolated. The history of ideas gives us innumerable examples of intellectual revolutions. Each of these is also a case study for change in the conceptual field.

A novel word which cannot be defined within the expressive field of a language may, of course, be *partially* explained using the existing language. Nevertheless, the crucial aspect of its meaning, which is new, will elude us. It is useless to study how the word is being used, for a new word has not been used often enough to provide clues. (And in any case, what does the first person using the word understand by it?) Nor is it useful to badger the person who is 'misusing' the language (by imaginative standards). Our problem suggests that this approach can have no satisfactory ending. Nor can we demand a complete enumeration of all the theories embedded in the word. There are too many of these. We can only require that the new theory be stated.

What we should do is to understand the need for novelty. What is the problem that prompts the new theory and the new word? This is the key to the possibility of communication, when there is growth in expressive capabilities.

ii. A Solution: New Theories and Their Terminology Can be Understood through Problems

It is to the *problems* that we must turn to understand how conceptual novelties are communicated. Somehow, problems must allow us to understand new theories and their terminology, if not completely, then at least well enough to be able to proceed to further inquire into the question. It is therefore necessary to understand how problems can help us do this. We can begin our study of problems by asking this question: what desiderata must a theory of problems meet in order to fulfil its role in our theory of language? A study of the difficulty we face suggests three desiderata worth noting.

The growth of language has intellectual endeavour as its progressive principle. Intellectual endeavour is what links the growth of language to human adaptation. But now it turns out that intellectual endeavour of the kind that leads to the growth of expressive capabilities of language presupposes the existence of problems. Whatever significance intellectual endeavour has for human adaptation must therefore also be a feature of problems. The first desideratum is therefore that *our theory of problems must locate problems in the context of adaptation.*

We see also that if language is to grow in spite of its natural sluggishness, the problems must somehow demand to be solved. There must be a need felt to consider and solve problems. The second desideratum of our theory is that *it must show the need to solve problems*, not just now and then, as a whim, but continuously as they turn up.

A theory of problems would be useless to us if it did not show us the way to understand conceptual innovations. New theories and new linguistic devices must somehow be indicated by the problems, if the problems are to help us 'take the leap' into the new expressive field. But if they are to do so, *problems must yield criteria for their own solution* (third desideratum). Only if our theory can give us this result can we hope to use problems as a steppingstone to understanding innovations. The growth of expressive capability in language depends upon the fact that problems come with their own criteria for adequate solution, which criteria cannot be satisfied by theories which are consistent with theories embedded in the meanings of words.

B. The Adaptive Value of Intellectual Problems

In order to pursue the study of problems we must distinguish between two kinds of problems that we face which differ from each other in their character—*practical problems* and *intellectual problems*. Practical problems must be understood in terms of aims or goals. A problem is a hurdle which we must surmount in order to achieve a goal. Surmounting the problem to get to the goal, or nearer the goal, or even to make it possible to get to the next hurdle towards the goal, is a solution. The more urgent it is to reach a goal, the more urgently it behooves us to surmount the hurdles, or the problems in our path. Since there is no need to expand on the importance of goal-directed activity in the adaptation of higher mammals, the evolutionary significance of practical problems need not delay us.

But intellectual problems are notoriously unlike problems in that their need to be solved hardly appears to be great. The goals or aims of intellectual activity do not seem to lend it the urgency which practical problems have. There are even those who believe that intellectual activity is a search for truth just for the sake of truth, without regard to the achievements of any ends or goals of a mundane or practical variety. Many of the most remarkable discoveries in mathematics and physics had hardly any application at the time of their discovery, though some have subsequently been used to solve practical problems.

In short, our first and second desiderata are fulfilled by a theory of practical problems. The need to solve practical problems, as well as their place in our struggle to survive, is clear. But practical problems cannot lead to intellectual growth, for, to solve them, what we typically need is action. Intellectual problems, on the other hand, do lead to the growth of ideas, and therefore to the growth of excessive capabilities, but unfortunately, they do not seem to have any practical aim or goal which they clearly block and which we desire. The typical intellectual problem is very often so impractical that the practical man in the street fails to sees its importance, and therefore sees the university as an 'ivory tower' in which useless questions are being discussed, while he must 'get on with it.' If we are to provide an adequate theory of problems, it must show how intellectual problems, like practical problems, can fulfil the first and second desiderata.

i. Logical Inconsistency and Adaptation to Reality

This difficulty which we face can be met by noting that practical problems are solved by us with the aid of our *expectations*. We must rely upon our beliefs regarding the world in order to surmount any hurdle in the way of our goal. If we put all our knowledge and beliefs and expectations, even those that we have but cannot state, into one system and call it the universe of our beliefs, then our difficulty can be met as follows. *Intellectual problems are logical inconsistencies within the universe of our beliefs.*

In this view one need not assume that we have *knowledge* of anything whatsoever. Even if there is something that we do know for certain, its existence is of little importance. Rather we see that our beliefs and expectations are necessary for our survival. They may all be mistaken. Or some of them may be true. But true or false, they are all we have and it is by them alone that we can live. Such beliefs are *useful* and even *necessary*, even if they are false. In accordance with this view, a doctor may tell a patient he will do the best he can; or an economist may advise a government that so far he knows a certain action is to be recommended.

The universe of our beliefs is not a closed one. We are always acquiring new ideas and changing old ones. In all this change there is always one danger. It is this. Some part of our expectations may contradict, or be logically inconsistent with, another part of it.

Now a logical inconsistency is a very serious business. There is no doubt that it indicates that some part of our views is false. We were willing to grant that it may be false in the first place. A logical inconsistency furthermore has a *systemic* effect. It destroys the effectiveness of our system of beliefs: *from a logically inconsistent set of statements any statement follows.*

This is an elementary result of logic. It does not depend at all on what we take to be the logical forms of sentences. It should therefore be acceptable to all. We need only reflect on invalidity to see why this is so: an invalid form of argument is one which may be exemplified by some argument with true premises and a false conclusion. But logically inconsistent premises are never true. So an argument with formally inconsistent premises is valid no matter what the form of the conclusion.

The fact that any statement or too many statements follow from a logical inconsistency does not mean that we cannot operate at all with inconsistencies. Most of us do in fact 'compartmentalize' our beliefs, so that incompatibilities between one compartment and another may never emerge, or be noticed. When we do detect an incompatibility, we can choose to ignore it, on the ground that since no two compartments come together in one set of premises, we need have no worry. But this has a disastrous result. *It means that we can never use our beliefs to draw new ingenious conclusions from them.* Let me explain.

Beliefs which are held explicitly are useful, of course, in virtue of what is explicitly said in them. But they are even more useful because of the other new and ingenious uses to which we can put them, as premises in unusual predictions, explanations, and arguments. Inferences from what we know (or what we think we know) are useful to avert disaster, and to achieve our goals. Hence, when a logical inconsistency afflicts our expectations, the whole system (or at least a functionally integral subsystem) becomes redundant. For if we could once have deduced clever, useful, and unexpected consequences for planning the next budget, from economics, psychology, sociology, and general commonsense put together, should our economics be inconsistent with some other 'compartment' of thought, we end up with advice like 'raise taxes next year' and equally well 'lower taxes next year', as well as 'do both of these' and 'do neither of these'.

Thus we see that intellectual problems are practical problems, in a certain sense. We wish to rid our expectations of their logical inconsistency only because we need to do so in order to achieve whatever goals we have. Hence our aim in solving intellectual problems is eminently practical. But, unlike most practical activity, intellectual activity does not try to remove impediments in our way to achieve specific goals. Rather, *intellectual activity removes impediments to goal-directed activity generally.*

The job of the intellectual is like the job of the 'maintenance' man at the factory. His product is only useful if what the factory produces is useful. His job is to keep the factory functioning.

Logical inconsistency might be a problem—must all problems be logical inconsistencies? (From now on we shall refer to intellectual problems simply as 'problems'.) We can think offhand of many problems or questions which have been posed in the history of our ideas that are not logical inconsistencies. The hypothesis that problems are logical inconsistencies seems to be refuted much too easily to be a serious hypothesis.

ii. Problems and Questions

However, the apparent difficulty of sustaining such a hypothesis is really a trick played on us by our unwitting acceptance of the widespread belief that *problems are questions.* Naturally, if that hypothesis is correct, and since questions are not logical inconsistencies, it seems ridiculous even to entertain the hypothesis that problems are inconsistencies. It might even seem to be a matter of *meaning*—the meaning of the word 'problem' might seem to equate it with a question. The Oxford English Dictionary does give question as one of its meanings.

I would like to dissociate problems from questions, however, for my purposes, since only then can we fairly consider the hypothesis that problems are logical inconsistencies. I might point out that the word 'problem' derives from a Greek word 'problema' meaning originally a shield or a bulwark or a hurdle—an impediment to some action of a person, or of water (as of a wave in the sea) or to some other physical action. Plato seems to be the first to use the word in an intellectual context, and Aristotle the first to use it exclusively in intellectual contexts. Aristotle seems to regard the impediments to our knowledge—the problems—as *questions.* '*Problema*' are a series of questions where what we call *problems* are '*aporiai*'.) We can say quite fairly that the hypothesis that problems are questions is Aristotle's. And since he might be wrong, we should be careful not to make a question part of the meaning of the word 'problem'. Let us think of a problem simply as whatever it is that creates an impediment to our knowing the world and which motivates us to look for the truth about that matter. Then our question is: is this something a question or a logical inconsistency?

My main argument for not regarding problems as questions is this. Even if we understand problems as questions, they still cannot be *any* questions chosen arbitrarily, because we can distinguish between *problematic* questions and *idle* or *unproblematic* ones. So not every question represents an impediment to our knowledge, nor is each an impetus to further acquiring knowledge. Not every young child who learns to ask 'Why?' in a repetitive and routine way is learning to do science or philosophy. The difference between *idle* and *problematic* questions is that the latter arise out of problems (which I propose to regard as logical inconsistencies).

The difference between regarding intellectual endeavour as answer to questions and regarding it as the resolution of logical inconsistencies is really a symptom of a more fundamental difference in explanatory strategy. The thesis that theories answer questions makes the best sense against a background of *Aristotelian essentialism* or the doctrine that all ultimate explanations are shared in terms of the *natures of things*. Thus, intellectual activity itself is understood in terms of man's *nature*—his inquiring or truth-seeking nature (cf., the opening sentences of Aristotle's *Metaphysics*). If we accept this sort of explanation, we need never wonder why a person asks a particular question. It is simply *human nature* to seek answers.

But the Aristotelian explanatory strategy is a poor one—this case being no better than the others that Molière made fun of in the seventeenth century. To say that human beings are by nature curious does not *explain* why we seek answers but merely says in other words that we do seek answers to questions.

Yet another objection is this one. Human beings do not ask questions all the time. In fact, we are extremely complacent about most things. Even the greatest of scientists seem to have been remarkably indifferent to all those aspects of the world that did not bear on their particular intellectual concerns. Different scientists at different times have different curiosities. So, clearly, an appeal to man's nature is insufficient, for this does not explain why, at a particular time, one particular question is found worth pursuing at great length, to the exclusion of a multitude of others, while at another time, another question is so pursued. (This is not to deny that we are curious about many things at many times, but just to say that curiosity is directed, or aroused.)

The explanatory strategy that is presupposed in the Aristotelian approach becomes unnecessary when we adopt the alternate hypothesis, for if all problems are logical inconsistencies, we need no longer depend on any special assumption regarding the *inquiring nature* of people. Rather, we can account for occasional curiosity by the existence of a logical inconsistency which prompts it and the usual lack of curiosity by the fact that there is usually no such inconsistency that provokes.

Thus the hypothesis that our curiosity is aroused by logical inconsistency explains our curiosity (or lack of it), whereas the Aristotelian point of view must accept as a mysterious inexplicable truth that man is a creature of curiosity. Unlike the obscurity of Aristotelian 'natures' or 'essences', logical inconsistency can be understood very well in terms of modern logic, and so provides a better theory of problems than does the Aristotelian approach.

In brief, we see that the problematic character of some questions, as opposed to the ideal character of others, is itself not a feature of erotetics, but of underlying logical inconsistencies. Secondly, we see that to regard problems as questions (albeit of a certain unspecifiable kind) is to depend on a woefully inadequate Aristotelian conception of the *nature* of man, which hardly explains why he is curious, let alone why he is sometimes curious and sometimes not. The hypothesis that problems are logical inconsistencies, however, explains why he is curious when he is and so goes far beyond what the other kind of theory can possibly do.

C. Problems and the Criteria of Their Solution

It remains only to show that problems can indicate the criteria for their own solutions. That they can do this has been denied, though in a different terminology, by Pierre Duhem, a denial which is followed by an influential modern philosopher, W. V. Quine.

i. Conventionalism: Duhem's and Quine's Theories

Let us begin with the picture of science given to us by Duhem.[1] Let us think of physical science, with all its empirical generalizations, abstract mathematical theories and its continuing experimental tradition. Suppose that some of the facts which are constantly being churned out in the laboratory become recalcitrant. Then there is a contradiction between what we believe on the basis of the laboratory experiments and what we believe on the basis of our theoretical understanding of things. Such a situation is an intellectual problem. We can generalize and say that an intellectual problem is any situation in which a group or a system of theories, together with statements of facts, and whatever else goes into the system, is such that its joint statement is incompatible. One of Duhem's most important contributions to our understanding of science was his discovery that theories face experimental refutation *collectively*. A recalcitrant experiment refutes a whole system of ideas, and not just a single hypothesis in the system of physical theory.

Duhem also argued that any single hypothesis in a system of (physical) theory can be formulated arbitrarily as far as observational knowledge is concerned. The only requirement for the acceptability of any single hypothesis is that the system of which it forms a part must deductively imply the observational laws which are known. Thus the only criterion of acceptability of any single hypothesis is a purely systemic one.[2]

> A physical theory is not an explanation. It is a system of mathematical propositions, deduced from a small number of principles, which aim to represent as simply, as completely, and as exactly as possible a set of experimental laws.
>
> All they (physicists) have been able to do is to confront the multitude of laws obtained directly from observation . . . , and to draw a symbolic representation of these laws, an admirably clear and orderly representation, but one which we can no longer even properly say is true.

Duhem maintained that the continuing process of choosing hypotheses is governed by considerations of order and symmetry and elegance, rather than their fitness to describe the world accurately.[3]

> Common sense rules in the dominion of laws of observation; it alone, through our natural means of perceiving and judging our perceptions, decides what is true and what is false. In the dominion of schematic representation, mathematical deduction is the sovereign mistress and everything has to be ordered by the rules she imposes.
>
> These principles ["hypotheses"] . . . do not claim in any manner to state real relations among the real properties of bodies. These hypotheses may be formulated in an arbitrary way. The only impassible barrier which limits this arbitrariness is logical contradiction either among the terms of the same hypothesis or among the various hypotheses of the same theory.

Let us call the thesis that 'hypotheses may be formulated in any arbitrary way' (constrained, of course, by the rules of mathematical deduction) *Duhem's Conventionalism.*

Quine has argued that it is not merely some theoretical systems of physics, but our entire world view which faces refutation as a whole.[4] There is then, nothing to which we can appeal *outside* our existing set of beliefs in evaluating different hypotheses, or solutions to a problem, since whatever we rely upon may itself be given up, conceivably, from some point of view. Hence, whatever solution we adopt is like a convention whose only value is that it leaves us with a more or less manageable system of useful beliefs. *Since theoretical choice is a matter of convention, it is rational to choose on the basis of elegance, simplicity, and other considerations of an aesthetic character.*[5] My own view is that Duhem and Quine are right in their analysis of problem solving for almost every (intellectual) problem. Any problem considered solely in terms of its logic, as we have done above, has to be solved by *ad hoc* measures, as best it can.

ii. A Refutation of Conventionalism

The crux of my view depends on the hypothesis that not all problems are so simple. Some have more structure. This additional structure over and above unit-structure is of a historical nature, and it gives rise to a typical methodology which goes beyond the simple Duhem-Quine model outlined above. Let me summarize this in advance by answering these two questions: is it true that theoretical choice must meet criteria of a systemic character only? Are the rules of deduction sovereign in matters of theory?

Duhem is quite right in maintaining that it is theoretical systems as a whole that are refuted. Let us even grant to Quine that an entire world view faces refutation as a whole. Nevertheless, Duhem's (and Quine's) conventionalism is false. The logic behind the idea that refutes conventionalism is this. Let us suppose that there are *two competing* theoretical systems which can each solve a common set of problems. Let us suppose furthermore, that one of these systems of hypotheses faces a new problem, say an experimental refutation, which does not face the other. In this case the choice between hypotheses is no longer constrained solely by systemic features of the theories in question. We must also consider how the acceptance of each hypothesis will affect the viability of one system vis-à-vis the other system. The desiderata of solving a problem therefore depend on the state of an intellectual debate. When there is no general debate surrounding the system in which a problem arises, then our choice of hypothesis may well be determined by taste, or by common sense. So Duhem and Quine's conventionalism is applicable to the extent that we consider problems which do not form part of a larger intellectual dispute. But science and other intellectual pursuits have long histories of debate, so conventionalism cannot be true of any problem in any intellectual discipline, but only of intellectual problems outside such disciplines as, for example, those of our everyday life. Let us now explore these contentions.

iii. The Structure of Problems

Suppose that some intellectual problem arises which is solved in different ways by different people. Let us suppose that they begin arguing about which is the correct way to solve it. *Now we have a problem with a simple structure which goes beyond the unit-structure.*

The vast majority of the problems we encounter have no more structure than the logical structure Duhem allowed, and *all these simple problems are solved with convenience in* mind. Therefore all such problems have to be solved by *ad hoc* methods. They have but the minimum (logical) structure that a problem can have.

Only a few problems have more structure than this, and these are the 'deep' problems whose methodology cannot be characterized in conventionalist terms. *The structure of deep problems is linked to a history of debates* (and the methodology is fallibilist).[6]

Both these theses require some explanation and illustration. Let us now consider the first of these.

(a) Conventionalist Problems

When we encounter intellectual problems in everyday life, we hardly ever try to solve them by first looking for the abstract features of a good scientific solution. On the contrary, we avoid any commitments that are not absolutely necessary. Our beliefs, therefore, may be somewhat 'trivialized' in the process. Let us look at one or two everyday examples.

Someone of our acquaintance begins to behave strangely. This is a typical intellectual problem of everyday life. (A practical problem would be what to do about it: this is not our concern.) Let us assume that the person is not close to us and that for our practical ends we need not bother with his behaviour at all. Yet we may be curious about him, because there is something peculiar about his situation. For years the person has behaved characteristically—indeed rigidly—and now suddenly he has changed.

More often than not, we solve such problems by saying that the person has become 'funny' or has 'lost his balance of mind'—if the strangeness of behaviour demands it—or else simply by saying 'I no longer understand him'. All these solutions presuppose, of course, that there has been a change in the person's disposition, and that the predictability which characterized the person's behaviour of old no longer applies. If we had to make a decision as to whether or not to trust the person concerning a delicate matter, we might well decide not to entrust him with the job. An old belief about the person's character will have lost *some* of its explanatory power, but we may not, of course, be too concerned with it.

If a person is close to us, and we feel loyal to him, we might well say that it is the *strain* of something affecting him that has temporarily upset the person, or his behaviour was quite to be expected *under the circumstances*. The more loyal one feels towards the afflicted individual, the less likely one is to entertain explanations that go beyond postulating purely circumstantial constraints on action.

What is evident in looking at such cases is our unwillingness to propose bold solutions, solutions involving new theories of human nature or new ideas regarding the normal and rational thing to do in various circumstances. We try to preserve our general conception of man and of the world, and make *ad hoc* changes where possible. We may be willing to give up our views regarding X's or Y's normal behaviour, but we nevertheless require some general views regarding how people as a rule will behave. Our understanding of people is so important an *instrument*, that we rarely tamper with it.

An example which is even plainer is that of an automobile mechanic who undertakes to repair cars. Clearly his ideas about how cars are built, how they run, and what various funny noises might be symptoms of, are *instruments*. He earns his living by making use of this knowledge of his. When, therefore, he comes across a car that refuses to yield to his ministrations, he will say that every car is different, but *this* one is peculiar. Or he might hazard an informed guess about some process that he cannot control. But he will rarely question his own theories and beliefs about how a car operates. If cars change over the years, retraining might be necessary.

In short, we solve problems by guesswork; but not by making very bold guesses. And we rarely look for refutations. ('Don't go looking for trouble' is the usual advice.) If refutations do arise, then we solve these problems—again by more *ad hoc* measures. There is no end to how complex our beliefs may become. We never seem to strive for simplicity, that cherished characteristic of good scientific theories. There are no revolutions in our everyday intellectual problems. There may be an evolution of our views, a slow, barely noticeable process of change in which significant difference can be seen only in retrospect, and over many years. But there will certainly be no noticeable discontinuities. This completes the discussion of the thesis that all simple problems are solved with convenience in view.

(b) Intellectual Problems

If we turn to look at intellectual problems in intellectual disciplines we find a marked contrast. Here the problems are often met with bold conjectures, and we find institutionalized criticism. For example, papers are read and designated commentators criticize them. Books are critically reviewed, and new ideas analyzed. No medical practitioner or automobile mechanic would be happy with such constant challenges to his beliefs. But in intellectual disciplines, like science or history, proposing and evaluating new conceptions of the subject matter is the norm.

I want to maintain that this activity is possible only because *in such contexts intellectual problems have a more complex structure*. They exhibit the logical structure (logical inconsistency) which is shared by all problems. But problems within intellectual disciplines are characterized by additional structural complexity. But this additional structured complex is, in my opinion, extra-logical.

1. The Structure of Intellectual Problems is Historically Determined.

If we call certain problems which arise within intellectual disciplines 'deep' problems, to distinguish them from the simple ones of our everyday life, then my thesis is this: *the structure of deep problems is historical in nature.*

The intellectual who understands the structure of such a problem must therefore understand some distilled history of the problem. This is certainly not to imply that all intellectuals must therefore be historians, any more than solicitors who understand Common Law need be historians of law, even though Common Law has an historical structure, insofar as it is based upon precedent. The scientist, like the solicitor, studies problems that have an historical structure—but with this difference, that the structure of deep problems is determined historically not by practice and precedent, but in a different manner altogether.

Problems are given their structures by the properties they possess, which I shall elaborate upon below. For one thing, there is more than one way to solve a problem, and a solution in its turn may generate more problems, and so on, although to qualify as a solution, a hypothesis must eliminate at least the problem which it purports to solve. These features of problems allow for the formation of *intellectual traditions,* in which rival lines of thought try to uncover problems associated with competing views, while solving problems for their own. Sometimes one line of thought may become defunct, or come to be dominated by some other. At other times several lines may flourish simultaneously. The relative feasibility of one line of thought in comparison with another may be called its 'standing in the debate'. I shall illustrate below how only discriminatory problems affect this standing, and so become part of the structure of later problems. I will also show how new demands are made upon those solutions proposed to solve problems which have acquired extra-logical structure through debating traditions. The central thesis to be argued is this. *Every reasonable methodological rule regarding the evaluation of scientific theories can be understood in terms of the adequacy of solutions to problems whose structure reflects an intellectual tradition.*

To illustrate how the structure of deep problems is historically determined, I shall resort to the use of some treelike diagrams. We could, for example show that the same problem has more than one proffered solution thus:

Schema 1:   Problems, Solutions (*Read upwards*)

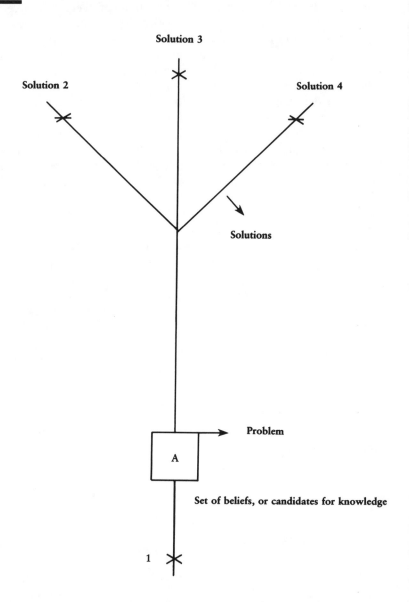

In this diagram, the straight lines with crosses on them represent solutions, theories, sets of statements, beliefs, etc., and the square boxes represent problems. The diagram illustrates three solutions, 2, 3, and 4 to a problem A which arose in some set of beliefs 1.

Schema 2: Multiple Solutions

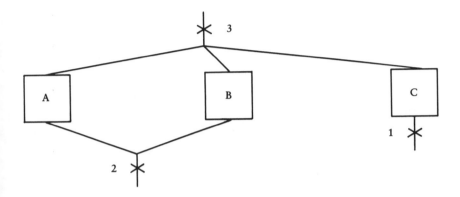

In this case, problems A, B, C are solved by one hypothesis, or a set of hypotheses, 3. A and B have arisen in the same theory 2, and C in another theory, 1.

The above diagram shows more than one problem being solved by one set of statements.

The importance of alternative solutions is that two such solutions to a problem may each spawn two to three further problems and more alternative solutions to each—and so on, leaving us with a treelike structure. But *it is an important feature of such trees, that if one goes along a line from any theory back to the first problem on that tree, then no problem will be repeated along that line.* Let us examine why this is.

From what we have seen in the second section of the paper regarding the unit-structure of problems, we can lay down that a problem which arises for a theory 1 cannot arise again in its solution.

Schema 3:   Nonrecurrence of Problems

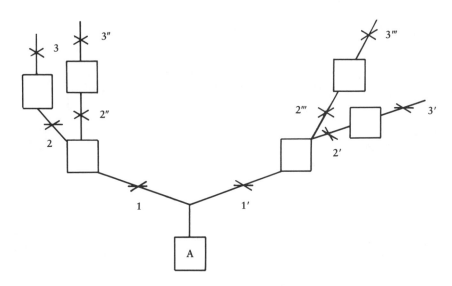

Very simply, what this diagram illustrates is that a problem once solved along a certain line simply never reappears in a later theory along that line. To see why this is so, consider schema 3. Theory 2 has tried to capture the intended explanatory power of 1 and 3 of 2, and hence by the class of all solutions. If 2 is one solution to A, then 3 must be another solution of A. A arises in 3, then there is a solution to A in which A arises. This is impossible. Hence one may say, generally, that along any line a subsequent problem includes within its structure all the earlier problems on that line. (By 'earlier' I do not necessarily mean temporally earlier. For it may turn out that a theory with a problem B is discovered long after 1. Then, after the discovery of B, and of the fact that 1 solves B, we will be able to 'put' B into the structure of A.) Whenever the 'same old' problem comes up again, we must take care to see that it is not a similar *problem with much more structure—i.e., really a new problem.*

2. Intellectual Traditions.   One of the most important structural features associated with problems is the formation of *intellectual traditions*. We have seen that a problem may sometimes be solved in more than one way. Moreover, the explanatory desiderata of each of these solutions may be different. Each of the solutions might in turn create more problems, which are solved by new theories. When this happens, we have the beginnings of *debates* in *intellectual traditions*. Any problem may lead to the development of such traditions. In particular, we may have subtraditions within primary intellectual traditions. (These complexities will not be illustrated.) The following diagram illustrates the formation of one intellectual tradition:

Schema 4:   Intellectual Traditions

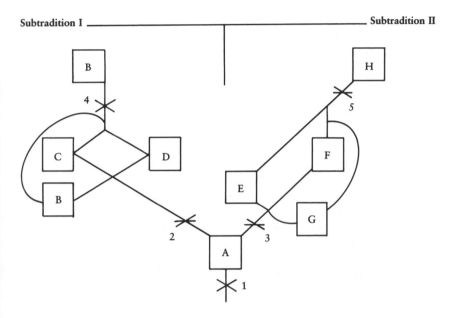

In this diagram, A is a problem which arises in 1 and which is solved by alternative means, 2, 3. Each of these in turn is afflicted by three problems. On the right-hand side, we have 5, which solves all problems of 3, and on the left-hand side, we have 4, which solves two of the problems of 2, namely C and D. But since it does not solve the problem B, it remains inconsistent. In the second intellectual tradition, however, 5 is prey to a new problem H.

Here we have an intellectual tradition in diagrammatic form. To understand how such traditions evolve, consider the example of the early debate regarding *matter and motion.*

The earliest formulation of the problem of motion can be credited to Parmenides. His preliminary argument in a modern guise goes like this: It is incoherent to say that nothing exists, since whatever exists must be something and not nothing. Therefore nothing does not exist. But a moving body moves from where it is to where it is not. (Furthermore two bodies cannot be in the same place at the same time, nor can one body be in two entirely different places at the same time.) Suppose a body moves. It cannot already be where it will be after having moved; but neither can any other body be there, since two bodies cannot occupy the same space. Hence, motion requires that a body move from where it is to where there is nothing. But, as we have seen, nothing cannot exist. Therefore, there can be no motion.

For those of us who believe that bodies do move this argument poses a problem. One solution to this problem was provided by the atomists, who boldly accepted the hypothesis that 'nothing', or the void, does exist. But motion may take place anywhere in the world, so if they are correct, it follows that there must be a void practically everywhere. Because bodies can change internally, the void must be inside bodies too. Furthermore, motion presupposes that there is something which moves. That which moves must also be where there is motion. Hence, the atomists proposed to regard the world as consisting of small particles of matter moving in a void.

Another solution to the problem was offered by the *plenists*. These thinkers accepted the premise that nothingness does not exist. Nevertheless they maintained that this does not preclude motion, for it is still possible for there to be cyclic motion. A great many things, for example, may be moving one behind the other, each moving into the place vacated by the one before it, and the 'last' one moving simultaneously into the place of the 'first' just as it leaves.

This intellectual debate of ancient Greece is part of the structure of every subsequent problem which has been studied in connection with matter and motion. We could therefore call the Parmenidean problem the fundamental problem of motion.

3. *Discriminatory Problems.*   Let us turn from the *formation* of intellectual traditions to their subsequent development. There is one thing here that I wish to stress. In an intellectual or debating tradition, *it is only discriminatory problems that are reflected in the structure of the later problems.* Suppose there are two or more solutions to some problem. A subsequent problem will be relevant to the debate between these rival lines only if, or so long as, it is a problem for some one line of the debate, and it is solved (or does not arise) for some other. *A common problem in a debate can be regarded as a problem of unit-structure.* (Notice, however, that a common problem in one debate may be a discriminatory problem in another. Hence, contextual considerations determine whether a problem is common or discriminatory; it can be labelled one or the other only with respect to some debate.

Schema 5 will give us a pictorial representation of the difference between a common and a discriminatory problem.

Schema 5:   Common and Discriminatory Problems

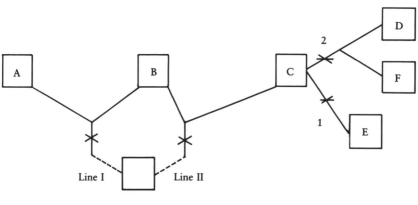

Fundamental Problem

B is the problem common to two lines, while A, C are discriminatory problems. Note that for 1 and for 2, D and E are discriminatory problems and if we consider the intellectual debate arising out of C, then D, E play a discriminatory role not very different from the role played by A and C with respect to the two main lines. F is a problem which does not discriminate between 1 and 2, but it does between the two main lines of the tradition.

It is not unusual to find that a problem which is common to the lines of an intellectual tradition becomes discriminatory when one of the lines is able to solve the problem in a way that is denied the other approach. In such a case, a problem with a unit-structure suddenly acquires an historical structure. In the history of our ideas, this is why a 'curiosity' or a 'novelty' becomes a deep or important or significant phenomenon. Let me take only one example. Double refraction is a phenomenon that was known at least since Grimaldi. As a novelty it is certainly interesting. Iceland spar or a crystal of calcite will refract a beam of light as two beams. A piece of crystal laid over the pages of a book will exhibit two letters for every one which lies beneath it. Yet if we put one or more crystals on top of this crystal, we do not get more than two images for each letter beneath. Those of us who believe that science answers 'why' questions might be surprised to learn that in the seventeenth century there was no great literature devoted to the explanation of this peculiar phenomenon, especially since it constitutes a *prima facie* difficulty for any seventeenth century geometrical theory of light—for how can one explain geometrically why a homogeneous beam of light is not refracted homogeneously? But the problem has a simple structure, for initially, nobody could solve it better than anyone else. It presented however, a serious problem for a wave theory of light, although it was easily explained by a particle theory. It was only with this discovery that the problem of polarization became 'deep'. I shall elaborate just a little.

It is not difficult for the wave theory of light merely to accommodate the phenomenon of double refraction. Huygens could do this in various ways. For example: a wave of light was, for him, a spherical wave of pressure that pushes outward away from the source (the centre). So he suggested that when a spherical wave meets the surface of such a doubly refracting substance, some of these waves become *deformed*. Such "deformed spheres" are refracted at an unnatural angle, as can be shown by simple geometrical reasoning. The deformation of light can be attributed to some unknown structural property of Iceland spar. We need say no more.

Note here, that the problem as it has been so far presented gives us no reason for testing the solution, nor have we any reason for being dissatisfied with it; nor for being particularly happy with it.

If we turn to a particle theory of light, naturally we cannot accept this solution. For one thing, the shape of a particle is not as readily deformed as is the shape of a wave. (After all, the particle must be hard enough to preserve its shape when it is refracted through all sorts of other substances. A wave, however, is a kind of motion and may therefore be modified as it moves.) According to a particle theory, we can solve the problem by appealing to a prior difference in two kinds of light particles. So we can tell whether the phenomenon of double refraction favours waves or particles as follows: if whatever it is about light that causes double refraction is an *original property of light* (particle theory) of if it is *acquired at the calcite crystal* (wave theory). How can we tell?

We might be inspired by a famous argument advanced by Newton. Newton showed that prismatic colours of light are original properties of light (and are not acquired at the surface of the prism) by showing that although white light going through a prism spreads into the spectrum, any one colour of a spectrum remains unchanged when sent through a second or further prism. White light is therefore a mixture of light with *original* colours. Colours are not a 'state' of white light.

But we can show that a beam of 'split' light fails to 'split' a second time when sent through subsequent crystals so therefore the splitting is in fact a *sorting out* of light of two different kinds. Hence, the property of light responsible for double refraction must be a property original to light, and not one acquired at the crystal of calcite. This argument illustrates the problem involved in the attempt to explain these phenomena with Huygens's version of the wave theory of light. And hence *for this reason double re-fraction turned out to be an important phenomenon, a discriminatory prob-lem and not just a curiosity.* Its role in the discrimination between Huygens's waves and Newton's particles immediately elevated it to the status of a deep problem with historical structure.[7]

This example is only one among many. Other curiosities that became deep problems by assuming discriminatory roles are: the problem of the perihelion of the planet Mercury, before and after Einstein's general theory of relativity; the problem concerning the 'turning-power' of a magnetic needle before and after Gilbert's hypothesis of universal magnetic forces; the problem of twitching frogs' legs before and after Galvani's theory of the electricity of life; Cantor's paradox of the universal class before and after Russell's refutation of the foundations of arithmetic. And so on and so forth. In short, a curiosity may well be a problem. As a problem it may demand no more than *ad hoc* accommodation. But when it is discriminatory, it acquires a structure which then rules out many of the earlier solutions precisely because they are ad hoc (in the pejorative sense). This brings us to a most important point, which has already been illustrated above.

4. Problems and the Status of Rival Traditions. The value of a solution in a debating tradition increases in proportion to the difference it makes to the relative 'standing' or 'viability' of the rival approaches in the tradition. For this reason, the criteria for solving a deep problem are more stringent and demanding than those that are involved in the solution of a problem with unit-structure. To explain I must turn to a discussion of the phrases 'standing' or 'viability' of lines in a tradition.

In an intellectual debate, proponents of each line will lay traps for those of others, criticize their ideas, try to refute their theories, etc. These efforts will be more or less successful depending upon how difficult are the problems they reveal. If line 1 has several problems, and line 2 has none (i.e., solves all its problems), it is up to proponents of line 1 to produce criticisms which create problems in line 2, by argument, testing, and so on. If line 2 does not acquire problems, it will end up by *dominating* line 1. This is an extreme case of maximal 'standing' or 'viability' of a particular line in a debate. In schema 7 below I have illustrated domination. Recall, however, that it is only *discriminatory problems* that the dominating line lacks; it will almost certainly be fraught with unit-structure problems.

Schema 6:   Domination

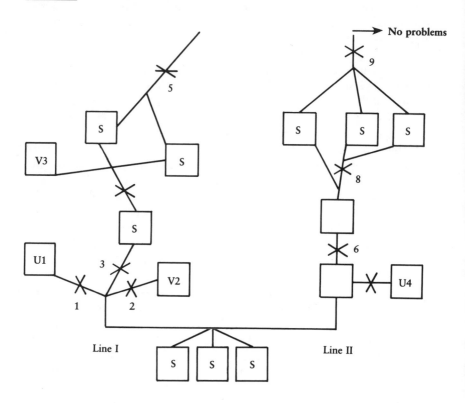

Schema 6 is a complicated model in which line 2 dominates line 1 and, within line 2, 6 dominates 7; more usual, and equable, relation between lines exists when both have problems. One can still prefer one line to another, depending on how intractable one takes certain problems to be. Opinions on this may differ, and intellectuals often find perfectly rational men whom they quite admire disagreeing with them over the tractability of certain problems. The 'standing' of a line with respect to another, then, is a function of its relative domination by that line. A line of thought is 'viable' if it is not dominated by any other. Naturally, the standing of a debate is affected whenever a discriminatory probelm is solved, or a new discriminatory problem is discovered or a problem which is thought to be common is shown to be discriminatory, or vice versa.

I suggest that *every reasonable methodological rule regarding the evaluation of scientific theories can be understood in terms of the structure of problems as this reflects intellectual debates.* The methodological rule that we need to adopt can be stated simply: *the greater the difference a solution makes to the standing of rival debating lines, the better the solution.* I shall show how this rule can replace some of the famous methodological rules which have been proposed by Karl Popper.

Let us look at a scale of values for proposed solutions. At one end of this scale are *ad hoc* solutions which give up explanatory power to 'solve' problems. They make little difference to a line's standing. Such theories— which preclude criticism—have, at their worst, been called "dictatorial strategies" (by J. Giedymin).[8] At the other end of the scale are those theories which not only solve their problems with a minimal loss of explanatory power, but whose 'lost' explanatory power turns out to be mistaken (or false), and hence constitutes a problem for the rival approach which subsumes it. Let me give two illustrations, one for each end of the scale. Consider the classical refutation of the wave theory of light. We shall first try to construct a poor solution to this problem. Then we can compare this solution with the magnificent solution of Young and Fresnel. I shall only be concerned with showing the contrast, and not the subtleties of the comparison of theories.

The wave theory of light as advanced in the seventeenth century is a very impressive theory. Using it, we can explain a great many puzzling phenomena by showing that they are simply manifestations of the geometry of a wave. Reflection, refraction, the prismatic colours, the existence and position and structure of the rainbow—all these can be explained. So if we look upon it as a set of expectations, we can see that it is a very useful set of expectations. As a theory it can be used to derive all sorts of wonderful sentences which would not be available to us otherwise. Hence, we would like to solve the problems of this approach. It is refuted by a rather simple consideration. From the very geometry that is used to explain all these different phenomena, we can also show that a wave of light *is not compatible with the existence of shadows.* For on the wave theory of light, light will travel *around a wall,* much as a sound wave will do. How, then, can we explain the existence of large and reasonably well-defined shadows?

A poor explanation of the problem is one which simply says this: 'light is precisely that sort of a wave which does somehow leave shadows'. This says nothing about *what* sort of a wave light is; and without that knowledge *we can no longer derive geometrically all the things that we could once explain!* We give up a lot and gain nothing. If on a particle theory such phenomena as refraction, reflection, colour, can be explained (and the attendant problems etc.), then we would have every reason to adopt the particle theory of light as the better one. We might as well not have solved the problem for wave theory by the *ad hoc* solution. Of course, we might still wish to see the wave theory *improved*. And in this sense we might still be partial to it. But at the same time, we would have to acknowledge the superiority of the particle theory to the wave theory in their best-known versions.

Hence a 'solution' which is as weak as the one that I have concocted would 'solve' a problem, but would make a minimal difference to the relative standing of two lines of a debate. This is generally the trouble with *ad hoc* solutions.

Consider, then, the beautiful solution to the problem of rectilinear motion given by Young and Fresnel. They argued that light that passes by an edge does bend into the 'shadow'. But a shadow is not what it appears to be. It does not represent an absence of light waves. Rather, it is an area where all those light waves which do arrive extinguish each other by interfering destructively.

Young and Fresnel went still further. For it remains to be explained why all and only the portion *behind a screen* is in shadow when a light is cast on it. Why does the light behave precisely in this way? To solve this problem Young and Fresnel gave up the explanatory power which helps us understand why all and only that area which is behind a screen is all shadow. By relinquishing the explanatory power, they were able to *predict* that it is reasonable to expect at least some light to show up in a shadow, at least when interference is constructive. And this, of course, turns out to be true! A small ball–bearing appropriately placed in the path of a beam of light will, as we all now know, project a spot of light right in the middle of its own shadow.

Now it is the other side which has the problem. If light consists of particles travelling in straight lines, how can any light manage to bend all the way around the ball bearing to the centre of the shadow? And if a particle can get that far, why can it not reach any other position on the shadow? Thus we see that Young and Fresnel's theory simultaneously solved its problem and created one for the opposing line. Moreover, it was the very 'loss of explanatory power' of the new wave theory that turned up as the biggest thorn in the flesh of the rival line! Actually, of course, the loss of explanatory power was really a prediction wrested from the theory of interference. But whether one looks at it as one or as the other is a matter of choice. Such a theory is a magnificent solution. It literally transposed the standing of the two lines.

If we analyze the success of such an ideal solution to a problem, we can see that it is characterized essentially by two methodological features. These correspond to two methodological features stressed by Karl Popper.[9] (1) Young and Fresnel's theory afforded predictions which contradicted the predictions of the other viable line. (2) These predictions of the wave theory turned out to be correct. The first feature of Young and Fresnel's theory can be explained by saying that it was *independently testable*. Popper's requirement that a really good new theory be independently testable can be generalized, in my opinion, to the requirement that a solution to a problem in one line of a debate affect its relative standing vis-à-vis another viable line. The second feature corresponds to Popper's idea of *corroboration*. In this case, wave theory is corroborated when its 'lost' explanatory power turns out to be false; or, which is the same thing, when those consequences which are unpalatable to the opposing theories turn out to be correct.[10]

5. *The Unifying Power of Problems and Their Solutions.* There is another requirement which Popper lays down as fulfilled by the very best theories. It is this. The new theory should "proceed from some *simple, new, and powerful, unifying* idea about some relation or connection . . . between hitherto unrelated things".[11] Popper adds that this requirement is a "bit vague", and that "it seems a little difficult to formulate it clearly". Looking at the structure of problems, we find that there are actually two sorts of solutions that satisfy Popper's requirements that theories be simple, powerful, new, unifying hypotheses. Both these types can be understood best by looking at the historical structure of problems. The first kind of solution which satisfies these requirements really depends on the character of the problem. *The historical structure of a problem itself often has an integrative or unifying character.* Hence, one theory that would satisfy Popper's requirement of simplicity, etc., would be *a good solution to a unifying problem.*

Schema 7:   Unification

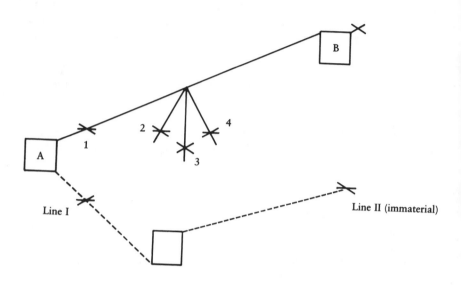

If a theory 1 solves a problem A along some line of some tradition, it can well happen that 1, together with some entirely 'new' hypotheses 2, 3, 4 yield a problem B. By 'new' I mean simply that these statements are not part of the intellectual tradition which is reflected in the structure of A.

Any solution to B in Schema 7 must *therefore preserve explanatory power not only in 1, but in 2, 3 and 4 also.* If 2, 3, and 4 belong to some *independent* intellectual tradition, then the problem B will unify the two traditions, and a solution to B will be a 'grand unification'. A beautiful example of such a unification is Einstein's unification of electrodynamics with Newtonian laws of motion. The clue to the unification is Einstein's realization that there is a problem in reconciling the two if we imagine a body moving at the speed of light. It is this problem which unified two traditions, and his solution, the special theory of relativity, was an aftermath of the unification. Similar is Planck's unification of thermodynamics and electromagnetic theory by studying the ('joint') problem of black-body radiation.

A second kind of new, simple, unifying, theory is one which *solves an old and fundamental problem of some debating tradition by a new (or revived) viable line of thought.* Such is the case, for example, when a historical or evolutionary explanation was proposed to explain the orderliness of living things. Such is the course, also, which Copernicus took when he set the earth in motion. It is *the ability to circumvent the standard, knotty problems of the opposing armies of intellectuals* which gives such theories their novelty, their simplicity, and their unifying power. Such new lines seem to capture valuable explanatory power from both the opposing lines that already exist. Such a theory, therefore, has profound consequences for the character of an intellectual debate. The very problems seem to change; desiderata for good solutions to old problems are suddenly much more stringent. It is this more than anything else which gives scientific revolutions their revolutionary character. The older the fundamental problem that is thus solved and the richer the old debate, the more astonishing is the change in the structure of subsequent problems. The example of the Copernican revolution, which will be sketched later, illustrates such a tremendous change in the structure of problems.

The most satisfying theories of all seem to be those that solve both a unifying problem and also a fundamental problem by a new and viable line of thought. Such is the case with Newton's (and Einstein's) physics, Descartes' epistemology, Russell's (or Frege's) theory of arithmetic, and with Darwin's theory of the evolution of species. Such theories unified fields that were till then unrelated, because *their problems* arose from putting two traditions together. At the same time, their solutions opened up lines that were new alternative solutions to hoary old problems. The influence that such theories have upon the standing of lines in a debate can hardly be surpassed.

D. The Growth of Language in the Light of Influential and Competing Theories

What is true of scientific traditions is equally true of other intellectual traditions. Problems acquire a structure only in the context of a debate. Hence, the later development of language after its earliest evolution, must have been in the context of intellectual competition of some sort.

It is important in this connection to distinguish *influential* theories from *widely held theories*. Not every theory which is influential is widely held. A view which is widely known, and rejected, has as great an influence on the development of thought as a view which is widely held and defended. The reason for this, as should be obvious, is that the problems of a theory, and criteria for judging their importance, as well as desiderata for their solution, depend upon clashes with competing alternatives. Hence, widely known but rejected alternatives have a great formative influence on the structure of problems—and consequently on desiderata for their solutions, and, as a further consequence, for the direction of the growth of ideas. To take only one example, Spinoza's philosophy was for a very long time universally despised. Even to this day Spinoza has found few disciples. Yet it is fair to say that his work has made a great difference to the development of thought in the last three centuries. His influence on thought has been positive not only in the immediate sense—forcing it to adopt an aspect of his own thought—but he has also forced those with opposed views to take account of his considerable arguments. The case of David Hume in philosophy, the thought of Gilbert in physics, and a host of others are similar. There are far more examples, of course, of people who influenced in *two or more* ways—by attracting adherents and at the same time compelling the attention of opponents.

The growth of expressive capabilities in language is closely bound up with intellectual traditions. To understand great novelties of theory or language, we must first appreciate something of the debate which is reflected in the structure of the problems for whose solutions the novelty is necessary. Once we appreciate the difficulty of solving a problem using only hypotheses that are consonant with our beliefs, we see why the new theory is necessary; and we see what features of the theory are used to go beyond our present expressive capabilities. New expressions are therefore, at first, only the prerogative of the few.

The development of expressive capabilities at the frontier is indistinguishable from intellectual debate regarding deep problems. But such is not the case with learning expressive capabilities at second hand. Students of thinkers who have proposed new theories do not need to understand the debate in depth in order to learn the language of the new theory. Thus Newton had to struggle with Descartes' theory to propose his views. But a few decades later, Newtonians could adeptly discuss what Newton struggled to state. By then, Descartes' theories were easily caricatured, and Newtonian theory understood by contrast with this caricature. In this century, Newtonian speech is taught in high-school physics with little or no reference to the momentous debates of the seventeenth century.

This difference between learning entirely new expressions, and understanding old expressions, which are new to the learner, is not hard to understand. After all, a young child learning a language has standards of correct speech that it can glean from its surroundings. When language is being extended, however, these standards have to be set aside. Until a few people can establish new speech patterns, every use of the new expressions militates against our intuition and linguistic comprehension.

On the other hand, it may be argued that to learn language at second hand—or even at third or fourth hand—is to miss some of the nuances of its original ideas. This may well be so. Expressions can be understood to a lesser or greater degree, and in different ways. But as we have noted already, to understand a new expression of someone's, we need not understand all that was originally intended in its total meaning. It is perfectly possible to communicate with only partial overlap between total meanings. The difference between extending language, and learning an existing language need not, therefore, pose a threat to our understanding of language.

In passing from the realm of intellectual debate to the common person, expressions lose some of their cognitive overtones and become elements of skillful linguistic behaviour—they become institutionalized. The relationship between abstract knowledge and skill, and the role of ritualization and institutionalization in language is taken up in subsequent chapters.

8
Empiricism from a Biological Perspective

A. Epistemology in the Light of Evolutionary Theory

i. Perceptions of Reality

In the twentieth century, the problem of knowledge manifests itself as the problem of the empirical basis of knowledge. Our hypotheses of science are statements. Our perceptions of the world have as their content qualities which are quite unlike statements. Yet, these perceptions are supposed to provide the basis for the empirical tests of hypotheses. If we do a logical analysis of tests, we are always left with a gap between a statement and the perception it purports to describe. This gap, which is a logical gap, can only be bridged by one of two methods: we must either give up the logical analysis of science, or we must find statement-like things in our perceptions.

What I propose to do here is to sketch, then elaborate, and then defend a relatively little known solution to the problem, to show that it is worth taking more seriously than it has yet been taken among epistemologists. The theory is a variant of one proposed by Konrad Lorenz, and it is inspired by the neo-Darwinian conception of the evolution of species. In some respects the points of view of Popper, Campbell, and Piaget are not dissimilar.[1]

Immanuel Kant sharply distinguished between things as they are perceived and things as they are in themselves. He did this to facilitate his famous critique of reason. It is a good starting point for us. Things as they seem to us, or the phenomenal world, are all that we can know. All that we know as a result of the investigations of natural philosophy must somehow be wrested from the phenomena. This is empiricism. The thing-in-itself is beyond human understanding. The most we can know of it, if at all, is that it must exist, but not what it is in itself. For to know anything about it we must fall back on experience. But then we fall back upon a redescription of something phenomenal.

In his paper 'Kant's Doctrine of the *A Priori* in the Light of Contemporary Biology' Lorenz suggested something new: since Darwin we know that species evolve by selective pressures from the environment, and thus adapt to it.[2] The environment consists of, in Kant's terminology, things-in-themselves. This is because features of the environment need not correspond to anything that is perceived or that is perceivable by any organism. But our perceptual abilities themselves are means for our adaptation to the environment. Our perception has also evolved to adapt to the way things in themselves are. We may conclude that the phenomenal world *does* reflect what there is. For if it did not we would not have survived at all. We know a great deal about the thing-in-itself. Moreover what we know of it may also be found in the phenomena.

It is important to note that Lorenz's theory of perception does not suggest that if an organism is to survive it must perceive the world exactly as it is. Phenomena are not "representations" of the world, in a sense reminiscent of John Locke. Lorenz suggests, rather, that our perceptions are tuned to pick out those features of a complex world which allow us to interact successfully with it. Our motor reactions, which are an enormously complex series of preprogrammed behavior, are triggered by our perception of simple signs.[3] So the environment is complex, and our reaction to it is complex, but the perceptual sign which triggers what must be the appropriate response is exceedingly simple. A tennis player's forehand cross-court passing shot is made on the basis of a split second perception of the movement of the tennis ball and of the opponent on the court. An analysis of what the tennis player does with his body in order to make his shot would fill a library. The complexity of his action stands in sharp contrast to the simplicity of the perceived signal to which he responds. The player's response suggests that he knows how the ball will bounce, where it will be at the top of its trajectory after the bounce, the angle at which to hit it to get it across the court, and where the opponent will be when the ball crosses the net, not to mention how the tennis player must position himself to meet the ball's return. He does not *see* any of this. His perception is simple, but it enables him to *function* on a court with all these and more variables.

Our perceptions give us a true description of certain aspects of the world. They are true because otherwise we would not be functioning effectively. But in what way are they true? Only in that the signals will not normally mislead us in a complex environment. We know the complex environment only indirectly, that is, to the extent that we can do what we do. Perceptual signals are not, therefore, *representations* of the complex environment, but are signs that it is such and so. One may regard it as a *hypothesis* that when a certain perception is present, a certain complex environment obtains. This hypothesis, it seems, must be true of the environment whenever organisms function effectively. On the other hand, there are times when they do not interact successfully with the environment. Organisms can have accidents, species may become extinct. Most species are eventually superseded by better adapted strains. So there must also be a great deal that they do not know about the world. Since we cannot predict exactly when organisms will go wrong, we may conclude that we do not know precisely what they do know, as organisms, about the world.

This, I submit, is a sketch of an interesting solution to the modern problem of epistemology. To summarize, there is a great deal that we do know about the world that is presupposed by our perceptions. We do not know the world entirely and precisely as it is, and we cannot say precisely which of our perceptual presuppositions are true. All the same, we do know that a great many of them are true of a great many circumstances. The 'truth' that we 'know' results, however, in our skill at doing things, rather than in the accuracy of what we perceive. Knowledge is not necessarily cerebral. The empirical basis of science is not necessarily perceptual.

B. Knowing That, and Knowing How

How can we reconcile the somewhat amorphous perceptual knowledge that we have with the geometrical world in which we live? And how can we know more about the world than our perceptions tell us if science is an *empirical* enterprise? The key to this, I suggest, is the interesting relationship between descriptive knowledge and skills, between, as Ryle puts it, knowing that and knowing how.[4]

i. Ryle's Theory

Ryle objected quite justly to the view which regarded all knowledge as intellectual. He argued that a good part of what we call knowledge consists of cases in which we know how to do something, rather than cases in which we know that something is so. Ryle argued, moreover, that we cannot reduce all 'knowing how' to 'knowing that'. Knowing how to ride a bicycle is quite different from knowing the theory of how it is done. One may not know how to play chess while yet being able to recite all the rules of chess, and all the known principles of strategy. No matter how many abstract principles we may know, we certainly do not know how to play chess until we know how to apply them. Nor can knowing how to apply rules be reduced to other knowings-that, because we would need to know how to apply that knowledge in turn. So we cannot reduce all cases of 'knowing how' to cases of 'knowing that', because this would involve an infinite and vicious regress. Ryle is quite right. Skills differ from descriptive knowledge, or propositional knowledge.

He is moreover right *in a certain sense* in regarding knowing how as primary, or a prerequisite to knowing that. More precisely, he says that the concept of knowing how is logically prior to the concept of knowing that.

For a scientist to know that something unexpected is the case, he must know how to find it out. For any of us to know that anything is the case, we must know how to use a language. We could even bolster Ryle's case with an evolutionary argument, although it is unnecessary: organisms possess skills in dealing with their environment even pretty low down on the tree of life. Propositional knowledge or knowledge that something is the case is found explicitly only in our species, so far as we know. The skill of the beaver in building a dam certainly does not depend on the beaver's explicit knowledge of the principles of hydrodynamics.

It is only in a certain sense, however, that Ryle is right. He is right so long as we restrict cases of knowing that something is the case to those in which one can in principle say that it is the case. But knowing that and saying that (or thinking that) are two different things. When someone knows that something is the case but cannot say it or think it, we may say that he knows it tacitly, or implicitly. It is an error to confuse knowing that something is the case with knowing explicitly that something is the case. A great many bridge players who know how to play bridge quite well will nevertheless be quite unable to recite the rules of contract bridge. Their knowledge of these rules may be quite complete, in the sense that in any given situation they are aware of what the appropriate rules imply. And yet they may be quite unable to tell us the rules, which are quite complex. It would be accurate to say that such a person certainly knows the rules in addition to knowing how to play bridge, but does not know them to recite.

Ryle, however, thinks that this "not unfashionable shuffle" not only tells psychological myths, but myths of the wrong type to account for the facts. "However many strata of knowledge-that are postulated, the same crux always recurs that a fool might have all that knowledge without knowing how to perform, and a sensible or cunning person might be able to perform who had not been introduced to those postulated facts." Where Ryle is perfectly right is in denying that all know-how is reducible to so many knowings-that. But once one concedes that the two are distinct, and even that knowing how is in some sense prior to knowing that, there remains the interesting fact that there is knowledge which is not explicit, and which in another sense is prior to skill, or knowing-how.

ii. Skills Presuppose Propositional Knowledge

Schrödinger in his classic, *Mind and Matter*, ". . . observed that consciousness is associated with the *learning* of a living substance, its knowing how . . . is unconscious."[5] Often, we acquire a skill by paying conscious attention to what is the case, but as we master the skill, the facts tend to fade from our consciousness. Let us begin by noting that, at least in the case where a learnt skill involves a knowing-that in the learning, the skill presupposes the knowing-that even after one has ceased to keep the descriptive knowledge in mind.

When I first learnt how to play squash, I took a few lessons from a seventy year old player, who continued to thrash me at the game long after I had learnt the rudiments. After I had reached a certain level of ability, he pointed out that my backhand stroke lacked authority when I played the ball too close to the body. If I tried to minimize my steps, he said, I would be able to use the outer circumference of my reach, thereby imparting more velocity to the ball. When I am out of practice, I have to remind myself of this fact, but when I am in practice I do not need to remain conscious of it. I was told many such facts about the game, most of which I do not remember, because I have no difficulty with them. I remember this particular bit of knowing-that only because it happens to be a recurring problem with my game.

There are cases when the person learning a skill does not remember a piece of knowing-that which later became implicit in a skill, although another person might remember it. At the age of four and a half my daughter Anandi could spell simple words, but confused the letters 'b' and 'd'. One naturally suspects a serious perceptual deficiency here, and it was worrying. I tried to analyze the difference for her (which comes first, the line or the circle?) but that did not do much good. I tried practicing different words with the letters in it. But practice is not much use when a mistake is not seen by the person practicing, because it is the wrong kind of practicing. How do you get a child to acquire a simple perceptual skill? My wife, Mira, solved the problem in this elegant way: she drew a bed thus:-

bed

She showed Anandi that the headboard and the footboard came at either end. Did Anandi remember how to spell the word 'bed'? Well, then Anandi knew that the letter 'b' came first, in which case the line came first, and the circle after. See how silly it is to spell the word like this, said Mira, who is both level-headed and a schoolteacher:

deb

The pillows and mattress do not stick out of a bed like that! I forget how many days it was before Anandi stopped making the mistake. The interesting thing is that she forgot about the bed in six month's time, and one year later I was telling her the story of how, when we were all young and foolish, we had to learn the difference between simple letters by using clever little pictures. Now she can tell the difference and also recognize the difference, but the two are quite distinct. One is a cognitive skill, the other is perceptual.

Playing squash and recognizing letters are both skills. But learning the skills can be aided by paying attention to pieces of descriptive knowledge. Once learnt, skills presuppose the descriptive knowledge. Another child may learn the difference between the letters 'b' and 'd' without paying attention to the rule about which comes first, the line or the circle. But in the ability to recognize the difference a child nevertheless exhibits the knowledge about which comes first, even prior to the ability to articulate that piece of cognitive knowledge. More simply put, Ryle confuses knowing-that with the capability of saying-that. One has a great deal of cognitive knowledge which is not explicit. All skills presuppose propositional knowledge. Even the best professional practitioners of a sport benefit from coaching. The relationship between the analysis made by the coach of a team and the improvement or deterioration in a player's game attests to the fact that skills presuppose cognitive knowledge.

At a less physical level of skill, we certainly cannot deny that knowing that something is the case has a great deal of influence upon what skills we possess. We could hardly be skillful at medicine or electronics without learning the appropriate doctrines. Not that learning textbook medicine is the same thing as being a skillful diagnostician—certainly not. But no one ignorant of facts about the human body can be a good diagnostician. In fact the importance of new knowledge from the point of view of social advantage is just this: without it, we could never go very far in improving our skills.

iii. Different Levels of Propositional Knowledge

When it comes to such new skills as those associated with endocrinology, or solid state physics, or economics, the relationship between propositional or linguistic knowledge and the appropriate skill is clear. Our skill presupposes that knowledge. It is less apparent, but equally certain that all the skills of an organism presuppose propositional if not necessarily explicit linguistic knowledge. This propositional knowledge is not even necessarily neural, or related to thinking, or to consciousness. The skill of an amoeba in distinguishing the acidity of its surroundings, and in distinguishing between organic food and sand, does not imply that it can think. In fact, in a thinking animal, such as man, the thinking may sometimes interfere with the performance of a skill, which, at another level, presupposes propositional knowledge.

Organisms possess knowledge at various levels. Level 1. Organisms have an uncanny ability to function in complex and hazardous environments. This ability may be read off by us as knowledge of the environment. Such knowledge may have no representation in an organism's consciousness—indeed, most organisms do not have consciousness. Level 2. If, in addition to a genetic store of knowledge, an organism does have consciousness, then this may be a repository of certain kinds of knowledge which modify the vast store of skills for the organism vis-à-vis the environment.

Normally, this store aids the organism, though sometimes it may hamper. Level 3. The social or linguistic ability of stating something is yet another way of knowing it. It is the most limited kind of knowledge in its scope. It acts upon conscious knowledge, and so upon the vast store of knowledge embodied in skills. Although these three levels of organization are all similar in that they may be analyzed as knowledge, their concrete embodiment is very different; and to that extent the associated learning mechanism, and cognitive status, are different.

We cannot state all the hypotheses presupposed by any one skill. But then we cannot state all the skills necessary to state one hypothesis. The two are in this respect complementary. If we do not restrict knowing-that to those cases where an organism is also able to say-that, then all living organisms know that certain things are so, even though some have no language in which to say so. If one can read off hypotheses from the possession of a skill, it is of great value, since hypotheses which are stated can be analyzed and stand in complex logical relations one to the other, whereas skills can only be named, or described in a rudimentary way.[6] I conclude that Ryle is right in denying that skills can be reduced to cognitions, but wrong in his claim that the concept of knowing-how is logically prior to the concept of knowing-that. (The question 'how is knowledge wired in an organism?' which may strike the reader as pertinent is dealt with in subsections C and D of this chapter.)

Organisms have innumerable skills. Each of these complex motor mechanisms seem to blend miraculously with complex features of the environment in order to allow the organism to survive. All these skills presuppose hypotheses. They involve propositions or hypotheses, though these are not usually explicitly stated.

iv. Limits of Propositional Knowledge—Relative to Econiches

The skills of organisms are not, of course, infallible. Comparative ethologists have created dummy signals which are carefully designed to evoke complex motor responses in what are biologically inappropriate circumstances. A cichlid fish has been coaxed to do a mating dance with a piece of cardboard. A bird can be coaxed to feed a painted box of the right shape, if a certain noise is made. A chicken can be frightened by a piece of paper of a certain shape at a certain height. And so on. If one knows enough about the behaviour, lifestyle and perceptual apparatus of an organism, one might, with luck, guess the hypotheses presupposed in some of the organism's perceptions, and thereby find situations in which the organism can be taken in by a dummy. One concludes that though the hypothesis presupposed in a given perception is general in nature, and false if stated generally, it is true of those situations which the organism ordinarily meets in its natural habitat. In other words, it is true within limited domains, and false outside of them. This is not unlike a theory in physics. Newton's theory of motion is false if stated in all its generality. Einstein showed us that at high velocities various peculiar things happen which would be noticeable, and quite uncomfortable, to a hypothetical Newtonian animal. But at low velocities, the skills, presupposing Newtonian physics, work quite well, if we ignore very low velocities at which other distortions appear. But all the skills related to terrestial locomotion can be performed merely by presupposing Newtonian physics. In logical terminology, we may say that false hypotheses may have true consequences which, if presupposed, enable us to function effectively.

Since hypotheses are general and the domain in which they are true is limited, we may note that the survival of any species, however tenuous, requires us to acknowledge that in the natural habitat of the organism, the hypotheses are likely to be true. That is to say, if a hypothesis is so modified as to apply only to such situations, then it is almost certainly true. If we call these environments or ecological niches 'econiches', then the hypotheses that are presupposed by skills are very probably true if they are restricted to apply solely to the appropriate econiches. Given the neo-Darwinian conception of life, each of our presupposed hypotheses, when restricted to apply only to appropriate econiches, has a probability close to one that it is true.

When a new hypothesis is proposed in science, or in any other context, for that matter, we depend upon the stock of skills we possess in our most familiar econiches to test it. When we feel sure that our perceptual skills function satisfactorily, the probability that we are wrong is very small. So all observations may be theory laden, but when we restrict ourselves to familiar situations, and to well honed skills, the presupposed theories are true, or at any rate so very probable that in the absence of very good theoretical reasons it would be foolish to question them.

If we could analyze completely all human econiches, we would know all the limitations of our perceptual skills, and so would be able to determine all and only those observations which may be trusted. But we do not know our econiches in their entirety, and that is for a good reason. An econiche is an environment within which our skills *almost* certainly work, but the possibility always remains that we may discover some feature of it which obliges us to modify our skills. Until I know where my presupposed theories do not work, I cannot be sure how to delimit my econiches to those which are absolutely trustworthy. Until Einstein came along, we did not know that Newton's theory is accurate only within limited velocities. Until impressionism came along we did not realize how what we see differs from what we think we see. Our perceptual apparatus does function extremely well for all the usual purposes in all the usual situations. It tells us the truth where we do those things which we do regularly. But some illusions are known. We also know that at a distance, or in dim light, or in other unfavorable conditions, we could be mistaken. These facts help us delimit our perceptual econiches somewhat. But until we know all the pitfalls of our perceptual skills, and all the hidden nuances of a world which may turn what seems a familiar environment into an unexpectedly treacherous one, we cannot *define* all our econiches.

The mathematical science of matter is quite compatible with our perception of an amorphous world, even for an empiricist. We do not base our understanding on, or test it against, the content of our perceptions; instead, we use our well tried skills triggered in familiar environments to test our hypotheses. We observe that though seeing may be believing, we cannot believe in everything that we see. We do not test our theories against our perceptions, we test them in familiar perceptual econiches. It is our perceptual skill, and not the content of what we see, that underpins empirical science.

Descartes tried to reconcile mathematical physics with the facts of perception by trying to refute the skeptics. If one could refute skepticism by argument, this is not a bad way to proceed. So interesting is this approach to the problem that the history of ideas is replete with such attempts, and with counter-arguments proposed on behalf of skepticism by philosophers who certainly do not doubt everything, and who perhaps doubt a little less than even their adversaries. But Hume is right. The skeptic cannot be met with an attempt to justify knowledge. We can show, however, that if we know a great deal about the world, then we can also show how science can improve upon what we know by intellectual endeavour.

There is no circularity in this reasoning. If Darwin's theory were based upon the content of our experience, then it could not tell us which experience to trust. But we do not interpret Darwin thus. All the statements of biology and of comparative ethology may be false, but their value still lies in the possibility of applying them in familiar econiches. If one of these hypotheses is false, we will learn its limitations, but there is no point in speculating on that until we find a better one, which tells us what its limitations are.

From another perspective, one might contrast all intellectual claims to knowledge with the sort of basic knowledge we have of the world when we are manipulating it more or less successfully, and find correctly or incorrectly that the former is deficient. In a way that Montaigne would approve, we might decide to abandon the serious study of ideas as being only one of many pleasant and instructive occupations which should not make disproportionate demands upon our time.[7] As instruments for acquiring knowledge our intellectual efforts seem to be decidedly inferior to our natural skills. How, for example, could Newton's *Principia* compete as a piece of useful knowledge with the skill of a fine horseman? From the skeptic's perspective Newton's work is neither clearly useful, nor clearly a piece of knowledge, unless we interpret the knowledge and its relationship to skills as I have suggested.

v. Evolutionary Interpretation of Pragmatism

The survival value of intellectual activity becomes clear when such activity is studied in the light of the relation of skills to their propositional presuppositions. Just as an empirical test obtains when a presupposition of perceptual skill stands in logical relation to a hypothesis which is being tested, so do hypotheses presupposed by other sorts of skills test our scientific hypotheses. The manipulative skill of an experimental scientist extends the empirical basis of science considerably. When an experiment can be performed routinely, i.e., when it is part of the repertoire of skills of the practicing scientist, one trusts the hypotheses presupposed in the skills more than even well established hypotheses if the latter happen not to be compatible with the former. The significance of the repeatability of an experiment performed not just by one experimenter but by any competent and trained experimenter, I suspect, is this: it is only the confidence in a well honed skill that gives us the courage to trust an experimental result, even, or especially, when it is a surprising one.

Let me repeat a point. The hypotheses presupposed by our manipulative skills are false if stated in all generality, as is the case with our perceptual skills. But they are true if stated in a way that restricts them to the set of econiches in which they are well tested (which set is not known to us except by hindsight, when we are proved wrong, as we have noted). When social structures or habitats change over a period of time, improved skills give us an edge in the competition for survival. In this competition it is the ability to improve upon the presupposed hypotheses in useful ways that sets off the more successful individual from the less successful. This then is the survival value for us of even our most esoteric science, that it aids us in technological and manipulative endeavors. Is not the reason that governments fund science that they value technology?

This constitutes an avowal of pragmatism of a sort on my part. The value of all human endeavour is eventually related to practice. This is also an endorsement of a sort of instrumentalism. A scientific theory, and science more generally, is eventually evaluated as an instrument for survival. The word 'eventually' is, however, indispensable here, because, more immediately, the value of hypotheses is not judged by these more remote considerations. I have suggested elsewhere that scientific hypotheses, and ideas more generally, may be regarded as pragmatic at one remove.[8] The hypotheses which we use to manipulate things and each other, whether these are explicit or tacitly presupposed, are sometimes beset as a whole by difficulties which may be represented logically as contradictory statements. This renders the set of our hypotheses functionally useless, because from logically inconsistent premises anything may be derived. Tinkering with our intellectual tools in order to repair them is being pragmatic at one remove. Our tools are certainly useful, even though the scientists' criterion for a successful resolution is the purely logical criterion of consistency (i.e. whether the tools are functional at all, as a whole). It has been argued in chapter seven that, armed only with the idea of avoiding logical inconsistency as the aim of science, we can reconstruct the development of science without invoking any methodological rules.[9]

The individual who takes up the job of intellectual tool repair must also use skills, which are special to that kind of task. This goes without saying. Every task calls for its own skills. But intellectual skills are particularly different in being the product of recent society: our primate ancestors in the wild clearly lacked such skills. One needs a reasonably well developed language to state, test and modify one's hypotheses. Even within linguistic communities, the skills of the intellect need to be taught and encouraged from generation to generation as a tradition. The tasks of preserving and furthering intellectual traditions have been the province of an élite subgroup within society, which is regarded with some awe by others in settled communities in times of peace. Modern science as it is taught in our universities is heir to features of many ancient and modern traditions, though the actual training that a student must undergo is constantly being modified, especially at more advanced levels. In short, science is a social activity not only because it presupposes many hundred millenia of linguistic and therefore social development but also because the practitioners must be "socialized" within a prominent subgroup within society, i.e. they must be educated.

In recent years much attention has been paid to the social aspect of skill acquisition and deployment by scientists, largely in response to the writings of Thomas Kuhn.[10] Kuhn has also drawn attention to the metaphysical and methodological theories presupposed by the repertoire of the scientists' skills at any one time. He suggests that these are normally tacit in science. He argues, like Polanyi,[11] that it is part of the characteristic value of normal science, as opposed to other sorts of intellectual activities, that metaphysical and methodological issues are tacit.

From our perspective this is exactly the wrong way to look at the matter, even though Kuhn and Polanyi are right as far as they go. Every skillful organism works with tacit hypotheses. In the vast number of cases of skill deployment that might be considered, it is intellectual activity alone which makes explicit a small portion of what is otherwise merely implicit. This is the secret of the flexibility of our responses to the variable and changing problems that we confront. So Polanyi and Kuhn are quite right to point to the scientist as a consummate craftsman, who uses his own intellectual skills without thought or consciousness of their presuppositions. For the bulk of the hypotheses which are brought to bear on the ongoing work of the scientist are implicit. But it is precisely in intellectual activity, and more particularly in science that explicit statements are at all possible, and arguments have some role in the evolution of tacit hypotheses. To miss the importance of logic and explicit statements in science is to miss its most distinguishing feature, the most important feature of science for our survival, and thus to reduce science to 'closet science'.

The old conundrum that the *pragmatic* value of doing science is best realized when scientists are allowed to pursue *truth for its own sake* is still surprising. If we study truth for its own sake, then our study can be useful only if all truth is pragmatic. The latter is a very doubtful claim. The most one can say is that any given truth claim *might* turn out to be useful; but most truth claims are hardly useful at all, and still less uncertain half-truths, which is the usual status of many of our hypotheses. Yet it is quite true that the scientist does not appeal to the criterion of pragmatic value to judge a hypothesis, except in technology proper. One does not judge a theory of the electrodynamics of moving bodies by its usefulness, but by its truthfulness.[12] Nevertheless it turns out to be useful. Scientific theories continue to be useful, to provide technological returns to any society with the necessary outlay to support science.

The apparent paradox is stark: society values science for its pragmatic results and therefore invests in it; scientists ignore pragmatic value when they do research; but miraculously, science continues to be of pragmatic benefit. There is, of course, no miracle here. The advance of science is accompanied by the growth of experimental testing. This expands the empirical base of science, and simultaneously improves our manipulative skills. We can add to our technology by using our superior manipulative abilities. This dissipates the apparent mystery. If we study the training of the superior scientist and the superior technologist in allied fields we find that their education is remarkably similar, whether in physics, chemistry, economics, biology, psychology or computer science. If we take any rapidly improving technology and look for products which exemplify the 'state of the art' and which are waiting to be exploited, then these will also be associated with institutions in which the testing of abstract hypotheses in related fields is most vigorously pursued.

In brief, then, the new empiricism is very much like an old pragmatism: it is not in what we see but in how we do things that our theories confront reality. It is perhaps unlike the old pragmatism in that truth is not defined in pragmatic terms—a manoeuvre which would rob us of the ability to explain why the truth is sometimes useless, and sometimes threatening to organisms.

C. A Model for Conceptual Change

i. Concepts Viewed as Prelinguistic Building Blocks of Language

It is a widespread belief that corresponding to fundamental concepts in language are natural kinds in the world. Perhaps we should begin with this.

To speak of a 'dog' is to speak of a sort of a thing. Similarly, 'lamp post', 'bark', 'gait', 'gray', 'health' or 'innoculation' pick out things, qualities, actions, etc. in the world. One way of looking at the relationship between concepts and the world is this. If all that exists is divided into different sorts of things with characteristic properties, and if any thing of a sort changes characteristically, then perhaps we can look at the concepts of our language as simply mirror images of the world, or aspects of it. The concepts of 'dog', or 'gray' or 'gait', one might say, simply only reflect the existence of dogs, gray things and certain ways in which creatures walk.

This way of looking at concepts is actually an ancient theory of knowledge, which is to be found in the writings of both Plato and Aristotle, though they differ in their account of the existence of 'sorts'. Concepts, in this view, transparently reflect sorts of things, all of which are part of an eternal ground plan for the cosmos. Needless to say, the ancient Greek worldview is not concerned with conceptual change, if only because, according to the Greeks, the divisions of being are eternal.

The scientific revolution, and in particular the mathematical and mechanical conception of the universe found in the writings of Galileo, Descartes and Newton brought a clear recognition that the physical world does not contain the sorts of things that common sense tells us must correspond to the concepts of our language. Descartes argued, for example, that where we see a rainbow, there is in fact only moisture and a certain amount of light refracted once or twice internally in spherical droplets of water. The water, moreover, is only a certain kind of space—indeed, the entire physical world is a collection of geometrical entities, called 'spaces', in relative motion.

Descartes did, of course, distinguish between three sorts of things which he thought were objectively different: God, selves and matter. Within the category of matter, however, there is little or no similarity between our concepts and what there is. The secondary qualities like colour or taste may be caused by primary qualities, but do not resemble them.

Since that time the way in which concepts arise in the mind has been an enigma. And opinion has been divided between those who at one extreme think that all our concepts must somehow be inscribed by the eternal world on the *tabula rasa* or 'blank slate' which is our mind, and to those who, at the other extreme, think that all concepts must be innate to the mind,[13] with several interesting possibilities in between.

We have described the meanings of words as a crystallization of theories. I suggest that we must also replace the old model of knowledge according to which the basic way in which we know the world is by identifying the kinds or sorts of things in the world, (i.e., by mental concepts). Instead, we must analyse concepts as themselves only products of something deeper and more propositional. For this, we have to abandon traditional models of knowledge.

ii. Traditional Models of Knowledge: Platonic, Aristotelian, Cartesian, and Newtonian Models of Knowledge

Almost anybody would understand what a model for a solar system might look like,

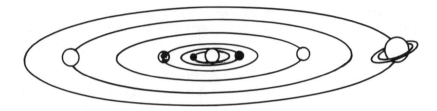

Or a model for impact.

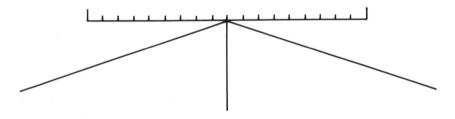

But what sort of thing is a model for knowledge? I can perhaps begin with three models for knowledge, which are very well known, to illustrate the sort of thing such a model might be.

For Plato, to know something is to know what it is, which is to know what sort of thing it is. To know courage is to be able to define it, as we would say today. And one of the characteristic features of Plato's theory of knowledge, is that to know the sort of thing a thing is to know it ideally, or to know its idea. Thus if we represent the objects of knowledge by symbols in small letters, and the knower by a circle, then knowing might be understood thus:

soul

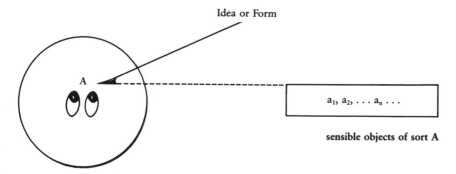

Idea or Form

A

$a_1, a_2, \ldots a_n \ldots$

sensible objects of sort A

The knower, one might say, has the reality in his soul in the form of Ideas, and to grasp them is to grasp the sort of thing which is its nonideal counterpart in the changing world.

Consider the Aristotelian model for knowledge. For Aristotle, to know what sort of thing something is, is to know its essence, which is not ideal but part of the thing itself. Things have material form, and it is this that the soul perceives when it perceives things. The way in which the soul perceives a thing is by taking on the form of the thing perceived. Being self-conscious it is able to apprehend the perceived object.

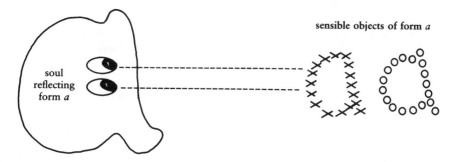

soul reflecting form *a*

sensible objects of form *a*

There is a similarity worth noting between these two models, and a dissimilarity. The similarity is that they both presuppose that things in the world constitute 'sorts', that everything in the world is one sort of thing or another. The difference between them lies in the determination of sorts. For Plato, a sort is determined by an ideal individual, in the soul, whereas for Aristotle it is determined by a form which is within all individuals of the same sort. So we see that a model for knowledge is invariably a model for a reality which is associated, or presupposed, or posited. This is hardly surprising, for how we know something must depend at least partly on what it is that we know, and partly on what we are, as knowers.

The ancient conception of reality divided reality into natural kinds or sorts which impinged themselves on the soul or mind. The rise of the mechanical point of view, or the conception of reality derived from the mathematical theory of motion dealt a severe blow to this view. The model of knowledge that we find in Descartes, who was one of the first to propose one in the light of the mechanical world view, may be represented thus:

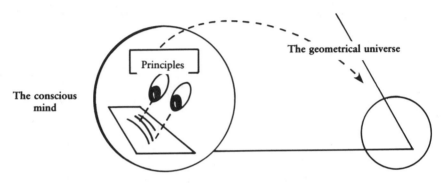

The mind is here represented by an inner cinema or screen; it sees a rainbow in all its glorious colours, when in fact the physical world consists of an achromatic geometry of moving space. In the diagram the square box called 'Principles' is that part of the mind which posseses the fundamental laws of motion. One immediately suspects that there will be difficulties with the relationship between the mind and matter, and of course there are several.

If we remove the innate Principles of Philosophy from the mind, we have a real problem, namely: how can the mind possibly fathom what is really out there if what is seen on the inner screen is so different from what physics informs us is real? The Newtonian model:

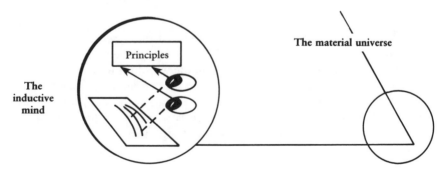

Numerous variants of this model have been proposed—from the solipsist model of a mind which is trapped inside itself, to the model of preestablished harmony, in which all the inner television screens are correlated by God's design.

iii. An Alternative Model of Knowledge: The 'Release Mechanism' Model of Knowledge

Let us turn to the very general and well known biological model of the relation between living organisms and their surroundings. I propose that knowledge is a special case of this model. This model may be identified as the 'trigger' model, also known as the release mechanism model.[14] As we have noted, according to this model, an organism which inhabits a complex and comparatively dangerous environment is adapted to the complex environment if in any given situation it reacts appropriately thereby preserving itself and its progeny. If we represent the environment by crosses, the behaviour by dashes, and the organism by a circle, then the model would look like this:

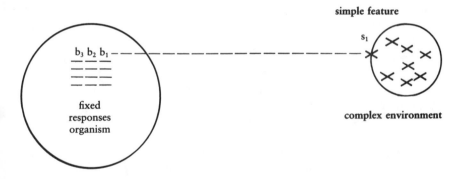

A pattern of response, b_1 is elicited by a simple feature S_1 of a complex environment E_1. It is important to note that the patterns of behaviour are fixed prior to being triggered by S, some innately, and some fixed through maturation or learning.

Several instances of complex environments $E_1 \ldots E_n$ will all elicit the response b_1 if they are all instances in which the simple feature S_1 presents itself to the organism. For example, a plant will respond characteristically to the rise in temperature during spring by releasing buds which will flower in the summer. A dog will respond characteristically to the sudden movement of a cat. A cat will respond characteristically to the movement of a mouse. Any experimentalist who is concerned to test the hypothesis that a certain simple sign will release or trigger a certain chain of responses can do so quite easily.

Now this model has several parts, which may be identified in different ways. The relationship between the class of an organism's responses and the class of environmental conditions which represent the natural habitat of an organism may be called the 'adaptation' of the organism. If we restrict our attention to its repertoire of responses to various simple signs, we may call these the skills, or abilities or capabilities of the organism. If, however, we look at the relationships between a simple feature of an environment and the environment, this may be called an expectation or anticipation or, in certain cases, knowledge. The relationship of the simple sign to a complex environment may be expressed by 'whenever S_1 obtains, E_1 obtains', which we may call a 'description'. In the case of behaviour which is pre-linguistic, or non-linguistic, there is still *tacit* knowledge. In the case of explicitly stated descriptions of the form 'All x are y' we have statements within language. It is useful to think of tacit and explicit knowledge as special cases of description, which is part of the general trigger model of the relationship of an organism to its environment.

The relationship between the trigger model of knowledge and the hypothesis that we possess concepts is not entirely antithetical, for in a trigger model there are special circumstances in which descriptions give rise to concepts, though in general the two are not equivalent. In what sense can concepts be special cases of descriptions?

This question has two components: (1) Under what conditions would we say that a concept (or the recognition of a sort or kind) is not presupposed? (2) Under what conditions would a series of triggered responses add up to the recognition of a 'kind'?

To take a simple example of a response which falls just short of being conceptual, consider the behaviour of the digger wasp as described by comparative ethologists. The female of this species leaves its larvae in several little 'nests', and then goes about looking for food to put in the nests to nourish her offspring. Moreover, she seems to know the difference between a full nest and an empty nest, for prior to her subsequent trips for food, she inspects each nest once. Now the interesting thing is that this wasp will not leave food in nests which are empty (say, if a predator has got at the larvae). Having inspected the nests, the wasp seems to be able to tell the difference between a full nest and an empty one. The obvious adaptive advantage of not wasting a precious food supply in empty nests hardly warrants further comment.

But an even more interesting fact about the digger wasp, as recounted by Baerends, is that it is not quite so clever.[15] If the biologist interferes by removing larvae from a nest just after the inspection tour, the wasp will nevertheless stuff food into it, even when she plainly sees that the nest is empty. It is as if the wasp can tell that a nest is empty when it is inspecting, but not when it is delivering. Now this attitude of the digger wasp, which is a trifle bureaucratic, leads one to wonder if the wasp really does know the difference between an empty nest and one which is occupied by its larvae. We are tempted to say 'yes and no'. It does not quite know the difference. This alerts us to an important fact about the recognition of kinds, namely, that kinds are recognised by an organism when various different signs of a thing of a certain kind trigger the appropriate response to it. To know what a dog is, is to know its bark, its physiognomy, its behaviour, its many typical appearances. A child that says 'dog' when it hears a bark, but not when it sees a dog does not quite grasp what a dog is.

In terms of the trigger model, in each appropriate response to a thing of a certain sort in the environment, we have called the relation of the trigger to the sort a piece of descriptive knowledge. Then we see that recognizing a kind adds up to a great many pieces of descriptive knowledge in all of which a certain array of responses is common. If we look at the recognition of sorts and descriptive knowledge in this general way it becomes clear that our descriptive knowledge far exceeds our ability to recognize sorts of things. Finding an invariant over the range of our senses is not the rule, rather it is the exception, and it is therefore the exception rather than the rule that the trigger model yields sortal knowledge of the world.

In human language, where descriptive knowledge may be explicitly stated, the situation is quite different. A language presupposes phrases, which have to be relatively invariant over time and between people to function as counters in communication. A linguistic description, then, would seem to presuppose the existence of phrases which stand for concepts. Sentences after all, must consist of phrases, and so we cannot have declarative sentences without phrases which pick out sorts of things. We see, therefore, that the relationship of descriptions to concepts is somewhat more complex than is commonly accepted. It is commonly believed that the concepts are somehow given to us, and we combine these to produce descriptions. This is, of course, a true description of language, so far as it goes. But it does not quite go far enough. For while explicit description may presuppose the existences of concepts, it has been my contention that concepts themselves presuppose the existence of tacit descriptions from which they are fashioned (in what is called a "proto-language" in chapter seven).

Turning finally to conceptual change, we see that it is not so mysterious after all. If we look at concepts not as unalterable atoms, but as intermediate molecules which are themselves composed of descriptive theories, then we can have concepts which are identical, or largely overlapping, or very different, depending on their composition. We have a measure for conceptual change. When we go from one fundamental theory in science to another, we are of course changing some descriptive knowledge around. Any of these pieces of knowledge, or their consequences, which are ingredients of concepts, will have to change. And consequently, concepts will also change. But when concepts change, it is not true that everything changes and we enter into a new and different world altogether, as Whorf would have us believe.[16]

Rather, what happens is that of the many different signs of certain sorts of things one or two are denied to be signs of that sort. Because other signs remain, we can usually still recognize a sort by means of all those other signs of it which have remained invariant.

Let us take an example. How does the concept of a 'species' change from Linnaeus to Darwin? Clearly, Darwin's theory depends on the existence of species, recognizable by any trained observer, but he does not believe in the existence of a *timeless order* of species. Thus the difference between Linnean and Darwinian botany is not so great that all the classifications change. It is rather that certain of our expectations regarding each of these classes change. We do not any longer expect immutability. Moreover, our criteria for a specimen being a member of a species may be modified by Darwin, to the extent that while morphology and reproduction are both good indications of a membership of species, for Darwin the latter becomes a more important criterion in certain situations than the former.

So we see that it is true that after Darwin the very notion, or the very concept, of 'species' changes. But the concept is nevertheless closely related to, and only a modification of, the old concept of 'species'.

D. Induction from a Biological Perspective

i. Hume's Skepticism

Having abandoned Kant's conception of the phenomena as an uncertain source of knowledge of the world as it exists beyond perception, we must face the problem of induction which has beset modern philosophy since Russell's philosophy of mathematics and Einstein's physics undermined the high *a priori* road. It is therefore necessary to turn to the problem of induction as Hume had faced it, to see how we may use the new model of knowledge to study this vexing problem of the Scottish Enlightenment.

Hume was convinced that there is no logical arrow that allows one to reason validly from our experiences of the past to hypotheses regarding the future. However, he suggested that while there is no logical reason for concluding that the sun will rise tomorrow from the experience we have accumulated in the past, there are good psychological factors which lead us to expect that it will.

In fact, Hume suggested that if we were to be perfectly rational and accept only what can be logically derived from earlier experience, we would be doomed, as skeptics, to inaction. Hume suggested he could be a skeptic for but an hour, for thereafter he would have to act, and in acting rely upon some expectation or other which went beyond what may be logically derivable from past experience. Hume's hour, if anything, is too long an estimate.

It is important to note that Hume saw the difficulty for induction in the realm of *action* and not of *thought*. I believe not enough attention has been paid to this shrewd assessment of his. If we pay attention to it, we can resolve the difficulty faced by Hume, without recourse to skepticism or to special pleading for inductive inference.

Hume sought to establish a Newtonian science of human nature, a psychology of man that would explain why we believe what we believe when we act as we do. But in the light of modern biology, we must conclude that human action is of a piece with that of animals, and the science that Hume needed in not the science of human nature so much as the science of living organisms, generally.

If a skeptic were to get up and walk, she would, according to Humeans, rely upon her expectation that the ground will hold firm, that her bones and muscles will continue to support her, and that her estimate of the distances of objects would not mislead. While all this may be true, it is nevertheless not peculiar to human beings that we walk, eat, sleep or make noise. In this we are very much like most other mammals. Any mammal that walks does so with an assurance no less marked than that possessed by the human. If we are to agree with Hume that in acting a skeptic must go beyond skepticism, then it is true that every organism succeeds as well as humans do in this respect, that they act in the world without skeptical worry.

In the case of human beings, we may say that they know that the ground will hold firm. Does a dog know that the ground will hold firm? Does a tulip bulb know that spring is in the air when it bursts out of the ground? Does a tomato plant know the direction of the sun as it turns its leaves in a certain direction to catch the sunlight best? Ordinarily we do not put it in this way.

Where we speak of human *knowledge,* we do not speak only of the *adaptation* of organisms to their environments. There is, however, that intimate connection between these two which I have mentioned above.

ii. More on the Trigger Model

The concept of adaptation in modern life science is of the first importance for philosophy. In the light of the 'trigger' model of action that is widely used in the life sciences, the analysis of the concept of adaptation yields us a solution to Hume's skeptical difficulty, which might give us a hint of a full fledged epistemology and philosophy of science.

On the 'trigger' model, an organism stores within itself a whole range of action patterns, with a releaser or trigger which sets it off. A more detailed study of this trigger reveals that it is often a de-inhibitor. To explain this I should add that a pattern of action which is stored in an organism will spontaneously manifest itself as often and as regularly as there is energy in that organism to fuel the action. Usually, however, a stored action pattern does not manifest itself because in the internal environment of the organism the right conditions do not prevail—there may be an inhibitor which prevents the action. If a chemical which temporarily suppresses the inhibitor is released in the body at the right spot, then the action will be released by 'the trigger,' or by the de-inhibiting chemical.

Modern molecular biology gives us a wonderful picture of organisms as chemical engines. Every living form of this biosphere for the past billion years has its basic blueprint worked out as a sequence of symbols in DNA. If we take any cell of any organism, its nucleus includes this long molecular string (a double string, as it happens) which is exactly a replica of the DNA of every other cell in that organism.

If a particular cell in the body produces insulin, for example, it is because a certain segment of the DNA has the instructions that allow for the production of this hormone. A copy of the instruction in the DNA, the RNA, traverses to a complex protein structure in the cell, the ribosome. In this structure of about fifty chemicals, the instructions for insulin production are worked out as the RNA goes through the ribosome like a magnetic tape through the head of a tape recorder.

But of course, the DNA in any organism is exactly the same in every cell, though the actions of cells differ considerably one from the other. Some cells produce insulin, some bile, some haemoglobin. All the vast arrays of cells in the body including bone, muscle, dermis, blood, and nerves act in their different ways according to the information which is contained in any one complete strip of DNA. If every cell has the same genetic information in it as every other, then the great variety of actions performed by different cells are functions of the different triggers which activate different segments of stored information in different circumstances.

Every organism begins as one cell, which divides. This process of meiosis produces in about thirty odd divisions all the cells necessary for any organism as complex as, let us say, an ape. Now this process is also governed by the information in the DNA. One cell forms the retina in an eye, another forms a ciliary muscle nearby, yet another forms a tear duct, and yet another forms a lens—all these and the bony socket in which the eye is set are produced by the same DNA interpreted in different circumstances as the cells divide. All the different kind of tissue, and all the organs, are produced by a pre-established harmony of triggers which produce the recognizable form of the ape. This pre-established harmony is only pre-established, I might add, by the process of evolution, as this matter is judged today.

Of this beautiful modern picture of the chemical engine, it is not at all true that the stored action patterns which are released by triggers are restricted to micro structures. Macro structures are, it seems, equally governed by such principles.

The muscles of the heart, if I may use this as an illustration, have an action which consists of a contraction and a release. Each muscle fibre will spontaneously and repeatedly act in this manner. In fact a heart attack which leads to cardiac arrest leaves the heart in a state of what is called 'fibrillation', where each muscle fibre in the heart is firing independently, and this will last until the muscles of the heart run out of oxygen. This will happen rapidly because the oxygen is fed to the heart by the blood which must be pumped by the heart, which has stopped. For the heart to function as a pump, an electrical signal runs down the heart, triggering the contractions of the muscle fibres in a co-ordinated manner, yielding the squeezing action of a pump. We see, in this case, how the trigger mechanism works in the physiology of organs in a body. We have already studied several illustrations of the trigger mechanism as it functions in the overall response of an organism to its econiche.

We see in fact that there is a whole hierarchy of action patterns stored in the organism, from DNA and protein structures at the micro level to physiological and even some social aspects of behaviour at the macro level. It is not my intention here to claim that all action is governed according to this model. Indeed, one of the interesting questions for this model is to show just how an organism gains insight into its surroundings if all organisms are basically chemical engines. This important question will be left unaddressed.

iii. More on Adaptation and Knowledge

If we wish to analyze the concept of the adaptation of an organism to its surroundings, we find that the trigger model gives us a useful way to do this. To say that an organism is adapted to its environment is to find that its actions are appropriate to that environment and conducive to the survival of the organism. Highly adaptive features of organisms are those which depend very precisely on very local or peculiar features of its normal environment without which the organism would not survive.

If we represent the organism and the class of its natural environments by two non-interesting circles, O and E, respectively, and if the vast repertoire of stored actions in O are deployed to be appropriate for E at just the right time, then it is by means of triggers T_1 which activate the right action pattern a_1, given the environment E_1.

O   E

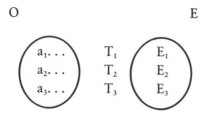

Given a complex environment E_x, the organism responds with the appropriate but complex action pattern A_y. How does this happen? Clearly, the complex environment has a simple feature T_z which acts as a trigger to activate the right action. Then any particular action A_y is adaptively suited to an environment E_x if and only if the trigger T_z which triggers A is a reliable sign of E_x. For an organism to be adapted to a class of environments, it must be activated in just the right way at the right times— that is to say it must respond to triggers in such a way as to anticipate the right environment.

Now this analysis of the concept of adaptation shows us that what we call practical human knowledge is a special case of adaptation. If I know that a car is approaching an intersection which I therefore do not cross at the time, then my 'knowledge' serves to govern my actions in a manner which can be analyzed just like other adaptive features of organisms. The visual and auditory signals together produce a trigger which inhibits my march down the street.

In the case of humans, we say that the human being 'knows' that if the trigger obtains, then the appropriate environment obtains, or 'whenever T_z obtains E_x obtains'. We could generalize this. Every adaptive feature of any organism has the tacit anticipation of nature of the form 'whenever T_1 obtains E_1 obtains', where T_1 activates the action pattern A_1 which is appropriate to E_1.

If we look at action patterns in the context of adaptation, then these may be regarded as skills, or 'technē' in the ancient Greek sense of the word. The stored repertoire of skills, the organism's 'technological repertoire', then presupposes an array of implicit hypotheses of the form 'whenever T_1 obtains E_1 obtains'.

Turning to the Humean (or 'moderate') skeptic who finds that his senses and reason can tell him nothing about the world, but nevertheless acts as successfully as he would were he to know a great deal, we see that his action presupposes knowledge no more and no less than any other organism. And if we accept the trigger model of modern biology, then the human being does know at least a large array of propositions of the form 'whenever T_1 obtains E_1 obtains'. It is only as an actor acting in the world that any organism knows such things, and this it knows only implicitly.

Turning to the problem of induction, we see that an arrow does exist in a direction opposite to the deductive arrow. If H is a set of hypotheses, and it is confirmed by a test T, where the statement T is derived from H and is found true,

$$H$$
$$\downarrow \ \uparrow$$
$$T$$

then we are looking for an arrow going back from T to H. *Logically,* Hume argued, there is no such arrow, but *psychologically,* Hume thought, there is such an arrow.

We can refine Hume's answer a bit. If we associate skills with implicit propositions, then corresponding to the test statement is a set of skills. When we examine a statement T and find it to be true, what we are doing is using our various skills which presuppose T, and if we can do what we expect to do, then we pronounce T to be true.

Even our simplest skills are themselves compounded from other yet simpler action patterns stored in the organism. Our skills consist of concatenations of action patterns which work in appropriate environments. It is only by starting with such an array of such patterns that we learn to put them together to form complex skills.

When I say skills are "put together", this is not intended to be a metaphor—I mean this quite literally. In order to do anything whatsoever, an organism can only reorganize action patterns possessed by it. It cannot do anything which it is genetically incapable of doing.

When human beings learn, therefore, they put together action patterns in various ways which, though mathematically finite in number, are practically unlimited in their possibilities.

Simple skills are therefore used to build more complex skills. Thus a scientist who is helping build an advanced gadget to go on a spaceship uses fine motor skills that he or she shares with the rest of us down here. In testing an apparatus with a strobe light, the perceptual skills used are common ones. What the scientists brings to bear are learnt skills, put together from fairly common ones, which are unique and appropriate to the task at hand only in the way they combine natural bits of action patterns.

The reliability that statements can provide other statements proceeds from the more general or composite to less general or simple elements of them, e.g. from (x)(Fx & Gx) or Fa & Ga to Fa, but if we place skills along such a scale

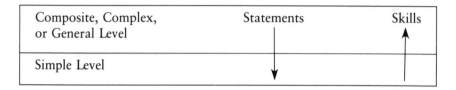

then corresponding to these would be a series of skills from simple to complex ones. What we see is that the inductive arrow does indeed hold among skills; in know-how and technology. A composite skill is only as reliable as the skills out of which it is composed. If a composite skill fails us, we examine the components to see where we failed, but if a fact is unexpected, it refutes the hypothesis which led us to the wrong expectation in the first place.

If I am right, the study of knowledge since Locke has made two basic errors regarding inductive processes. It has tried to find the source of all knowledge in perception, which I suggest is an error. At best our knowledge lies in our perceptual skills, and not in the images of perception, but more generally it is also to be found in other kinds of skills, too. (For example in experimental skills.)

The second error has been to look for an index of reliability among statements, where, if we only pay attention to Hume's arguments, this cannot exist. But if we study Hume's difficulty, we find that it is one concerning *action,* namely how does the skeptic do what must be done for his or her daily living? Here we see that there is indeed an inductive direction— complex actions are built up by practice and repetition from simpler actions. Ultimately, our most advanced knowhow derives all its reliability from the reliability of our well honed skills in our natural stomping grounds.

A test, on this model, is a test only if it looks for a consequence of a hypothesis in an environment which is familiar to us, or where we can use skills about which we feel no doubt. The laboratory is a controlled environment, a test procedure a well honed skill. This is why we use the laboratory, and why we fall back on established procedures—whether in physical experiments, in mathematics, in banking or in social activities generally.

9
Essence versus Evolution in Language

A. How Can Language be Used Creatively in Communication?

Noam Chomsky has proposed a very remarkable theory of language learning. It is so much better than its competition that it dominates the work of a great many linguists today. I shall contest this theory and propose an alternative. If Chomsky's theory remains the best available, at least it will not have won its place by default. Chomsky's approach to language is inspired by a solution to an intriguing problem of language learning: How can a language be used creatively when we communicate? We do communicate creatively. Yet there are strong theoretical grounds for holding this to be impossible. Let me explain.

A fluent speaker of a language is capable of producing new meaningful sentences. Moreover, another native speaker is able to understand a particular sentence which he may never have heard before. How can this be? Well, they do know the meaning of the words which are, after all, finite in number. A new sentence is a combination of old words. But (here is the problem), a finite number of words can be combined by a finite number of rules into a denumerably infinite number of word strings. There are also a denumerably infinite number of random strings which are meaningless. How do language users pick out the meaningful strings from the rest? Let us call this ability to pick out meaningful sentences the 'knowledge' or 'possession of a grammar'. This grammar 'generates' all the 'new' sentences for us. But how do we learn a generative grammar?

Consider the miracle that anyone can understand anyone else. The set of sentences a person has heard is always different from that heard by another, and no one has heard more than a finite number of the infinite number of word strings possible.

Each speaker has incomplete or 'degenerate' evidence of the grammar. The evidence also differs from one person to the next. Yet, to communicate, two people must generate the same strings of words as meaningful. How do people come to the same generative grammar based on different pieces of degenerate evidence?

i. Chomsky's Solution: Universal Grammar

Chomsky's solution to this riddle is to go back to an intellectualist theory of language learning. Chomsky proposes that human language cannot be understood except as a manifestation of a special intellectual ability, or reason. He suggests that all humans possess an innate universal grammar.[1]

> The principles that determine the form of grammar and that select the grammar of the appropriate form on the basis of certain data constitute a subject that might . . . be termed 'universal grammar'. The study of universal grammar, so understood, is a study of the nature of human intellectual capacities. It tries to formulate the necessary and sufficient conditions that a system must meet to qualify as a potential human language, conditions that are not accidentally true of the existing human languages, but that are rather rooted in the human 'language capacity' and thus constitute the innate organization that determines what counts as linguistic experience and what knowledge of language arises on the basis of this experience.

Chomsky has actually solved two problems at once with his theory of universal grammar. He has solved the problem of the creative use of language. But he has also solved another problem, namely: How is it possible that any human being, when put into an appropriate linguistic society, can learn to speak and understand the unique language of that society?

Chomsky's answer is that all humans, without respect to race, have one thing in common, which they bring to the learning of the language. All of us have the same rational capacity. This innate organizing capacity, then, is modified by the particular linguistic forms of a particular society to enable us to speak the language.

The universal grammar may be thought of as the essential grammar of our thought itself. The particular grammar of any language then is an *appearance* signifying the reality of reason, the universal grammar, which lurks in the background. Inspired by this remarkable vision of language and reason in man, Chomsky has looked for deeper levels of language, and has made many unusual discoveries. He has discovered, for example, that there are identifiable grammatical forms of a language that are different from apparent, or 'surface' forms of sentences. Our grammar is able to pick two meanings for 'John filled the box' even though the surface structure of the sentence does not tell us one or the other unambiguously. That John filled the box with something, or that the box was full of John are different *thoughts*. These two different thoughts are the unique interpretations of two different 'deep structures'. The deep structures are generated by a grammar, not of the English language as it appears to us, but by a more abstract grammar which yields the surface forms as transformations.[2]

He goes further.[3] Our deep grammar can yield limitless new meaningful sentences. But our brains are not limitless. How then can we possess such a grammar? Borrowing a leaf from the mathematicians' book, Chomsky suggests that what we possess are generative rules. The number of the generative rules we possess is finite, but since these rules are recursive they can generate an infinite number of sentences. The search for these generative rules is, of course, *generative linguistics.*

Naturally, when we find the universal grammar, we will have explained and understood the basis for understanding *all* languages. In this sense it would be the ultimate rational explanation. So linguists look for elements of it. The study must be absorbing, because they seem to need little moral support from others. Perhaps this is because of the great success of Chomsky's Aristotelian (or 'essentialistic') revolution in linguistics. So linguists may search and wait for the final word. But what if it is not there? Are professional linguists then waiting for godot? This is the disquieting question.

.

B. How Could Language have been Invented, and Once Invented, How Can It Develop?

Let me now summarize, for convenience, my own views. My own interest in language is prompted by a different set of problems. I am intrigued by a riddle which has come down to us from Rousseau, Herder and Beattie. This problem, my first, is simply this: (1) How could language have been invented when its invention (and teaching) would itself presuppose the existence of language prior to it? Here is how Beattie saw this riddle:[4]

> If there was a time when all mankind were . . . a dumb and brutal race of animals, all mankind must, in the ordinary course of events, have continued dumb to this day. For first, to such animals speech could not be necessary; as they are supposed to have existed for ages without it; and it is not to be imagined, that dumb and beastly savages would ever think of contriving unnecessary arts, whereof they had no example in the world around them.

This can be generalised to a second problem. (2) It is not only puzzling how language could have come to be, but also how it could develop once it came to exist. If someone innovates, not simply by making a new string out of old words according to set rules, but by making a grammatical departure, then it is something of a miracle if he is not misunderstood. How did the first one to use a pronominal expression convey the pronominal force of his word to someone who had never envisaged pronouns? How did the first preposition convey its propositional character to the unwitting listener?

Turning from grammatical questions, we can ask something else which Chomsky does not consider, a third problem. (3) How does one convey the meaning of a new word—a really new word, not just a new mark for a combination of known words? Insofar as it can be explained in terms of other words in the language which we already know, the word is redundant. Insofar as it cannot, it is mysterious. Yet we do know of the introduction of words for new concepts, words like 'field of force', 'complex number', 'cardinality of a collection or class'. These, when first introduced, were new, puzzling but expressive.

i. New Expressions

The proposed solutions to these problems, which are summarised in reverse order, include an extension of what is known as the Sapir-Whorf hypothesis.[5] Whorf argued for the view that a language is not merely a vehicle for expressing thought, but itself embodies a point of view, a *Weltanschauung*. Studying the Hopi language, for example, Whorf discovered a remarkable difference between Hopi concepts and ours: their concepts seem to presuppose a world unlike the one English speakers would recognize. This is fascinating, and very credible. As a young bilingual, I myself used to associate two different 'moods' with the two languages that I knew best.

One must avoid a supposed consequence of the Whorfian hypothesis which has made it very famous, the so-called 'linguistic relativity' hypothesis. Perhaps because they wondered how one could rationally discuss what is presupposed by the very language being used, some concluded that ultimately a language and its world-view must imprison the native speaker. Languages like Hopi and English are never quite inter-translatable, one might conclude.

Languages do bring with them world–views, categories of thought, grammatical structures which exhibit certain embedded ontologies. But they do not imprison us. They do not imprison because they come not with one world–view but with several, which compete, and also with problems of each world–view. When solved these problems might yield not only a modified world–view but novel concepts, and even, sometimes, new categories of thought. The need to improve our understanding of the world is a continual one, if we live in a healthy intellectual community. Language, moved by this force, is constantly changing its concepts and its categories, even if we ignore the influence of contact with new people.

But this progressive force in language is counteracted by another one, which is conservative.[6] So long as we try to communicate a new idea, it is necessary to be modest in our linguistic demands—otherwise we will be misunderstood. So the need to communicate acts as a conservative force. (This conservative force of the need to communicate has been appreciated by Wittgenstein and his followers.) These two forces—the progressive and the conservative—create a dynamic balance, one which leads to the gradual but sustained growth of language, a growth marked by changing categories of thought and the increasing expressive power of the language.

Let us now turn to the third problem, the problem about concepts. To understand why we have the concepts that we do is not a simple matter. Each new concept arises out of a need felt in a specific intellectual and linguistic context. This context is always one of intellectual ferment, where new views are being considered and perhaps being accepted. Most of our words and all their roots, unfortunately, have their origins in a past without record. This plight of the linguist is much like that of the paleontologist, only a little worse. To know why our language is as it is, we would have to know how it evolved, just as knowing why we have the anatomy we do involves a knowledge of the descent of man.

We have to turn to more recent linguistic history to test the hypothesis that really new expressions grow out of intellectual ferment, and not, as some have argued, out of rustic speech habits, or laziness, or out of an aimless 'semantic drift'. Regarding this history it would seem that the emergence of new concepts has as its background the transformation of our understanding of the world, and the need thereby felt to express novel things.

ii. Grammatical Evolution

A solution to the second problem, the problem of conservatism, can be indicated by showing how there might be grammatical evolution. New ideas often bring new categorial frameworks with them, and these may not sit well with the grammatical categories entrenched already in language. This can lead to the modification, and even the creation of new grammatical structures or forms. One example is the modern proliferation of abstract substantives. We can see the beginning of this grammatical form and the need felt for it in the writings of Plato. In Plato's early dialogues, Socrates always has some difficulty explaining what he wants when he asks 'what is the virtuous?' or 'what is the beautiful?' The words that Socrates needs are the abstract substantives 'virtue', 'beauty'; to distinguish the Form itself, as Plato might have said, from those things which merely participate in it.

My friend and colleague, Allan Cobb, has given me a striking piece of corroboration for my view that new grammatical tools are forged in intellectual kilns. He has shown that a very well-known and hitherto unaccountable difference between Classical Greek and Koinē or New Testament Greek had its origin in a most remarkable place: in Aristotle's metaphysics. Cobb has been able to show that Aristotle, who was the first ever to make use of the present progressive ('I am walking' rather than the older form 'I walk'), was led to make this grammatical innovation by his metaphysics, namely his conviction that becoming has a certain kind of being.[7]

The existing surface grammar of a language must therefore be interpreted as an evolutionary residue from grammatical stages of the language in its past. Deep structure or grammar incorporates categories which we are willing to accept today as part of our understanding of the world. Our 'deeper' grammatical intuitions are therefore merely the product of our world view, as it may be reflected in our concepts, especially if this world view does not agree with the categories of surface grammar.

iii. Origin of Language

Finally we come to Rousseau's problem, itself regarding the possibility of the origin of language. This is a real difficulty, for though apes have expectations and problems, and though they have a system of communication, they do not have even the beginnings of a symbolic or conceptual language in which they might express their expectations, or their problems. How did the first symbol come to be? This is such a serious problem that I had often despaired of finding a way out of its difficulties. Only recently, however, I have been lucky to find a possible (though probably not a true) explanation of how language might have *originated*. This solution does not depend on a unique first feature of man, but is thoroughly evolutionary, or neo-Darwinian. The basic idea is that man learnt language by imitating himself. Language must have begun as an extended tradition among children of the playful imitation of adult communication. For the elucidation of this point I must refer you to the next chapter.

C. The Evolutionary View of Language

The two main models of language sketched out above are designed to solve very different problems. Chomsky's problem is a static one, about the structure of language. Those with which I start are dynamic. So one is tempted to think that these two views may be held together, to solve both problems at once. But they are not complementary theories, to be easily combined; rather they are deeply divided rival approaches. The basic difference between them is that Chomsky's theory is *essentialistic* while the one I propose is thoroughly *evolutionary*.[8] The evolutionary theory does not have to postulate a structural property common to all languages by virtue of which they are languages (which is essentialism). All languages, of course, have some structure in common. (This is trivially true.) What is common, however, is not a structural property that explains their grammar, or how we can learn it. What accounts for their similarity, and their being languages is a combination of two things: they have one origin, and they have evolved in circumstances which are not entirely different. They have, so to speak, some common *hereditary characters* which have evolved under very similar but not identical *selective pressures*.

The evolutionary view provides somewhat different answers to Chomsky's problems concerning language learning. (The problems: (1) How is linguistic creativity possible in communication? (2) How is it that all humans have access in principle to any human language?) The evolutionary view also postulates something innate to man, which is common to all men, in order to solve these problems. Unlike Chomsky I do not have to postulate that what is common to and innate in us is a rational universal grammar. The Chomskyan problems of language learning can instead be answered by putting together and extending some ideas of learning proposed by Konrad Lorenz and Karl Popper.[9] Let me sketch this alternative in summary.

i. Outline of the Theory

Language and our expectations are closely connected, as Whorf and Sapir have argued. Add to this Popper's idea that our expectations improve as the problems which come with them are solved. A change of theory as some problems are solved in turn, leads to the evolution of the concepts and grammar of the language. Let us now use these same ideas to solve the problems of language-learning. What is innate to man and common to all men is a system of expectations which are brought to the world at birth. These are not merely innate capacities but fully-fledged innate expectations, somewhat like Lorenz's innate patterns of behaviour as opposed to innate capacities to behave. The problems facing young children in a human society are fairly stereotyped, most of them having a social dimension. Some of the social cues trigger responses which later develop into language. These responses, e.g., "babbling", imitation of social role, demanding attention from adults, etc., in the second year of life become cognitive tools.[10] After this stage the language and ideas develop along more individual lines, except to the extent that social, environmental and particularly institutional pressures within a language community create less diversity than that which is found between communities.

But the common background of innate responses, similarity of social requirements, the effect of pre-existing similarities between linguistic traditions, (from a genetic point of view) solve the second problem—namely why all humans have in principle, access to any human language.

The problem of creativity in language is merged with the problem of creativity more generally. The problem of understanding a new combination of old words (Chomsky's problem of creativity) is only a less extended version of the problem of understanding new concepts, new syntactic combinations or grammatical innovations. Such understanding is possible only because and to the extent that we can appreciate those cognitive needs in each other which oblige us to be creative. Of course, we do understand grammatical rules, perhaps of the kind that Chomsky has in mind. But the rules we accept do not constitute our understanding of language. Rather, we use the rules as conjectures to test how the language is used by others, by seeing them broken. Rules of grammar and syntax are heuristic tools and not the end-state of learning a language.

We are able to communicate not because we share precisely and exactly the same grammar and concepts, but because our complementary cognitive and social interests oblige us to recognize that there are many ways (closely related, perhaps) of using a language. We make allowances for this. Without this tolerance communication would be very poor, indeed. The mechanism by which we make allowances, and improve upon our approximate understanding of each other's language has already been dealt with.[11]

Like Chomsky we must accept a modified doctrine of innate ideas. The only thing to add to this doctrine is that our innate ideas (expectations) are usually among the first to be discarded, or modified; they are not simply possessed by us as an unalterable essence. If all the speakers in one community speak the same language it is because starting from roughly the same innate base, they face similar problems in a society with certain kinds of traditions, including the language. The problems do however differ from stratum to stratum in the society, and from profession to profession, and naturally this will have some diversifying influence. In this way we can do without an essence of language, by turning to its evolution. Darwin, similarly, showed us how to do without appealing to the essence of each species, by relying on evolution instead.

ii. The Evolutionary Theory of Language
versus the Essentialistic

The evolutionary theory of language is free of the main difficulties of an essentialist theory; these fall into three categories: linguistic, psychological and biological.

(a) Linguistic Difficulties.

Most evidence from synchronic or diachronic linguistics will not be useful for this debate, having been gathered for different purposes. But there is a linguistic difficulty facing the Chomskyans, which arises from the fact that they are looking for universal elements of grammar, which (in my opinion) are not there. There is a strain felt in everyday Chomskyan linguistics which comes from this search for the non-existent. Let me explain.

Our ability to understand each other is supposed to be rooted in our possession of a common grammar. So two native speakers must be able to pick out the same strings as grammatical. In fact this never happens. This is a serious problem for Chomskyan linguistics which is often easily dismissed. If there is no such grammar there are no word strings, *as such* which are meaningful. If something does not strike us as meaningful, we look for a meaning that the speaker intended to convey. We may even try to find out why the expressions used were not the usual ones. In the end we rule on whether a sentence is grammatical only within a known context.

The search for context-free grammars (which Chomskyans and Structuralists must presuppose) has been well criticized by all those who favour contextualism in linguistics.[12] A great many expressions which a Chomskyan linguist might regard as 'deviant' or 'ungrammatical' are, within some context, reasonable ones to make. No doubt there is a serious problem that contextualists must face. It is a problem of telling generally but precisely *how* contexts influence meaningfulness. But this does not save Chomskyan linguistics.

(b) Psychological Difficulties

If language-learning consists of a mere filling in of an innate grammar, then there should be no reason why a feat of language-learning performed by a child for the first time should be very different from the learning of subsequent language as an adult. In each case it is the same innate grammar supposedly being modified in different ways. The facts seem to suggest that there is actually a great difference between learning a language as a child does, and learning as it is done by an adult. This is naturally explained on the evolutionary view, since learning the first language or group of languages is part of a general cognitive development; a subsequent learning of a language is different because it occurs by falling back on the learnt language, or it occurs in terms of the learnt 'cognitive structures'. Evolution implies some irreversible developments.

Other indications of what seems to be a difficulty of the essentialist's position are the facts concerning the ability to learn language by those who lose the ability to speak or understand language—for example, due to damage to the brain (*aphasia*). In such cases, possibilities of relearning seem to be definitely related to age, the younger you are the better the chances.[13] This also favours an evolutionary approach, according to which languages are learnt for the first time as an integral part of learning about the world.

Finally, Chomsky's theory of language-learning (unlike mine) seems to be compatible with considerable independence between the learning of language and other cognitive development, since his theory does not require a close connection between beliefs and grammar. We could test this by making correlations between the grammatical and cognitive developments of children, and comparing these for a large number of children. There is a serious problem for the evolutionary theory of identifying the cognitive and grammatical stages which are correlated.

(c) Biological Difficulties

The essentialistic theory is firmly and unalterably un-Darwinian. This creates severe biological problems regarding the descent of man. This is a decisive argument against Chomskyan theory.

First, let me show that from an evolutionary point of view *the universal grammar itself, if there is such a thing could not have evolved.*

Imagine that it has. Then two geographically separated subspecies of man would have different universal grammars, since it is most unlikely that two lines of independent evolution would lead to exactly the same result. But a grammar is a system of rules. Being a system, it would become vastly different in its effect if it were even slightly changed in its generative structure. (Imagine a random change in the axioms of a mathematical system, be it ever so little!) If so, it is most surprising that members of different races who now speak one language find themselves capable of picking out the same well-fashioned sentences. Since we have no such inter-racial problems, 'universal grammar' could not have evolved, whatever it may be (and if it exists).

Another feature of universal grammar as a hereditary human character is that *it could not have evolved from any character* of any primate whatsoever. Because it is the essence of human language, and because no such essence can be found associated with animal communication, Chomsky is forced to deny any connection between language and primate communication. (Notice, though, that if we believe that species have essences, then we could not accept the evolution of species, either.) To quote Chomsky,[14]

> There is no more reason for assuming an evolutionary development of
> "higher" from "lower" stages (of human language from animal
> communication, that is) . . . than there is for assuming an evolutionary
> development from breathing to walking. The stages have no significant
> analogy, it appears, and seem to involve entirely different processes and
> principles.

In fact if the essence of language is a universal grammar, then there is nothing in animals which could possibly have a 'significant analogy' to it.

Since language, according to Chomsky, presupposes a universal grammar which has, first, not evolved since it has come to be, and second, not evolved from any complex of primate characters, one can only conclude that it is a single mutation that has come about very recently, say twenty or forty thousand years ago. Although this seems to be the only way out of the difficulties facing Chomsky's universal grammar considered as a hereditary character it does not escape further difficulties.

Firstly, if universal grammar is a single allelomorph (or new form) of recent origin, then we should still see quite a few of the original humans with a total inability to learn a human language, (a sort of superintelligent ape). This just does not happen. That, of course, is because man and language have evolved together for at least half a million years, if not more.

Secondly, if a certain strain of men suddenly developed which had an innate grammar, it is quite incredible that they survived. The reason is that the first language speakers who were spending their time developing a language were at a considerable disadvantage as compared to those fellow members of the species who were doing adaptively useful things. This argument is conclusive, *unless the first beginnings of language were adaptively useful*. Now we know that language in its later development was useful. But if at first it was not there would have been no further trials. So languages must have been useful right from the start.

Notice, furthermore, that Chomsky believes that language presupposes rational thought. It is therefore even harder to find an advantage that men might have found for the first beginnings of language, if they were already rational, anyway. On the evolutionary approach, there is no further need to explain why the first beginnings of language were adaptively useful, since language is the basis and the result of improved expectations, and better expectations lead to better adaptation.

Thirdly and finally, there is evidence from physical anthropology which tells against the view that language *presupposes* a fully formed innate reason. If the abstract intellectual capacity of man came to exist over the million or whatever years preceding the very recent language, then one would expect that the human brain would have developed before the simian jaw disappeared. But *homo erectus* or *pithecanthropus erectus* as he used to be called, has only a partially developed cranial structure. His jaw would have held a true human tongue. The importance of the human tongue for speech is enormous. Because our tongue is tied down near the tip, we have greater control over its use. A primate which has its tongue held up near its throat can only use the tongue for gross movements. (Imagine holding a ten foot stick to turn on a light switch, as opposed to a stick which is six inches long.) The considerable difference in the structure of the human jaw, especially the absence of a 'bony ridge' in the lower jaw for several million years, suggests that man has been speaking more delicately than other primates for as long. The ape-man with the parabolic dental arc and without a bony ridge in the lower jaw is said to be several million years old, but the new brain arrived no more than half a million years ago. We must have spoken for many million years before we found out what we were saying.

In conclusion, I should add that while I have challenged Chomsky's rationalism in linguistics, I do not wish to add my name to the long and growing list of anti-rationalists; rather I wish to disagree with Chomsky's essentialistic idea of reason and propose that reason (rationality) is a feature of how we *develop* our thought and language—and not a feature of what we are structurally.

10
Mind and the Origin
of Language

A. The Origins of Mind and Language are Distinct

i. Introduction

I shall defend two theses in this chapter:

Thesis No. 1: Human language, insofar as it is a system of communication, and the human mind, which is capable of thought, have independent biological origins, even though thought and word are not easily separable in the evolved state of a human conceptual language.

Thesis No. 2: A symbolic language came first. Its presence triggered the development of our abstract understanding in the mental structure that man already shared with all primates.

The contrary view, that language presupposes mind, has already been criticized in the preceding chapter in the form in which Chomsky supports it. The main argument used to criticize it was that *this view is incompatible with our understanding of the evolution of species.*

In order to maintain the numbered theses above, especially the second, I shall have to consider certain difficulties. I treat these as hurdles to be overcome by a good model of how language came to exist. The crux of this essay is a model of the independent beginning of conceptual language which presupposes a background of mental behaviour which man shares with the apes. This model will overcome the hurdles without presupposing that the primates who evolved into men were already gifted with a human abstract understanding. What the model is designed to do is this. It shows that one need not abandon Darwin's theory of evolution, or assume an exceptionally lucky mutation, or believe in a harmony which is pre–established by any forces other than those of gradual evolution. This new model of the origin of language is a variation of the old 'imitation' theories. Language, on this model, arose from *man's playful imitation of his own prelinguistic cries.* And it is this which ultimately led to the development of the peculiar mental capabilities of man, the rational animal.

Which came first, the human language or the human mind? This riddle of the chicken-and-egg variety is an intriguing one. It is of great interest to us because *Homo sapiens* can be characterized either by its conceptual and descriptive language, or just as well by the propositional or linguistic character of its thought.

In the *evolved* state of human thought and language, it is hard to isolate one from the other. One might even be tempted to think that the very attempt to distinguish between the peculiarly human language and the special structure of the human mind is misguided. But these two features of man can, I believe, be very usefully distinguished. There are two arguments to show that their origins are quite distinct:[1]

ii Evidence from Biology and Psychology

(a) From an evolutionary standpoint, we are descendants of an ultimately simian source; we should look for the origin of our characters in the features of the primates. Among the nonhuman primates there is certainly a sharp distinction between *intelligence* and *social communication*. Köhler's chimpanzee, Sultan, has been photographed putting two sticks together to make an ingenious new double-stick.[2] The extra length was used to draw objects otherwise out of his reach. This, one might say, is a sign of intelligence. At the same time Sultan could intimidate or pacify a fellow chimpanzee, and this is certainly evidence of social communication among chimpanzees.

The difference between the ingenuity of Sultan and that on which humans pride themselves is this. Humans have learnt to use language in a special way. The intelligence of a human is manifested most clearly in his language and in the use made of it. By contrast, no reliable intelligence test for a chimpanzee can depend predominately on features of the chimpanzee's ability to communicate socially. This shows clearly how distinct are thought and language among the nonhuman primates—and by contrast how closely intertwined are the intelligence and linguistic capabilities of a human community

(b) A second argument showing the distinct origins of thought and language comes from child psychology. Karl Bühler, in *The Mental Development of the Child,* has given an excellent account of the independent development of thought and language in the child.[3] In fact, the developing intellect of the child until the twelfth month is called the 'chimpanzee age' by Bühler to distinguish it from the development after it begins to speak. At the same time, the human child develops strong communicative bonds, for example with the mother and, to a lesser extent, with other humans. Thus, we see that even in the human infant there is a stage when communication and ingenuity are not fused together in a human conceptual language.

Even more emphatic is the difference between autism and mongolism. An autistic child is quite intelligent, but is unable to develop normal communicative skills. But a mongoloid has a retarded intelligence rather than any inability to communicate, though the retardation inhibits communication.[4]

Let us then accept that intellect and communication somehow get together in our history, and in the history of the mental development of the child; there is no difficulty then, in seeing that a human conceptual language is an evolved institution. Its later state and character can be understood in terms of the earlier state and character of the language as used by intelligent and motivated individuals. The question is: How did these two distinct forerunners of our language come to meet?

iii. Traditional Theories

If we look at theories of language, and of intelligence, we find that both of the following views have been held regarding the origin of human language: (a) Generally speaking, *linguists* who have gone so far as to ask how a language is possible, find that it is a special human intellectual organization that underlies human language. Chomsky, for example, believes that humans have a rational intellect which, when combined with the linguistic tradition of a particular society, will give an individual the ability to use the language of that society.[5] (b) *Psychologists* like Wolfgang Köhler or Karl Bühler, who have been more interested in the nature of thought and reason, have tried to show that the human mind is not unlike that of another primate, but for the singularly liberating influence of our conceptual language.[6]

iv. Mind is a By-Product of a New Mode of Communication

I shall argue, in what follows, that the origin of human language lies in an innovation in an earlier system of communication. The resultant new system has liberated our intellects, and, over hundreds of thousands of years, has given us our uniquely human mind. *Our special mind is a by-product of a new system of communication.*

Let me first meet two important objections to this theory. These objections consist of two apparently damaging arguments that seem to show *that human language could not have evolved from social communication among the animals.* In answering these two objections we will have to come up with a hypothesis about how language was first invented. I shall not deal here with the other hypothesis—that human reason or the human intellect precedes human language—other than to say that it is *pre-Darwinian* (i.e., that it is incompatible with the neo-Darwinian picture of the descent of man).

B. The Origin of Conceptual Language

i. Some Difficulties

As evolutionists, we must accept that language has a beginning. I would like to consider two arguments to show that humans, or some hominid ancestors, *could not have invented the typically human conceptual language.* Since from this it would follow that we do not have a conceptual language—which is palpably false—I have no wish to accept these arguments uncritically. On the contrary, I hope to criticize them, and in this way search for a good answer to our earlier conundrum, as to find a way around these two particular objections.

The first argument is this.[7] If a particular species of ape develops a conceptual language, then this is due either to a unique feature of the species or to features it shares with other primates.

If it is the latter, then the other primates within the same ecological region would also develop the language. But, as we know, they have not. Therefore the feature which enables an ape to develop language must be unique. If it is unique then, once again, we have the same dilemma. The unique first feature is in turn due to something unique or shared. But since we can rule out a miraculous agency or a superordinary beneficial mutation for our purposes, we can rule out a unique *first* feature.[8] But it cannot be shared. This leaves us with a vicious regress, which is incompatible with the idea that man has evolved and inherited his characters from some ape. This argument leads to the conclusion that if the neo-Darwinian theory of descent is true then we have not developed a conceptual language.

The second argument is a more special one. Animal communication among primates has three features of importance. Given these features we can show that any species evolving toward a language like ours would long ago have perished. These three features, which have been discovered by students of animal behaviour, are as follows:[9]

a) Communication among primates performs crucial functions, without which a primate community could not survive. For mating, feeding, care of the young, and for a host of other functions, their specially adapted system of social communication is indispensable.

b) The system is a rigid one, depending on few expressions which are clearly distinguishable from each other by strong contrast. Thus, appeasement and aggression are strongly contrasted. The significance of this contrast is that it makes signals clear and unambiguous, as the difference between aggressive display and offering to be mounted for appeasement. Of course, behaviour can vary indefinitely *between* two opposites. But like the knob of a radio which can control only volume, each range is linearly definable by the two end points ('loud' and 'soft').

c) These relatively few and easily recognizable signals govern a highly complex pattern of social behaviour whose precise performance makes community life possible.

Human language regarded as a system of animal communication is clearly *degenerate*. All its symbols sound remarkably like each other, *and depend on syntax rather than contrast* for their identification. (i.e., human language is a *degenerate contrastive* system even though it is a *sophisticated syntactic system*.)

Any primate evolving from a highly integrated, rigid and delicate system of communication to one whose system of communication is largely degenerate in this sense, can survive only if contrastive communication itself is superfluous from an evolutionary point of view. Analogously, a creature with a degenerate tail can survive if the tail has ceased to play a crucial part in the adaptation of the species. But social communication among primates is manifestly unlike the nonfunctioning tail. Social communication among primates is, if anything, more important for survival than it was with some of its forerunners. In other words, if *contrastive* communication played an essential role in the life of primates, and was replaced by a *syntactic language,* how does, or how can, the latter take over the functions of the former without loss of efficiency?

Human language could, therefore, never have evolved, because any species that lost its rigid system of communication either fully or in part would have been superseded by strains that preserved the vital system.

It is of no value to argue that the degenerate system *in the end* turned out to be superior to the rigid one. For no species would survive the experiment long enough to await these later developments.

ii. Desiderata for a Theory of the Origin of Conceptual Language

These arguments are problematic ones for us. The problem is to find out how human language could possibly have come about. Let us first find out how the difficulties could be avoided. Then we shall have *an abstract set of desiderata of a satisfactory theory of the origin of language,* dictated by the need to avoid the difficulties. When we learn how to avoid the two unhappy conclusions, we will know what to look for in a good theory of the origin of conceptual language. Let us do so.

The first difficulty is easily resolved. We say that the features which enabled our ancestors to develop language are unique to our species, and are also features that *Homo sapiens* share with other forms of life. That is to say, each particular feature is shared with other species, their particular combination is unique.[10]

The second difficulty can be resolved by saying that humans developed conceptual language from a system of communication which was *already freed from its social obligations*. This flexible system has to be similar to the system of communication which performs the necessary functions; but this flexible one must coexist for a long while with the rigid one, without interfering with the vital functions of the original communicative system. (And if so, why is it not selected against? . . .)

In addition to satisfying these desiderata, our theory must also be able to explain the important differences between social communication among the animals and human language. I continue below with a list of the most important of these differences which we can take as further desiderata of a good theory of the origin of language.[11]

Human language is symbolic. That is to say, it is representational in much the same way as the language of the bees is representational.[12] In this respect it differs from most social communication among animals in so far as most animal social communication can signal or can express without necessarily representing anything whatsoever. How could the symbols have come to be?

There is a clear distinction between the imperative and the indicative in human language.[13] Among other primates it is certainly possible to interpret a piece of communication as an imperative or as an indicative, as we like. Besides, it seems rather difficult to say what exactly is the difference between understanding a primate call as a demand or as a description of a wish, or as merely a description. A hungry child who is crying may be said to demand milk or to express a wish for milk, or describe (signal) its internal state of needing and/or desiring milk, or even to ask a question 'Why do I not have milk?' The difference between human language and that of a chimpanzee, it seems, is that human language can not only have imperatives and indicatives but that these are very clearly separated. How could this difference have come to be?

There is a clear proliferation of the phonetic and other bases of human language, as compared to animal communication. One might say that humans have succeeded in making use of a wider range of phonemes in their language than have the primates, or for that matter members of any other species that make use of social communication. Whence this flexibility?

Nevertheless, human language is a *system* of communication, rather than a set of discrete symbols, however many they may be. Anyone who has doubts on this score, should turn to the works of Noam Chomsky, who has strongly argued for the importance of the systematic character of human language, to explain how it can be used creatively by us in ever new situations.[14]

The last feature of human language is that it varies from one group to the other. Although there may be some common thread that runs through all human languages there is certainly also variation. As we see, this desideratum immediately rules out the possibility that there is one inborn language which is carried genetically from parent to child. A child who would normally learn French from its parents will, if brought up in appropriate surroundings, learn English.[15] Our model must allow for cultural influences.

C. Characteristics of Early Man and the Origins of Language

Let us now ask: What features do humans share with the apes, and even with other living organisms, which combine in a singular way to enable them to develop a conceptual language? It is my belief that the answer is a combination of the following six elements, the first four of which may be regarded as critical features of the human mind shared with the apes.

i. Playing and learning
ii. Imitation
iii. Social traditions
iv. A system of communication
v. A long childhood
vi. A recent change in diet and lifestyle.

Let me first describe these features of animal behaviour, and show that each of them applies not only to humans but to other animals as well. Then I shall show how the six of them taken together do, in fact, give us a combination which uniquely allows for the development of a conceptual language. In this way we will be able to explain why humans have a conceptual language, while no other life forms do. I shall also show how the second difficulty mentioned above will be automatically avoided, and how the other desiderata regarding the difference between human as opposed to animal social communication can also be dealt with.

i. Play and Learning.

We share with the other animals the ability to learn and to play. Wolfgang Köhler has suggested that there is a strong connection between the two, and in this he is followed by modern students of animal behaviour.[16] The higher vertebrates are able to *learn*. This means they are able to modify their behaviour. But since patterns of behaviour have been naturally selected, a mere breakdown in these patterns would not lead to any survival value for the species whose patterns are thus broken up. In other words, *any* modification is not learning. If modifications of behaviour are to be adaptive, there must be, as a compensating feature, a centralized coordination of the loose or loosened patterns of behaviour which can be combined and permuted to produce results appropriate to a changing environment. Moreover, the centralized coordination must possess a pretty fast feedback mechanism viz. the sensory nervous system.[17]

If we compare feedback mechanisms in the evolution of life as a whole, and the feedback mechanism which is especially associated with learning, we see that with the life process there is a feedback mechanism which operates over the generations by genetic mutation, and some form of natural selective pressure. In the case of learning, however, the feedback mechanism takes place through certain receptors, the sense organs, which enable the organism to change its position or its attitude at short notice, at a pace which a plant cannot match.

If an organism can recombine elementary patterns of behaviour to form new patterns, then it seems that the following must also be true. Normal stimulations which would automatically elicit a certain pattern of behaviour must be substitutable by alternative means within the organism. Thus, if a pattern of behaviour is normally evoked by seeing a certain colour, and if an organism has to learn to perform that very activity without seeing the colour, then it has somehow to respond to a new internal signal in the way it responded to the old colour signal. For example, if it had to learn to gather food when it was not hungry, then it had to have the ability to internally simulate the signals which elicit the response to collect food. In this way an animal that has no instinctive direction to store food (unlike a bee or an ant) might nevertheless succeed in doing so if it can gather food at a normally inappropriate time. Finally, the ability to simulate appropriate stimulation would allow novel, chainlike, complex patterns of behaviour to be arranged from pre–existing elementary ones by making an earlier element of behaviour a signal for the next one in the chain. We can call this 'coordination', a form of habit formation.

An organism which is capable of all this is therefore capable of exhibiting a certain complex chain of behaviour even when not stimulated by the appropriate object. Thus, a cat might hunt a ball of wool, even if the latter does not behave like a mouse. A child might play nurse-a-doll, and put it to bed, even though the doll itself may be no more than a cloth dummy. In other words, any animal which is capable of learning is capable, under special circumstances, of producing its patterns of behaviour *inappropriately*, and is therefore capable of play. What is characteristic of play, however, is that it helps exercise patterns of behaviour when they are not elicited by the normal objects. This makes the chances of a fatal mistake less likely when the serious situation arises.

One of the peculiarities of playful behaviour is this. Though it is characteristically like normal behaviour in some respects, it is characteristically different in others. "All forms of play have the common quality that they are fundamentally different from 'earnest'; at the same time, however, they show an unmistakable resemblance, indeed an imitation of a definite earnest situation."[18] Two puppies, or two children fighting, do fight, and yet they do not fight in earnest. The simulation of stimulation, learning, and play, are all of a piece, making the modification of behaviour an adaptive feature of mammals.

It is a corollary that the greater the plasticity of behaviour, the greater the range of simulation of stimulation (or, what we might ordinarily call 'imagination'). Among humans the plasticity of behaviour is so marked that even sexual behaviour is normally elicited not by the original object but by surrogate signals of the imagination. Sexual perversion, as Jean Genet has observed, is almost natural to humans, perhaps for this very reason.

ii. Imitation

Play, as we have seen, is imitative, in the sense that play actions imitate the 'earnest' ones. But strictly speaking they are not so much imitations as exercises or rehearsals. Imitation, such as that produced by a mynah bird when it imitates the cry of another bird, is quite a different process. It is true that a child's exercise and play, being similar to adult behaviour in some respects, is easily confused with imitation. Strictly speaking, however, a true imitation or mimicking occurs when a child picks up *idiosyncratic* behaviour from adults and incorporates it into its behavioural patterns. For example, speech accents and mannerisms are so often picked up by children from other children and adults.

Imitation is also evident among primates. A good deal of the teaching of the young by a parent relies on the mimicking of the adult's action by the young. Lions raised in captivity also exhibit similar behaviour. They are unable to hunt effectively; whereas those young lions that have been hunting with a proficient lioness will normally be able to hunt well. Examples such as these can be multiplied. But it is not surprising that animals which have some plasticity of behaviour also have the ability to mimic behaviour. For in a certain way the greater the plasticity, the greater the need for social controls which guide the right type of behaviour, especially those forms of behaviour which have to be performed exactly for survival.

iii. Social Traditions

Imitation of quirks of one member of a species by others can lead to a chain which we can call a tradition. So, in a certain sense, traditions can and do exist among those animals which can learn and which can imitate. But in this sense, traditions are superficial in some cases, since a tradition which is 'lost", such as hunting among lions, can be picked up again after a short period of trial by an individual lion. In a similar way many imitative chains which serve the functions of *facilitating* the production of certain important patterns of behaviour may not strictly be traditions insofar as they will soon reassert themselves if we cut the thread at any time.

A true tradition is one in which typical patterns of behaviour develop which cannot be explained without reference to some accidental learning. 'Accidental', of course, is meant from the genetic point of view. In this sense, *homo sapiens* may be thought to be unique in possessing social traditions, but studies have shown that many animals also possess true social tradition. Eugene Marais discovered that the chacma baboon has such traditions;[19] Konrad Lorenz has shown that jackdaws possess true traditions; ethologists Kawai and Kawamura have made extensive studies of new social traditions which have evolved among the macaques in Japan.[20]

iv. A System of Communication

One of the important features of the animal kingdom is *social behaviour.* The very fact that mobility involves a variable distance between organisms requires that there has to be a system of communication between them if they are to get together to propagate their own species. At the same time, if they are not to starve because of overpopulation even when food is plentiful, there must be some communication among them to keep each other far enough away to ensure a decent average supply of nourishment. Social communication among the primates bears a strong resemblance to the corresponding kind of communication in *homo sapiens.*[21] It is hard *not* to know when a non-human primate is threatening and when it is appeased, even though it is a human who is looking on. *Homo sapiens* even shares a part of this language with other animals. The fact that a dog will learn to look where one points, and to tell when one is angry or happy, is an excellent indication that, with a little adjustment, one can learn to communicate with most animals. The very fact that one can so very easily anthropomorphize animals and pets shows that systems of communication have not altered so drastically that we have lost touch entirely with the language of the animals—what Lorenz has called "King Solomon's Ring".

v. A Long Childhood

One of the features of *homo sapiens* that is rare, but not unique, is that human children go through a long period of pre–adulthood. Even if the length of his childhood is a product of the evolution of man after he acquired language, I believe we would be safe in supposing that even before this, his childhood was a comparatively long one. A comparatively long preadulthood is a feature of importance to a species with great plasticity of behaviour—great enough to allow for the existence of social traditions, for example, and of play. The reason is simply that if an organism is born with great potential for solving the varied problems which it will face, but very poor actual answers, then it needs time to develop its good actual answers before it faces the real tests of life. It needs a period of protection. An organism which has rigid responses to its environment needs comparatively less time in a pre–adult stage.

vi. A Recent Change in Diet and Lifestyle

One final respect in which human beings are unusual, but not unique, is that humans, among all the primates, have a modified diet. Initially fruit-eating vegetarians, humans have become carnivores who depend for the significant part of their diet on hunted prey. Not all have given up fruits and vegetables. But few would question that our ancestors had turned predominantly to hunting quite a long time ago. The fact that since the Neolithic Age humans have changed their diet again to grains and other cooked foods which were previously inedible, shows that one of the greatest adventures of this particular species has been a gastronomic one.

But ours is not the only species to have changed its diet. On the contrary, almost every major evolutionary change has usually involved a change of diet as well as a change of internal structure. Even among the primates we have witnessed the change of diet among macaques (who have learnt to eat potatoes dipped in salt water), and a similar change can also be observed among the baboons, some of which eat scorpions, while others do not.

D. Language Originated in Playful Imitation

Let me now state my thesis as briefly as possible: *A species which has all the features we have mentioned above would more likely than not develop a conceptual language.* What would develop into a language as we know it now, would be *a tradition, among the young, of a playful imitation of the adult social communication in its own species.* The children of an early ancestral ape or perhaps early human children, developed a certain tradition of playfully imitating adult social communication. As this tradition developed, it 'caught on', and evolved into our present language.

Let us say a little more about it. Since this is play, it would not be in 'earnest', and would therefore not be mistakable for a real piece of communication. A playful imitation of a real cry is quite unlike a real cry: a mother must know when a child is really alarmed, rather than screaming 'for fun'. A play threat must not be confused with a real threat, or the child would quickly get punished. The soft-voiced imitations of real communication would *stand for or symbolize* the situations which would normally evoke the real call, even though the imitative play-call would neither be like the full-throated normal cry, nor be evinced by the truly appropriate object. Thus, two kittens 'hunting' each other are neither hunting in earnest nor are they in a real hunting situation.

It is not enough, I may add, that there be play-communication between children. It is in addition necessary that this be *playful imitation of adult communication.* The point of this is that a play-imitation differs from other play in so far as play-imitation involves a symbolic relation or make-believe which is not present in the other. Thus, a game of hide-and-seek involves no symbols for the child, even though it may be related to patterns of behaviour which naturally have different objects. But a game *imitating* or *mimicking* a scream of fear is another matter. It is like a scream in earnest, as when one screams on seeing a real snake. But a mock cry involves the relation of a specific *symbolic* character of the mock cry to the natural object of the real cry.

Consider a game, for example, where children give a mock scream looking at the root of a tree. In this game the children pretend that the root of a tree is a snake. But the mock scream does not depend on the root of the tree being *mistaken* for a snake. If it were mistaken for one, then the scream would be real. So when a child gives a mock scream, its communication has the effect of making the play-object stand for or symbolize the snake. In general terms, the play-imitation of social communication involves the existence of an ineradicable symbolic relation. The symbolic relation lies between the imitative cry and the object which would normally elicit the real cry, with a dummy object which may or may not be present to stand for the supposed real one. In the example we have looked at, there is a dummy object. But children may well put a baby to sleep when there is nothing in their hands.

Play, then, might be similar to 'pieces' of adult behaviour. But play-imitation involves an additional awareness of the relation between the real cry and the object which normally elicits it. The symbolism in the relationship of the mock-cry and the real object depends on the awareness of this relation. At the same time, mere imitation of sounds is not enough to explain the development of language. A parrot can imitate many of our sounds, but it cannot imitate our sounds as a response to appropriate situations. What a parrot learns it can only repeat arbitrarily, or 'parrot-like'.

It is not enough, I may also add, for there to be play-imitation of our own social communication, unless it be *a tradition*. For only if the play-imitation becomes a traditional game will it gradually begin to capture the truly systematic character and all the nuances of the social communicaiton of adult hominids or humans; so that each succeeding generation of children will improve the game, to the point where it becomes a sophisticated social pastime. For this to happen, the hominid who started this process must, of course, also have a long childhood. And succeeding children who participate in this sort of traditional pastime must also have a fairly long childhood. The long childhood ensures the continuity of traditions from children to other children without involving adult or mature intermediaries who have little opportunity to play. But luckily that is an important feature of *homo sapiens*. Members of any species that have a childhood long enough to develop as subtle a game as cricket, one might say, should have no difficulty in developing an imitative play-linguistic tradition.

All we have to add to this is to say what made a play-language take over as the dominant language of society, and then our story will be complete. But the answer to this question is plain. Humans changed their diet and their whole style of life in the million years before this language took root. Our instincts could hardly keep up with our ambition! In strength and in agility the human is no hunter. Our communications are most suited to chattering among the fruit trees. Whatever our hominid ancestor learnt to do, it had to be done with inadequate instinctive endowments. The great flexibility of the play-language would soon be found to be useful to pursue new and flexible aims. What the new language did was to fulfill a need that would otherwise have been filled only by a slow genetic evolution of a different system of social communication. This play-language, however, turned out to be, in many respects, even more advantageous than a new instinctive system of communication. For one thing it enabled us to achieve something no other animal has done, namely to conceptualize. It enabled us to refute theories abstractly, and so learn from our mistaken theories without actually acting upon those mistakes. A human being learns from the experience of those before by means which are faster than genetic or even nervous learning. The symbolic character of play-imitation turned out, in the end, to more than compensate for the inappropriate human instincts which were brought to the new life.

Let me add, finally, that the new play-language is a flexible one in a most important respect: *its special elements do not serve a social function that is vital for survival.* A modification of the real social communication would soon lead to chaos. But the use of soft-voiced play-calls in new situations cannot interfere with the real calls, which are naturally distinct. The mere fact that they are play guarantees this. The new language can exist side by side with the old one, and evolve to a sufficiently fine state of complexity, until it can take over whatever tasks are found to be better handled by the new communicative system *without disrupting the social structure*. In fact, we still retain the ancestral forms of communication, though their use is usually not found to be civilised.

Let us now see how this model satisfies the desiderata we laid down for our model.

(1) It is unique to humans but combines elements each of which is far from unique.

(2) It does not disrupt or threaten the social structure of the species.

(3) It comes equipped with a symbolic rather than a natural relation to the objects which elicit that response—making conceptualization possible.

(4) The imperatives (the real calls) are clearly distinguished from the indicatives (the play-calls). Later, of course, the play-language also developed to the point of incorporating many of the functions of the imperatives.

(5) The freedom from normal social duties allows for greater freedom of experimentation, and for the necessary *diversification* of language, and multiplicity of linguistic symbols.

(6) Nevertheless, it starts as a *system* of communication and develops into a more complex system. It never loses its systematic character.

(7) Since language, according to this view, is an evolving social tradition, there is no difficulty in explaining or undersanding why different languages can exist—these are just variant subtraditions.

In short, my thesis is that language came before conceptual thought, before the rational mind. What is unique about the human mind today is that after millions of years of linguistic evolution, we are able to learn language quickly and naturally. The neurological foundation of this ability of ours remains a mystery.

11
Stages in the Development of Language

A. Evolution of Syntactic Structures

What we have in the preceding chapter is at best a model for the origin of language. Its purpose is merely to solve one problem—how is it possible that man alone among all the species of animals developed the ability to create symbols and to communicate his world view (or aspects of it) to each other? But the proposed model for the origin of language is a model for the origin of symbols only, and not for either syntax or grammar, or what we would recognize as a semantic field. There is a difficulty here.

The difficulty is this. The earliest play-language can be called a language only in the sense of Karl Bühler: it has a symbolic, conceptual, descriptive or representational element. But it cannot be used to argue, or even state anything.[1] And it can hardly be called a language in the Chomskyan sense since it lacks a syntax.[2] It does not lack *system*, since it is an imitation of something systematic. But it has a zero-level syntax or no syntax in the sense that units which bear meanings (statements) cannot be broke up into elements (words) which recombine into other units to form new symbolic expressions. The language is atomic. Furthermore, it lacks a device for the concatenation of atoms to form larger meaning-units. There is only a finite number of things one can say with it, and even these must have been few to begin with.

Our problem is *the problem of syntax*. How could it have come about? It is particularly problematical if we distinguish deep and surface structures in our modern language and believe that beyond both is a linguistic universal which is innate to man. In this view, grammar is like a deductive system. *In this form* (as we have seen), the problem is insoluble within an evolutionary framework which does not presuppose either a divinely pre-established harmony or lucky mutations.

The problem, then, is: how can we reinterpret syntax, and the difference between deep and surface structures? And how can this interpretation allow for the evolution of syntactic structures?

i. General Thesis

The grammar of a language is an evolutionary residue of outdated forms of speech which have found new functions. Language as a social institution is in this respect no different from other social institutions and traditions. What might once have been done deliberately and with a definite purpose in view, if it becomes a widespread form of behaviour or activity, will often persevere as a ritual or as a redundant form of activity for some time after the original purpose has become obsolete. The original use of table knives and forks displayed good manners largely because they obviated the use of lethal weapons like swords and daggers to cut food. But long after such weaponry has disappeared, the use of knives and forks is the ritual mark of well-bred European people. Even when fingers have to be inadvertently used at table, one excuses oneself—as if knives and forks were invented solely for the purpose of avoiding contamination of our guests' food. It is no secret that bare fingers are used in the kitchen, and no one makes it a practice to excuse oneself about that.

Here we have a typical ritual which has a new function, and even a new rationale, at variance with its original purpose. Similar institutional residues of our past can be found in our dress, our manners, our political system, our economic institutions (like the stock market), our legal systems, in fact, in every aspect of our social life. Every social institution evolves in this interesting manner. When compelled to find new forms of social functioning, institutions do not always simply discard old and redundant forms, but instead they incorporate them, giving them new and flexible uses. Much of the richness of a civilization lies in the pluralistic institutions which it supports, institutions in which there are enough redundant and 'recycled' forms of social activity to allow individuals a great deal of freedom of action, a freedom of action that would be severely threatened in a society in which institutions merely functioned (however efficiently) to perform only their *intended* purposes.

Language is the one social institution of all social institutions which evolves precisely in this manner. The rules of grammar and of syntax are like scar tissue left from the revolutions of world views in the past which led to new forms of speech. The structures which lost their original significance were capable of being used in ingenious ways to facilitate new uses of the language—giving us eventually the syntactic and grammatical entity that might even seem in some respects to have a Chomskyan character.

ii. Functionalism: Durkheim's and Wittgenstein's Theories

The fossilization of old views, or the formation of grammar, has a most important consequence for the study of social anthropology, or sociology as conceived by Emile Durkheim.

Durkheim came to the study of our ideas from a Kantian standpoint.[3] He believed that Kant was fundamentally correct in believing that the basic categories of natural science are not extracted by empiricist or inductive means. He was convinced that they are *a priori* preconditions of perception. But a study of the viewpoints widespread in cultures other than our own suggested that these categories are in some respects not universal. Durkheim recognized that our own conceptual framework evolved out of these more primitive ones. And since categories are preconditions of experience and reason, even primitive societies must have categories which afford them reason and the ability to cope with the phenomena.

Convinced of this, Durkheim argued that the categories are not universal, but socially determined. Thus Durkheim argued that man has a double aspect—an individual and a social aspect, where the social aspect is precisely the *a priori* that society imposes on each of us as a precondition of experience. Consequently, Durkheim was led to the view that in order to understand the peculiar rites of primitive societies we must understand the categories which socially determine the perception of a community. Furthermore, Durkheim maintained that these rites and these beliefs, and the forms of perception which underlie them, cannot be founded upon lies, or on a tissue of misunderstanding, but must have some truth in the manner in which they function. To dismiss them as irrational would be simply not to understand them.

Nowadays few people are in sympathy with the origin of Durkheim's views on sociology. But his hypothesis that we must study a society in terms of its own conceptions, that we must see the truth as its members would, is very widely accepted as excellent advice. The doctrine that we must understand the activity of a community in terms of the way in which it functions in the society and as it is understood by that society, can be called *functionalism.*

Functionalism is one of the two most influential methodologies in the social science that we have. With regard to language, the best representative of this approach is the later philosophy of Wittgenstein.

Wittingstein began by supporting an intolerant view of natural language. He tried to argue for the advantage of certain logically correct ways of expressing things over other sloppier ways (especially in philosophy).[4] But in his later years he came to hold a diametrically opposed view, for reasons which have already been mentioned. He came to believe that the apparently irrational features of language (from a logician's point of view) are in fact quite functional, and therefore that one must seek the meaning of expressions not in abstract logical theories, but in the usage of the words. Wittgenstein thereby became, without announcing it, an anthropologist who supported a functionalist interpretation of the social institution we call language.

Durkheim is a precursor of Wittgenstein in this respect: Durkheim recognized that one must understand the apparently irrational features of any institution in any society as exhibiting the rationality of the participant from his point of view as he is involved in the social activity. Furthermore,

Durkheim, like Wittgenstein after him, saw a certain necessity in the way institutions function. This necessity emerges in Wittgenstein as the injunction not to misuse language. For the misuse of language leads to a typical confusion which Wittgenstein believed to be the root cause of fruitless philosophical perplexity.

Now it is clear why the functionalist point of view cannot hope to adequately account for the *growth* of language.[5] Even though Durkheim and Wittgenstein are both aware of institutional change, and both write about it, there is something in their very method which precludes the possibility of understanding evolution.

An anthropologist looks at a society and asks—what are the beliefs which make its rites rational and reasonable? Naturally he finds an interpretation of the (implicitly held) beliefs and known rites which are in perfect consonance. Society seems to be in perfect equilibrium. It is a myth firmly held among some social anthropologists that primitive societies are static, that they do not evolve. But it is not the societies that are static so much as the functionalist interpretation of society which leaves society in unchanging equilibrium. (Some societies have this image of themselves also, which complicates matters somewhat.)

Any society which has a language and a grammar, if I am right, has evolved conceptually. Let us assume for a moment that I am right. Would a social anthropologist be able to see it? Never. For the institutions which do remain in a society naturally have some functions. In trying to locate these functions the social anthropologist will consider the current world view in terms of which the activity of the subjects under study appear to be rational. And thus he will see the institutions, the beliefs, the rites and the socially compulsive categories as being in perfect equilibrium. But a little thought shows that if in fact the social institutions inherited by a society did not have a *prima facie* peculiarity there would be no need for social anthropology. If our language had a transparently rational structure we would not need Wittgenstein to point out the value of the actual usage of words in our language.

Wittgenstein's own reason for maintaining that there is a need to study language in this way is that it saves us from philosophical perplexity. This kind of perplexity, which he thought violated all attempts to state philosophical theses, had to be countered by constantly travelling in the no mans land between sense and nonsense. This sort of therapeutic activity, he thought, is philosophy as it ought to be practised because it respects the contrast between the framework which language provides for description and the description itself. Philosophers, he thought, will too often violate the border by trying to state theses as if they were descriptive of the world when they were really interested only in the framework, or aspects of it.

Wittgenstein's descriptions of ordinary language, therefore, are in one important respect unlike modern social anthropology as practised by functionalists. A functionalist would try to interpret all the statements of a tribe as meaningful in terms of their use. Philosophical statements would be especially singled out for analysis, particularly of the sort that Wittgenstein finds so paradoxical. With regard to them, Wittgenstein's dilemma will concern a social anthropologist only when he is studying his own tribe. For ethno-methodologists, who have taken up this task in our society, Wittgenstein's worries are of central concern.

When we consider large scale changes in our practices, which do occur now and again, and do lead to the establishment of new routines, the relationship of framework and content becomes less important. If philosophy is perplexing at times it might be because it is sometimes at the cutting edge of progress. All subjects, if I am right, will exhibit features which perplex us in a philosophical way as Wittgenstein describes it when they are in the throes of conceptual change. We must not forget, moreover, that wherever there is conceptual change, or change of social custom, there is residue available for recycling.

If we ask whether in fact I am right that grammar is the product of fossilized patterns of speech left behind by revolutions in our thought, it is difficult to find more than a piece or two of evidence for it. But in other social institutions, fossilized forms of behaviour can be clearly shown to be related to old and discarded modes of thought.

Thus Aristotle held the view that the world which we seek to understand can be neatly divided into ontological compartments. Corresponding to each compartment was a subject of study which inductively gathered the truth. Universities can easily be modelled on this structure. Today, we no longer believe Aristotle's world view and ontology, but our university department system is still modelled on Aristotle's ontology, though with deviations and modifications. In fact, it is not unusual for a lecturer in philosophy inveighing against Aristotle to dispose of a question by saying 'This question does not belong to my field which is x, but to y'. Here is an institution—the institution of the division of subjects—which dominates us even while we reject it.

B. Conflicts are Inherent in Social Institutions

i. Evolutionism versus Functionalism

This brings us finally to a fundamental difference between functionalism and evolutionism—the recognition of possible tension or contradictions inherent in the presuppositions of social institutions.[6] Just as there may be an incoherence between the presupposed views of a language and what we use a language to say, so, too, may there be incoherence between presuppositions of different institutions, or between the views of a person and the presuppositions of some of his activity.

Consider the ritual, on the other hand, which is associated with the conductor of a musical symphony. It is hard to imagine one not performing with his whole body, as if he were possessed. And the institution of conducting as it developed in the days of romanticism did in fact demand that to properly conduct an orchestra, the conductor must indeed be possessed—by the genius inherent in the music. As a result, a modern conductor who conducts a postromantic symphony with no pretensions of being an inherent genius will continue to behave like a man possessed. An anthropologist from another society might well be puzzled by the discrepancy, but we are so accustomed to this institution of music that few of us would even notice it.

This brings us finally to a fundamental and irrevocable difference between functionalism and evolutionism—at least the evolutionism of this kind. While the evolutionism that I am outlining does recognize that our world view provides a significant background which is necessary for understanding social activity, it also leaves room for the deposit of history as an irrational given in society. Irrational givens are *of course* put to use if they are to survive and so acquire some new rationale. Furthermore, their very structure might involve an original purpose. Yet their original purpose and their use in the present activity might not necessarily be in harmony. This, then, is the heart of ritual, of grammar, of the sheer weight of tradition in society. This is the process which I call fossilization, for just as dead animals leave behind fossils as indirect evidence of their erstwhile existence, so concepts leave institutions, rites, and grammar as a record of their demise.

Furthermore, it is worth noticing that it is not only between the original conceptual underpinning of an institution and our present world view that there may be logical conflict. There may also be conflict between an individual's views and the views actively presupposed by institutions, or between institutions themselves. Thus, a hypothetical National Energy Board and a Board for Protecting the Environment not only have frequently conflicting aims and policies, but are deposits (fossils) of conceptions of social engineering which are quite different. So, too, the Englishwoman, wanted by the police, who married scores of would-be immigrants to the United Kingdom, had personal views which were at variance with the conceptual underpinnings of the legal and civil customs of that country.

Conflict between what one thinks is the reasonable thing to do, and what one believes is the expected thing, i.e., that which is in accordance with institutional rules, is far from uncommon. Too little flexibility in these rules, or too much infringement can both lead to breakdown. But the conflict is definitely there in hundreds of typical situations in society.

In short, to understand the rationality of a person's activity one must indeed understand it in terms of the person's beliefs. But one must not lose sight of the fact that a society is never simply a consensus of coherent views.

Rather, every society has institutions with different conceptual presuppositions. While an anthropologist studies a society to find the functional value of its rites and its peculiar institutions (and show how rational they are) a member of the society may still rightly find the institutions peculiar and inexplicable, and be only reasonable in recommending a reform.

C. Neo-Darwinist Considerations Regarding Linguistic Evolution

It is considerably more difficult to give a systematic account of the evolutionary progress of language than it is to criticize the view which regards custom as sacrosanct. It is also considerably more speculative to give an evolutionary account of language than of the descent of man. For the latter there is the help, however slim it may be, of physical evidence in the form of fossils, which may be dated, and analysed to help us decipher the past. These fossils help differentiate between various options that our initial understanding leaves open to us. In the case of language, it is not only the theoretical study but the 'palaeontology' that is yet to be developed, if I am allowed to extend the metaphor of fossilization in language somewhat further.

I do not believe, though, that this metaphor is taken too far when so extended. The process by which forms of speech turn into ritual forms of speech (and lie, stratum upon stratum, in our language) is not a physio-chemical one of the kind that produces stone images of past organic forms. But there is a hidden presence of the past in our language. If, however, we mean to go beyond the metaphor to look for the operative mechanisms in the evolution of language, we have nothing to go by but our perplexity.

Our perplexity, it turns out, has a great deal more to teach us than we might suppose. For if we combine this perplexity with the idea that language is a product of great importance to man's survival, then we can also bring certain neo-Darwinian considerations to bear upon its evolution.

On evolutionary grounds, we must begin with man as an ape, living in one of the various social forms of the apes as we know them (or a variant not to be found among today's apes, perhaps). In this society, we have already concluded that language as we know it must have evolved independently of the normal social communication of the society, in the form of a tradition of a certain peculiar sort. The peculiar tradition would be a kind of play, or a game, in which there is an imitation—an imitation within an imitation, as it were. In a strange way this produces symbols.

A kitten might play with a ball of wool just as if it were a mouse. For this to happen, the ball of wool elicits some of the responses that the kitten has in its repertoire which are functionally appropriate to hunting mice. In this situation, we may regard the ball as a *substitute* for a mouse, but not a *symbol* of a mouse. A kitten which has never seen a mouse, and has no idea of what a mouse is like, responds to a ball of wool in a way which remind *us* of a cat mousing.

If we turn to the phenomenon of imitation, there is no symbol here, either. A child that imitates its mother's actions incorporates certain idiosyncratic features of the mother's action patterns into its own, but these idiosyncracies do not symbolise anything. Where then do symbols begin?

A symbol, we recall, stands for the thing symbolised as a *convention*, or a product of our *history*. When a sambur bounds away because of a slight but unusual rustle in a bush, the rustle need not be a sign of a tiger. If it is, however, it is a natural sign, because the tiger causes the bush to rustle. If in a suitable location a human were to spot a tiger, and to whisper 'tiger' to a companion, the whisper would have the tiger as one of its causal conditions, but another would be the history of the culture in which the person learnt the language, in which the word 'tiger' is well-formed.

Play, as we have seen, substitutes familiar objects for unknown or far-flung objects that we may have to deal with in 'real life'. Imitation, especially a chain of imitation from individual to individual, leads to tradition, or history, and therefore culture. If a particular substitution which, let us suppose, is idiosyncratic, is initiated and then perpetuated for generations, it becomes a *convention*. We come finally to communication. In communication of any kind, the one communicating utters a sound, or makes a gesture, which is a sign (of appeasement or aggression, of invitation or rebuff of warning or of well-being). If a tradition of play-imitation is formed, then we have *conventional signs* of the same things for which in normal communication there are *natural signs*. This is how symbols can arise in communication.

These symbols which have arisen in play lack any system or syntax. Each symbol exists all by itself as a conventional sign of something or other. If we call one such vocal symbol a 'word', it may be equally called a 'sentence', and if a sentence then equally an indicative sentence, or an interrogative one. It is perhaps best to say that simple symbols are not one or the other, but ancestors of all the speech forms that evolved.

A social ape which has developed a juvenile form of play which is capable of being passed along *as play* from generation to generation is still an ape. What is special about it? From a neo-Darwinian perspective, it is only this which is surprising—that the game survives. What advantage could it be to those who play the game? This is always the crux of the matter. If a group of juveniles plays a game at which some individuals do better than the others, *then this must lead somehow to a differential advantage for those who play well*. We cannot assume here that it is the power of language which helps them, for this would be circular—we want to know what gave this primitive language power.

On general considerations we do know the abstract form of the answer to this question—it must be that the play better prepares the adept juvenile to perform better in real life. Moreover, we realize that since the general function of play from a neo-Darwinian perspective is the composition of action-patterns into sequences that are adaptively useful, we must suppose that play language from the first co-ordinated some crucial action patterns of apes in an adaptively superior way.

Nor is this a one-shot affair. If a particular change in action-patterns began with juvenile discovery, then that would preserve that change, but not necessarily the form of discovery. For a juvenile form to have become useful enough to us for at least four million years, it must have continued to give a superior advantage to those who were most adept at it. It seems to me that this could only have happened if a rapid change of social relations made this particular ape's normal social responses less adaptively useful than the ones it could learn from convention. Although in one sense of the word 'natural', the new conventions are as natural as the older social forms, what I am suggesting can be put in another way by saying that language of this most primitive sort could only have been adaptively useful if some features of human social organization made artificial (or conventional, or juvenile-inspired) behaviour more successful within the group than the natural (or the older, adult-type) behaviour.

Putting it in this way it seems quite a small thing, but from an evolutionary perspective, this represents a tremendous shift. We have seen that traditions exist among birds and other apes. If we are right, then it is characteristic of humans that the traditions became an environment within which human beings began to evolve—in which respect, as far as we know, we are unique. The importance of this is that for the first time an organism is able to transfer information to offspring not genetically, but directly. In human beings acquired characters came to be adopted by offspring even though they were not inherited.

Some more theoretical light may be shed on this great shift if we look at language from the point of view of game theory and evolution. The characteristic feature of language (and conventional behavior generally) is that it is a co-operative rather than a competitive game. If two people play such a game and one violates a rule, both suffer, and so it encourages co-operation rather than competition. On abstract grounds, one suspects that the social situation which encouraged this sort of primitive language might have been one where we had a natural tendency to compete, but a new (artificial) tendency to co-operate, within the general social fabric of this society of apes.

Language must have become established as a socially valuable form in such a way, from an adaptive point of view. The effect, of course, would snowball. If human beings are adaptively selected by their own conventional environment, they become self-domesticated. Moreover, their 'natural' responses to social situations are modified in time, but never as fast as the changes in convention, because the latter may be modified often in one lifetime, where the former may take several generations to produce even one such change. If a change in social form were to make a set of conventional action patterns adaptively superior, then rapid social change (as compared to genetic endowment) becomes a general feature of this particular ape. Rapid change, in turn, would make this ape a prisoner of its conventions, for they alone could allow the ape to find a way to adjust to its own traditions.

Language is in a certain sense the main social tradition, the one which led to social change, and hence to the patterns of traditions which are characteristic of human societies today. It is also our primary means of adapting to our own society.

D. Mechanisms in the Evolution of Language

i. The Problem of Syntax

Keeping the evolutionary considerations of the last section in mind, we can turn to certain perplexities regarding language and ask how they might be resolved. How, in particular, did the most primitive symbols develop to the point that they have a *syntax?* We have noted that, as Chomsky describes this, it has a mathematical structure, with a few rules allowing for an infinite number of possible sentences of our language which are not equivalent one with the other. How could this have come about?

We note, particularly, that if we describe the anatomy or the physiology of an organism in evolutionary terms, we are not left with a mathematical structure to explain. What is special about language?

While the most primitive language, of the sort I have suggested, contains only symbols, and the symbols somehow help a society of apes to co-operate where they would otherwise naturally compete, these symbols are of very restricted value from an adaptive perspective until they can be used to *describe* something, it would seem. If they could be combined to give a description, however primitive, this would make the adaptive value of language that much more important. Once we have a syntax, we can describe things, and this is certainly of great adaptive value. How, though, does syntax begin?

It seems to me that to be consistent with neo-Darwinian constraints, we have to assume that the first stage of language, in which there were just symbols, which were constantly being multiplied in juvenile play, and a few, perhaps, finding use in adult forms, may be the basis of four-stage hypothetical evolution of language.

ii. Stages of Linguistic Evolution

Although the following stages are arbitrary in that others may intervene between them, we can solve our problem regarding the origin of syntax by supposing that the following types of language were precursors of our developed form (to summarise the preceding):

(a)   The Atomic or Cumulative Stage;
(b)   The Stage of Presyntactic Differentiation;
(c)   The Recycling Stage; and
(d)   The Reflective Stage.

(a) The Atomic or Cumulative Stage

The atomic or cumulative stage led to the accumulation of vast numbers of useful symbolic devices which could be used within hominid communities, as much as four million years ago. At this stage the symbols are atomic and independent.

(b) The Stage of Presyntactic Differentiation

This would be that stage at which the use of language would be a well-established fact, and hundreds of symbols would have evolved. In this situation, as a technique for learning, or as abbreviation, or both, making two symbols (analogical) variants of one basic root would be an innovation both simple and profound. Notice, however, that this is *a presyntax, not a true syntax:* there are no general rules for the combination of elements. A particular symbol may be varied one way to give another particular symbol, but a third symbol may be varied in yet another way to yield a fourth.

At this stage, we can describe the structure of language as a broken-up, finite, lattice-structure, in which symbolic transformations *may* exhibit some order in some cases and not in others. That is to say, 'shaking-tree' and 'climbing tree' may with the same affix be made to mean 'shaking' or 'climbing' respectively. Or there may not be a common affix. It would be a matter of accident, and perhaps *some* design, but certainly not very much.

The most significant feature of this stage of language is *redundancy.* To use the previous fanciful example, 'shaking-tree' and 'climbing tree' might both yield 'tree' with the application of the same (or different) affixes.

Normally, one would expect the community not to use the two inter-changeably at first. But with increasing sophistication, with more abstract interests, one of these two would soon become *redundant*.

(c) The Recycling Stage

The redundant elements get recycled, or become new symbols. This is the most significant stage of all, because this gives language a quasi-syntax.

First of all, one might ask, why don't redundant elements just disappear? The answer to this is twofold: first, language is a social tradition, and therefore has a dead weight which is not to be denied. How many of our own social traditions are redundant, even though we live in a dynamic, self-critical age? The second reason is this: the very structure of the language at this stage points to the redundant symbols. The symbols are *functionally* redundant, but *structurally* they are still very much there, like the lapels on our coats.

These redundant symbols became recycled as syncategorematic expressions, as generalized affixes, prepositions, pronouns, generally as those expressions and grammatical parts of expressions which one can call 'formal' rather than 'conceptual' words.

Notice that this development of formal elements is essential to the formation of noun phrases, adverbial phrases, quantifiers, and so on. It is these recycled symbols that allow us to construct statements of varying size and differing structure. But we must not assume that all of them or any of them become general linguistic regularities all at once. Thus, the ability to make an abstract noun out of a verb remained restricted until very recent times.

This stage of language must have been present at least a million years ago. The development of the size of the human brain about half a million years ago and our facility for learning quasi-syntactic structures (I call them quasi-syntactic in deference to Chomsky's claim that true syntax is not finite) must both have been selected because of a preexisting linguistic environment in which quasi-syntactic structures flourished. The considerations from a neo-Darwinian perspective mentioned before would seem to suggest, more-over, that self-domestication must have been accomplished long before this, because only then can language have such a decisive role in the selection of human characters.

We note, furthermore, that in all respects except that of syntax, the language at this stage is expressively as capable as ours. Theorising, dis-cussing, quarrelling, questioning, requesting, ordering or lying could be differentiated within the language, in later stages, perhaps even by the users.

(d) The Reflective Stage

The last stage is the *reflective stage,* or the stage when human beings began to reflect on their own thought and language. This was a great liberating influence, because various devices which were previously restricted to a few symbols could now be applied generally. The proliferation of abstract substantives in modern times is, I believe, a result of our reflections on the nature of thought and language (in this case the reflections of Socrates—see Chapter 1).

I should mention that not only do these four stages blend into each other, but each stage which comes later is superimposed on the previous one, while the earlier kind of development carries on unimpeded. Thus differentiation does not impede accumulation. It even encourages it, by making more room. Reflection does not prevent recycling but only encourages it by stimulating inventiveness.

iii. The Emergence of the Mathematical Structure of Language

The apparently mathematical structure of our present language is, I believe, the direct result of self-reflection on language. It is only after language was rich enough to allow for discussion of language itself that this stage could begin. But once it begins, it is not difficult to see why certain grammatical devices which are initially restricted to a few isolated symbols can be applied more generally to language. These also require revolutions in thought, but the revolutions are much more potent in their effect on the entire language if the members of the society are self-conscious in their use of the language.

How recent is the fourth stage of the development of language? Since every stage of development carries into the present time, what we want to know is how late did the fourth stage start?

It is extremely difficult to estimate the time, for the clues are meagre. But we do know that phonetic writing was invented four thousand years ago. And for it to be invented there had to be an astonishingly good understanding of the different kinds of sounds that we produce. This suggests that speculation about language must have had an enormously long history if it is to have developed to such a stage as early as four thousand years ago, and therefore suggests that it must be a late neolithic achievement at the latest.

iv. Deep and Surface Structures

Where in this evolution can we fit *deep,* and *surface structures?*[7] To do this we must look more closely at individual structures. My main thesis here is this: Syntactic structures develop under the influence of crucial beliefs which are widespread at the time. After a certain structure develops, these beliefs may change. This requires that the language be used in a new way. This new use may become part of the structure of language, or it may not. If the new view is the received view, then the new structure which is super-imposed on the old, traditional syntax is the 'deep structure', and the irrational-looking crystallized structure of the same language is the 'surface structure'. Thus, genders for inanimate objects are part of the *surface structure,* because we no longer accept the underlying views.

Imagine a time when 'fills' was used ambiguously in the sense of 'oc-cupies all the space' and 'causes to occupy space'. Thus 'fills a hole' was understood generally in an active-passive sense.

Then someone invented the theory that not all matter is active. We can cause things to happen, the sky can, the lion can—but this stone, and the water in this hole, cannot. So a new distinction was drawn between *active* and *passive.*

The old uniform verbs started falling into new patterns. Some verbs came to be distinguishable by the difference in their 'deep' structure. Thus 'John filled the glass' came to be distinguishably different from 'wine filled the glass'—the former being active and the latter passive. John can fill a glass both actively and passively at once. Water can only fill a glass passively.

We can see that this depends on a theory of action because those verbs which could not be both passive and active do not exhibit this ambiguity. Thus 'John died in his bed' and 'the wine died in the bottle' do not differ, because death was never taken to be a voluntary act. That is why the active sense of 'die' is the cumbersome 'commit suicide', a phrase from a more reflective post-Latin stage of English. If, at an early stage of development, English-speaking people had come to believe in a normal form of voluntary death, then we would almost certainly have had two forms of 'die' as we have of 'fill'. If today I come to believe that most of us die because we really want to die (though we may not admit it to ourselves), I could start talking of two senses of 'die'.

In brief, we can describe the surface-deep structure distinction, thus: structural laws of language which seem irrational (because our beliefs have changed) are 'surface structure', while the corresponding superimposed lin-guistic habits of beliefs that we still uphold are the corresponding 'deep structure'.

A difficulty remains. Having described the mathematical structure of language as one imposed by grammarians, but which then gives us new expressive capabilities, we are left a very general question unanswered: What about mathematics as a whole? Does it also result out of self-reflection? And if so, how does it, and what are its antecedents?

Notes

Notes

Notes to Chapter 1

1. For a description of how ideas are proposed in response to problems, and why that is an appropriate way to approach the subject, see Chapter 7.
2. This is dealt with more fully in Chapter 10.
3. Feyerabend, P. K., *Against Method* (London: Verso 1975).
4. Chomsky, N., *Language and Mind* (New York: Harcourt, 1968) is a very well written and clear essay giving Chomsky's view.
5. Whorf, B. L., *Language, Thought and Reality* (Cambridge, Mass.: M.I.T. Press, 1956). For its difficulties, see Max Black's "Linguistic Relativity: The Views of Benjamin Lee Whorf", in *Philosophical Review*, 68 (1959) pp. 228-238.
6. Collingwood, R. G., *An Essay on Metaphysics* (Oxford: Clarendon Press, 1940).
7. Chomsky, N., "A Review of B. F. Skinner's *Verbal Behavior*", *Language*, 35 (1959) pp. 26–58.
8. Gellner, E., "Concept and Society" in *Cause and Meaning in the Social Sciences* (London: Routledge and Kegan Paul, 1973), is a classic exposition of this interpretation of Wittgenstein's *Philosophical Investigations* (tr. by G.E.M. Anscombe; New York: Macmillan, 1953).
9. See Chapter 7 below for a discussion of incommensurability of theories which is supposed to infect such changes of meaning.
10. Chomsky, N., *Aspects of the Theory of Syntax* (Cambridge, Mass.: M.I.T. Press, 1965).
11. Strawson, P. F., *Individuals: An Essay in Descriptive Metaphysics* (London: Methuen, 1959).
12. Quine, W.V.O., *From a Logical Point of View* (Cambridge, Mass.: Harvard University Press, 1953).
13. Hintikka, J., *Models for Modalities* (Dordrecht: Reidel, 1969).
14. D. Davidson's views are similarly unsatisfactory for relating meaning too closely to truth rather than to something like 'sense'.
15. Einstein, A. and Infeld, L., *The Evolution of Physics*, (New York: Simon and Schuster, 1938).
16. See Whorf, *Language, Thought and Reality*.
17. Whorf, *Language, Thought and Reality*, p. 134.

Notes to Chapter 2

1. There may be exceptions to this rule, too, to the extent that 'dead' languages evolve in the hands of grammarians, becoming more 'regular' over the years.
2. Lewis, David K. *Conventions: A Philosophical Study* (Cambridge, Mass.: Harvard University Press, 1969).
3. I take the expression from Konrad Lorenz, who attributes it to one of his instructors, Otto Heinroth. A surprisingly close approximation to this idea, and also to the idea of 'pleasure' being a release from tension, may also be found in Freud, S., *Beyond the Pleasure Principle* (tr. by J. Strachey, New York: Norton, 1911).
4. From Hattiangadi, J. N., "Meaning Reference and Subjunctive Conditionals", *American Philosophical Quarterly*, 16 (1979) pp. 197–205.
5. The *locus classicus* is Russell, B. "On Denoting", *Mind*, 1905; also Russell, B. and Whitehead, A. N., Preface to the *Principia Mathematica* (Cambridge: Cambridge University Press, 1976; first published, 1910).
6. Hempel, C. G. "Empiricist Criteria of Meaningfulness" in *Aspects of Scientific Explanation* (New York: Free Press of Glencoe, 1965).
7. Wittgenstein's views on usage can be interpreted differently, to imply that each use of the word changes the usage, so that the meaning constantly changes. But such an interpretation cannot accommodate the possibility of the misuse of language, which is understood by Wittgenstein as a use made of words which does not conform to common usage: if every use is a new use, then all uses are meaningful (or all meaningless) on the criterion of usage alone. Moreover, no investigation such as Wittgenstein's *Philosophical Investigations* can be possible if every usage is new, because his introspective method would have to be replaced by an empirical one to investigate whether philosophical and metaphysical locations really are meaningless, such as suggested, for example, by Arne Naess, *Interpretation and Preciseness: A Contribution to the Theory of Communication* (Oslo: Universities forlaget 1953).
8. Cf. Gellner's view expressed in "Concept and Society" (in *Cause and Meaning in the Social Sciences,* London: Routledge and Kegan Paul, 1973).
9. Whitney, D. W., *The Life and Growth of Language* (New York: D. Appleton and Company, 1898).

Notes to Chapter 3

1. Frege, G. "On Sense and Nominatum", translated by H. Feigl in Feigl, H. and Sellars W., (eds), *Readings in Philosophical Analysis* (New York, Appleton, 1949).
2. Hintikka, J., *Models for Modalities* (Dordrecht: Reidel, 1969).
3. Frege's (op. cit.) and Russell's ("On Denoting", Mind (1905)) respectively.
4. See van Fraassen, B., "Singular Terms, Truth-Value Gaps, and Free Logic", *The Journal of Philosophy*, 63 (1966) pp. 481–95, which validates Strawson's criticism of Russell in his essay "On Referring", *Mind*, 1950, pp. 320–344.

5. Carnap, R., "Testability and Meaning" In *Readings in the Philosophy of Science*, by Feigl and Brodbeck, eds., (New York: Appleton-Century-Crofts, 1953).
6. See Chapter 4, Section E, on Kripke's analysis of proper names.
7. The idea, originally from Leibniz, has had considerable influence on K. R. Popper's *Logic of Scientific Discovery*, (London: Routledge and Kegan Paul, 1959) Appendix X, pp. 420–441 and David K. Lewis's "Counterpart Theory and Quantified Modal Logic" in *Journal of Philosophy* (1968) pp. 113–126.
8. Quine, W.V.O. *Word and Object*, (Cambridge, Ma.: MIT Press, 1960), p. 222.
9. Quine, W.V.O. *Word and Object*, p. 223.
10. This example is K.R. Popper's. *Logic of Scientific Discovery*, Appendix IX.
11. Chisholm, R.M. "The Contrary-to-Fact Conditional", Feigl, H. and Sellars, W. (eds.), *Readings in Philosophical Analysis*.

Notes to Chapter 4

1. The distinction was made by Kant, and has been challenged by Quine, in "Two Dogmas of Empiricism" in *From a Logical Point of View* (Cambridge, Mass.: Harvard University Press, 1953) The challenge from Quine concerns analyticity as *a priori*. In my defense of the notion of the distinction, in the text below, I use a notion of the analytic *a posteriori*.
2. The idea of "implicit definitions" had considerable influence on the philosophy of H. Herz and E. Mach, who therefore regarded a law like F = ma as empty since it only served to define F.
3. For the use of 'inadequate restricted meanings', and for the method of drawing distinctions the reader is referred to Section C, below.
4. In Quine's paper "Two Dogmas of Empiricism" (op. cit.), there is no argument against the analyticity of theorems of the predicate calculus, only against the extended theorems obtained from "meaning postulates".
5. The hypothesis that ordinary words do not have a determinate meaning, and that attempts to state material adequacy conditions cannot therefore succeed was made famous by Wittgenstein in his *Philosophical Investigations*. That we cannot think of sub-conditions is perhaps true in most cases, but it does not follow that there is no feature that can be found which is common, if the search were diligent enough. This is precisely the issue which separates true followers of Wittgenstein from those, like me, who find only some things congenial in his writings.
6. Kripke, S. *Naming and Necessity* (Cambridge, Mass.: Harvard University Press, 1980).
7. I suppose that my view is to be assimilated to the cluster concept theory, note 8 below and accompanying text.
8. Kripke, *Naming and Necessity*, p. 64.
9. Kripke, *Naming and Necessity*, p. 29.
10. Kripke, *Naming and Necessity*, p. 49.

Notes to Chapter 5

1. Popper, K. R., *Logic of Scientific Discovery* (London: Routledge and Kegan Paul, 1959), p. 107.
2. Russell, B. *Problems of Philosophy* (London: Home University Library, 1912).
3. Gibson, J. J., *The Senses Considered as Perceptual Systems* (Boston: Houghton Mifflin, 1966).
4. Cf. Chapter 8.
5. This example is cleverly discussed, with a few others, by Feyerabend in his *Against Method* (London: Verso, 1975).
6. Popper, K. R. *Logic of Scientific Discovery*, Appendix IX.
7. Cf. Chapter 8 below.
8. Duhem, P., *The Aim and Structure of Physical Theory* (tr. P. Wiener, Princeton: Princeton University Press, 1959) and Popper, K. R., *Realism and the Aim of Science*, Volume 1 of the *Postscript* to *The Logic of Scientific Discovery*, W. W. Bartley III, ed., Totowa, N.J.: Rowman and Littlefield).
9. See Chapter 8, pp. 159–162.

Notes to Chapter 6

1. Lorenz, K., "Innate Bases of Learning" in *On the Biology of Learning*, Pribram, K. ed., (New York: Harcourt, Brace and World, 1969).
2. Lorenz, K., "Innate Bases of Learning", pp. 30–31.
3. Baerends's study ("Fortpfanzungsverhatten und Orienterung der Grabwespe") is reported by N. Tinbergen in *The Study of Instinct* (Oxford: Oxford University Press, 1951).
4. That thought patterns may show the same structure as motor patterns has evinced some surprise among my readers, but I find it plausible given the fact that it is such a common model for the entire biosphere. See Monod, J., *Chance and Necessity* (tr. Austin Weinhouse, New York: Alfred A. Knopf, 1971).
5. Monod, *Chance and Necessity*.
6. Monod, *Chance and Necessity*, p. 83.

Notes to Chapter 7

1. Duhem, P., *The Aim and Structure of Physical Theory* (tr. P. Wiener, Princeton: Princeton University Press, 1959).
2. Duhem, *The Aim and Structure*, p. 19 for the first passage and p. 266 for the second.
3. Duhem, *The Aim and Structure*, 266 for the first passage and p. 21 for the second.

4. Quine, W.V.O. *From a Logical Point of View.* (Cambridge, Mass.: Harvard University Press 1953).

5. Of particular importance is the fact that all our beliefs collectively face empirical discrimination and when it occurs, it is a matter of convenience which course of action we are to adopt. But if we adopt a methodology of science along these lines, we have difficulty explaining why there are conceptual revolutions which are inconvenient in many ways. It is to answer this difficulty that conventionalists appeal to 'simplicity'. New theories which are adopted are much simpler, they say, and hence, in a curious way, more convenient. When I speak of the conventionalist character of casual intellectual problems, I do not include the unfortunate theory of simplicity which is tacked on to conventionalism, since I believe that the methodology for solving scientific problems is not conventionalist at all. For nonscientific problems, where revolutions do not occur, convenience (but not usually 'simplicity') is an important issue.

6. By a fallibilist methodology I mean one that encourages bold, new hypotheses, crucial tests, institutionalized criticism and the avoidance of *ad hoc* solutions to difficulties—all of which contrast with a conventionalist methodology.

7. The problem of 'novel' facts, which is raised by I. Lakatos, can be solved without remainder by my analysis of the discriminatory character of problems. The problem is this: Lakatos argued that significant cases for a theory are those which are novel, and not those to explain which the theory was proposed. E. Zahar, in "Why did Einstein's Programme Supersede Lorentz's?" *British Journal for the Philosophy of Science,* 24 (1973), pp. 95–123, 223–262, showed that there are facts which are well known before a theory is proposed which are nevertheless significant. (Unfortunately, the word 'novel' was used to mean 'significant', creating an apparent paradox that old facts are also sometimes novel.) Zahar proposed that any facts which are not intended to be explained by the theory but which follow from the theory, are 'novel'. Alan Musgrave showed that this implies the view that biography is part of what one must study in order to evaluate the worth of a theory, in "Logical versus Historical Theories of Confirmation" (*British Journal for the Philosophy of Science,* 25 (1974) pp. 1–23). This is unacceptable, for the following reason: If Darwin and Wallace propose the same theory of evolution to explain different facts, would we assign two different values to the same theory?

   This problem is solved without remainder by my analysis of problems: A significant ('novel') fact is simply that which discriminates between two lines of a debating tradition. All the examples that I give from optics above illustrate how debates lend significance to facts. The problem of 'novelty' which, as we see, is a problem of significance can be solved on a pluralistic theory. For an amusing application see "Novelty, Creation and Society" in *Interchange,* (1985) pp. 40–50.

8. Giedymin, Jerzy, "A Generalisation of the Refutability Postulate", *Studia Logica,* (1960).

9. Popper, K. R. *Conjectures and Refutations* (London: Routledge and Kegan Paul, 1963) ch. 10, p. 241.

10. Popper requires that a theory must pass at least one—the first genuine test (in ch. 10 of his *Conjectures and Refutations*) a point which has raised some

protest from Agassi (*Australasian Journal of Philosophy*, 39 (1961), 90). But Agassi is wrong, in this case, for any significant solution to a problem, because corroboration is always automatic. When one view is refuted another is automatically corroborated if the refutation is to be significant (i.e., discriminatory). Science is debate just as surely as chess is a two-person game. (If one man plays chess, he must play for two.) So a new theory, to be viable, must have some fact or other which discriminates in its favour, which automatically is a problem for another line, and hence 'unexpected' (from that point of view) and therefore a corroboration. It is also the first because if not, the new theory is not viable, but is dominated, hence not even relevant to the debate.

11. Popper, *Conjectures and Refutations,* chapter 10.

Notes to Chapter 8

1. Popper K. R., *Objective Knowledge: An Evolutionary Approach.* (Oxford: Clarendon Press, 1972). Campbell, Donald, "Evolutionary Epistemology." In P. A. Schilpp (ed.) *The Philosophy of Karl Popper,* Vol. I in the *Library of Living Philosophers,* (LaSalle, Illinois: Open Court, 1973). Piaget, J., *The Principles of Genetic Epistemology.* Tr. Wolfe Mays, (New York: Basic Books, 1973).

2. Lorenz, K., "Kant's Doctrine of the A Priori in The Light of Contemporary Biology." *General Systems, Yearbook of the Society for General Systems Research,* Vol. VIII (1962).

3. 'Pre-programmed' behaviour includes learnt behaviour which has become habitual.

4. Ryle, G., "Knowing How and Knowing That." Presidential Address, *Proceedings of the Aristotelian Society XLVI (1946).*

5. Schrödinger, E., *Mind and Matter.* (Cambridge: Cambridge University Press 1959), p. 105.

6. The tendency among developmental psychologists to restrict their study to children's skills, (operations, 'schemata') and to abstain from studying cognitions is one of the basic reasons why the process of going from one stage to another ('equilibration') is so mysterious. They look at that aspect of skill which naturally makes the process of development mysterious, as opposed to the fact of it, which they illuminate quite brilliantly.

7. Montaigne, M., "On the Education of Children". In J. M. Cohen (ed.), *Essays,* Ch. 26. (Harmondsworth: Penguin Books 1957.)

8. Hattiangadi, J. N., "A Methodology Without Methodological Rules", In R. Cohen and M. Wartofsky, eds., *Language, Logic & Method, Boston Studies in the Philosophy of Science* (Dordrecht: Reidel 1982).

9. Hattiangadi, "A Methodology Without Methodological Rules".

10. Kuhn, T. S., *The Structure of Scientific Revolutions.* (Chicago: University of Chicago Press 1962).

11. Polanyi, M., *Personal Knowledge: Towards A Post Critical Philosophy* (Chicago: University of Chicago Press, 1958).

12. In this example, Einstein published his paper in 1905, but its most significant practical impact (nuclear energy) was not seen until the second world war, when its positive as well as negative impact was recognized to be enormous. Einstein, Albert, "On the Electrodynamics of Moving Bodies", In W. Perrett & G. B. Jefferey, Trs., *The Principle of Relativity* (London: Dover Publications, 1952).

13. Fodor, J. A., *The Language of Thought* (New York: Powell, 1975).

14. Lorenz, K., *Evolution and Modification of Behavior* (Chicago, University of Chicago Press, 1965) points out that one must not suppose that learnt behaviour is not triggered, or that it does not have an innate base.

15. Tinbergen, N., *The Study of Instinct* (Oxford University Press, 1951) who reports on this excellent study of G. P. Baerends' "Fortpfanzungsverhatten und Orientierung der Grabwespe, *Ammophilia Campestris*" in *Tijdschrift voor Entomologie* 84 (1941).

16. Whorf, Benjamin L., *Language, Thought and Reality* (Cambridge, Ma: MIT Press, 1962).

Notes to Chapter 9

1. Chomsky, N., *Language and Mind* (New York: Harcourt, Brace and World, 1968), p. 24.

2. Chomsky, N., *Aspects of The Theory of Syntax*. (Cambridge, Mass.: The M.I.T. Press, 1965).

3. Chomsky, *Aspects of the Theory of Syntax*.

4. Beattie, J., *The Theory of Language* (Menston: England Scholar Press, 1976; rpt. of 1788 ed.) p. 96. This problem of the origin of language is of course, a refutation of the social contract theory of society. For a social contract presuppose a language, which presupposes society—and so society cannot presuppose a social contract.

5. See Whorf, L. *Language, Thought and Reality* (Cambridge, Mass.: M.I.T. Press, 1956.) especially the section entitled "Some Verbal Categories of Hopi".

6. See Whitney, W. D., *The Life and Growth of Language*, (New York: D. Appleton and Company, 1898).

7. Cobb, R. A., "The Present Progressive Periphrasis and the Metaphysics of Aristotle", *Phronesis* 18 (1973), pp. 80–90.

8. The innate universal grammar is either the essence of human language or the essence of human grammar, but in any case, an essence (or unchanging core) is presupposed by the various versions of Chomsky's theories.

9. Lorenz's idea that learning must have an innate base, and what might be the form of innate and instinctual behaviorism, can be found in Lorenz, K., *Evolution and the Modification of Behavior* (Chicago: University of Chicago Press, 1965). Popper proposed a not dissimilar conception of learning. One of the best later expressions of his view can be found in Popper, K. R., "The Bucket and the Searchlight", in *Objective Knowledge: An Evolutionary Approach* (Oxford: Clarendon Press, 1972).

10. The crucial stage that enables a child to appreciate the cognitive value of language will parallel, in my opinion, the stage when language was first invented. There will be a play-imitation of adult communication, and the first inkling of which a "symbol" is will develop from this. See Whitney, *The Life and Growth of Language.*

11. See Hattiangadi, J. N., "Meaning, Reference and Subjective conditional", *American Philosophical Quarterly* 16 (1979), pp. 192–205.

12. See King-Farlow, J., "Pronouns, Primacy, and Falsification in Modern Linguistics", *Philosophy of the Social Sciences* (1973) pp. 41–60.

13. Lenneberg, E. *Biological Foundations of Language* (New York: John Wiley, 1967).

14. Chomsky, N. *Language and Mind*, p. 60.

Notes to Chapter 10

1. See Vygotsky, L. S., *Thought and Language,* ed. and tr. E. Hanfmann and G. Vakar (Cambridge, Mass.: M.I.T. Press, 1962), Chapter 4.

2. Köhler, W., *The Mentality of Apes,* rev. ed. and tr. Ella Winter (London: Routledge and Kegan Paul, 1927), p. 128.

3. Bühler, K., *The Mental Development of the Child,* tr. Oscar Oeser (London: Kegan, Paul, Trübner, Trench and Co., 1930).

4. My thanks to E. Akin for suggesting such a succinct summary of the previous point.

5. Chomsky, N., *Language and Mind* (New York: Harcourt Brace and World, 1968), see especially the early part of the second section entitled "Present".

6. Köhler, op. cit., argues in the Introduction and in the rest of his work for the similarity of intelligent behavior in ape and man. Bühler, op. cit., finds that language with a representational function (what we would call 'conceptual language') separates man from the ape. The phrase 'conceptual language' was suggested by J. Agassi.

7. Here I am indebted to J. Agassi for this formulation of the problem in the form of a dilemma with an infinite regress on one horn.

8. This point could be amplified as a criticism of Chomsky's intellectualist theory of language.

9. For points (a) and (b) below, see Lorenz, K., *On Aggression,* trans. M. Latzke (London: Methuen and Company, 1966) from the German edition of 1963. Point (b) was already known to Charles Darwin, *The Expression of Emotions in Animals and Man* (New York: D. Appleton and Co., 1898). The general problem of the emergence of 'hopeful monsters' is discussed by Popper in his 1961 Herbert Spencer Lecture (in *Objective Knowledge,* Oxford: Clarendon Press, 1972) in a new inspiring way.

10. Thorpe, W. H., "Animal Vocalization and Communication", in F. L. Darley, ed., *Brain Mechanisms Underlying Speech and Language* (New York: Grune and Stratton, 1967) has provided this solution in its essentials in his treatment. As Chomsky points out, he does not thereby succeed in providing a satisfactory answer (*Language and Mind*, pp. 60–61).

11. The list I have made only identifies a *prima facie* good candidate—if it is to work, a theory will have to show how every difference between primate communication and human language can be understood in terms of the origins, the evolution, or a combination of origin and evolution, of primate features inherited by man.

12. See von Frisch, K. *Bees* (Ithaca: Cornell University Press, 1950); Lindauer, M. *Communication Among Social Bees* (Cambridge, Mass.: Harvard University Press, 1961).

13. Greenberg, J. H., *Anthropological Linguistics* (New York: Random House, 1968).

14. Chomsky's powerful attack on theories of language which depend on behavioristic claptrap like the catch phrase 'stimulus generalization' makes it unnecessary to consider behaviorist and associationist theories of meaning in this context. We can similarly dismiss the idea that language is a set of conventions.

15. This rules out a genetically determined language, but not all languages with a genetic base.

16. Köhler is followed by K. Lorenz, *Man Meets Dog* (London: Methuen, 1954) Ch. 16, and I. Eibl-Eibesfeldt, *Ethology* (New York: Holt, Rinehart and Winston, 1970), pp. 238–248.

17. The idea that learning must have an innate base is emphasized by K. Lorenz in his *Evolution and Modification of Behavior* (Chicago: University of Chicago Press, 1965). K. R. Popper gave an excellent explanation of this in his theory of *genetic dualism* (or pluralism) in his 1961 Herbert Spencer Lecture "Evolution and The Tree of Knowledge", reprinted in *Objective Knowledge* (Oxford: Clarendon Press, 1972). See also Piaget, J. *Principles of Evolutionary Epistemology,* tr. Wolfe Mays (London: Routledge and Kegan Paul, 1972).

18. K. Lorenz, *Man Meets Dog,* p. 155.

19. Marais, Eugene, *The Soul of the Ape* (London: Anthony Blond, 1969). This is a curious but unreliable book that anthropomorphizes a little too much.

20. M. Kawai, "Newly Acquired Pre-cultural Behavior of the Natural Troop of Japanese Monkeys on Koshima Island", *Primates* (1965); S. Kawamura, "The Process of Sub-cultural Propagation among Japanese Macques", in *Primate Social Behavior,* ed. C. H. Southwick (New York: van Nostrand, 1963).

21. Charles Darwin, *The Expression of the Emotions in Man and Animals* (London: 1873).

Notes to Chapter 11

1. Popper, K. R., *Conjectures and Refutations* (London: Routledge and Kegan Paul, 1963), chapter 12.

2. See Chomsky's critique of Popper's views in *Language and Mind* (New York: Harcourt, Brace and World, 1968), pp. 59–62.

3. Durkheim, E., *Elementary Forms of the Religious Life* (tr. by J. W. Swain, London: Allen and Unwin, 1976).

4. Wittgenstein, L. *Tractatus Logico-Philosophicus* (tr. by D. F. Pears and B. F. McGuinness, London: Routledge and Kegan Paul, 1961; first published 1921), and in *Philosophical Investigations* (New York: Macmillan, 1953) he repudiates many of his earlier views, though not the one regarding the meaninglessness of philosophy as traditionally pursued.

5. I refer the reader once again to Gellner's classic "Concept and Society" in *Cause and Meaning in the Social Sciences* (London: Routledge and Kegan Paul, 1973).

6. The word "contradictions", used by Hegel, Marx and their respective followers presupposes the idealism that they both inherit from Kant—though by 'idealism' in this sense one does not wish to preclude materialism (in Marx's sense) from it. This usage is not adopted here, because I see no reason to confuse logic and reality.

7. Cf. Chomsky *Aspects of the Theory of Syntax* (Cambridge, Mass: Harvard University Press, 1953).

Index